ALSO BY JOSEPH O'CONNOR

Novels
Cowboys and Indians
Desperadoes
The Salesman
Inishowen

Short Stories/Novels
True Believers
The Comedian

Non-Fiction
Even the Olives Are Bleeding: The Life
and Times of Charles Donnelly
Sweet Liberty: Travels in Irish America
The Secret World of the Irish Male
The Irish Male at Home and Abroad

Stageplays
Red Roses and Petrol
The Weeping of Angels
True Believers (adaptation)

Screenplays
A Stone of the Heart
The Long Way Home
Ailsa

Participation in Collaborative Works
Finbar's Hotel (ed. Dermot Bolger)
Mysteries 2000 (version of the Chester Play Cycle)

Editor
Yeats Is Dead! A Novel by Fifteen Irish Writers
for Amnesty International

The Last of the
Irish Males

JOSEPH O'CONNOR

review

For Edwin Higel

CONTENTS

INTRODUCTION

How The Irish Male Destroyed My Life

All of man's misfortunes derive from one single thing, which is his inability to remain at ease in his room.

Blaise Pascal *Pensées* (1670)

Way back in the Twentieth Century, I wrote a little book that was to change countless lives. It began as a cult, but grew to a trend; the sequel became an international best-seller, then a television sitcom and a West End musical. After the successful transfer to Broadway, there followed the triple live album, the Playstation game, the line of men's cosmetics, the guest appearance on *Seinfeld* and the launch of the X-rated internet site (www.irishmale.com). I was profiled in the *Tribune*, praised in the *Independent*, pursued by the *Mirror* and probed by the *Sun*. My magnanimous face adorned the cover of *Time*, my magnificent haunches the centrefold of *Playgirl*.

But my great success didn't change me one bit. Not for me the false Gods of fame and fortune, the blandishments of that fickle old slapper, Dame Celebrity. I kept on writing, no matter what. Books, articles, pamphlets, speeches, tragic operettas and terse haiku. There were stage-plays and novels and syndicated columns, expert theses on philosophical questions. Literary awards rained upon me in golden showers, among them the Pulitzer Prize for *double entendre*. I was seen in the company of glamorous women, by no means all of them professional escorts. No book launch, charity bash or night-club opening was really complete without my presence. I was dressed by Armani, undressed by Elle McPherson. Tea with the President was a regular occurrence; late-night calls from

Government Buildings came often, seeking my counsel on affairs of state.

Nor was this adulation confined to Ireland. The people of Italy took me to their ample, if figurative, bosom, the Australians, Germans and Dutch the same. The Spanish bestowed on me honorary citizenship, the French their supreme literary accolade, *Chevalier Grand de le Coq Sportif*. Steppes, pampas and wide-open prairies resounded with the echo of my noble name. At the insistence of my hordes of grateful British admirers I was even decorated by Her Majesty over beyond. Naturally, as a proud citizen of the Republic, I declined the full knighthood she beseeched me to take. Instead, as the cheering crowds surged against the palace gates below, I accepted a special title (*Royal Male*) and an honorary toe-suck off the Duchess of York. Elsewhere the offers just kept flooding in.

In those now lost-and-faraway days, I truly didn't think of what I was doing as writing. Neither did anyone else, for that matter. No, no, for me it was *giving*. I gave and gave until it hurt. And even then I gave some more.

As time went on I had to franchise myself. I simply couldn't keep up my work-rate any longer. For four entire months in late 1996, every single word that was published under my own name was in truth written by a team of highly-trained dwarfs I kept on a FÁS scheme in the cellars of my vast and tasteless mansion in Killiney. My 1998 novel *The Salesman* ('Best Irish Novel of the Year' — *The Sunday Independent*) was actually penned by Dermot Bolger; my stage play *The Weeping of Angels* ('the absolute low point of the Dublin Theatre Festival' — *Sunday Times*) by a chap who used to come in once a week to train my falcons. The output of wordage was simply phenomenal. My agent had to get more staff. Before long, my agent had to get her own agent. Then Hollywood beckoned. The rest is all too painful history.

Since the lawsuit arising out of my infamous Tinseltown sojourn is still pending, I am not at liberty to go into the details. Indeed, I am lucky to be at liberty at all. Suffice it to say, my newfound riches proved hard to handle. As many of my regular readers will know, I was raised on the bad side of town. My parents worked in the iron and steel industry — she did the ironing, he did the stealing[1] — and all those royalties generated by *The Secret World of the Irish Male* simply turned my head and brought me low. I was arrested one night on the corner of Hollywood Boulevard, accused of propositioning an off-duty policeman. But the details leaked to the newspapers were almost all wrong; vile slanders put about by my enemies and the envious. The facts of what passed between myself and Officer Martinez on that fatefully steamy night beneath the bougainvillea will all emerge in the fullness of time. For the moment I have been advised to say only this: It wasn't a chicken. And I *never* suggested we use a bowling ball. And it wasn't mayonnaise; it was Thousand Island dressing.

In any event, the strain of the publicity became too much. I was torn up inside, I craved privacy. I craved it in *Hello!* and *OK!* and *Woman's Own*; on Letterman, Leno and Larry King Live. I craved it on my own mid-morning chatshow on TV3 — *Cream In Your Coffee With The Irish Male* — but nobody was watching, so that wasn't much use. I craved it and craved it, but my public wouldn't give it to me.

I lost my home. I lost my first wife. She kept finding me, unfortunately, but I kept on losing her again, despite the squads of detectives and bloodhounds she employed. Finally, cunningly, she tracked me down. In the Divorce Court she accused me of being sexually odd, of asking whether she'd mind if I thought about someone else while we were making love. Under cross-examination she said she *didn't* actually

---

[1] Traditional fourteenth-century joke.

11

mind — since at least it made a change from me thinking about myself. The judge then woke up and went on the offensive. He said she had behaved like a Rottweiler to me. But I had to demur. That wasn't true. When a Rottweiler savages you, it locks its jaws *shut*.

In the court papers she had listed her occupation as 'housekeeper', a startlingly accurate designation, it turned out, since following the divorce she indeed kept the house, in a manner more Ghengis Khan than Zsa Zsa Gabor. But the hard feelings have gone now, despite the Viagra. We married in haste, but repented in Leitrim. These things happen. What can I tell you?

After the divorce I moved into a gutter, but was evicted by the rats for being untidy. For three long months I lived in a kind friend's compost heap, subsisting on rainwater and bits of grass. During the bitter days of that freezing winter, my publishers would sometimes allow me to come into the splendidly appointed offices of New Island Books to keep warm. I felt I was entitled. After all, my massive royalties had paid for the extensive refurbishment, not to mention the Robert Ballagh murals and the golden chandeliers. But when five o'clock came, it was the street again. If I refused to go, there were terrible beatings.

Around that time there was a shamefully high number of squalid and meaningless encounters with women. But there were bad times too; I have to admit it. My close friend Woody Allen is of the view that 'sex without love is an empty experience, but as empty experiences go it is one of the best'. I am not so sure. In my own case, such an approach soon lost its novelty. After a couple of months, not to mention vodkas, one supermodel looks much the same as the next. It was often a case of bed and bored.

A bitter-sweet dalliance did briefly flower with a hefty Ban Garda from down the country. An enthusiastic devotee of bondage and sado-masochism, she was, she modestly told me, 'a submissive'. But she dumped me after one short month. And that did hurt. I have to admit it. It is not every day you get dumped by a submissive.

Most romantic relationships begin with a drink, perhaps, and a nice chat about the price of eggs; followed by kissing, canoodling and heavy petting, eventually building up to frantic, uninhibited bonking in assorted gymnastic positions. My own liaisons, invariably, went the other way around. My idea of safe sex was getting out the next morning without leaving my phone number behind. Thank God I was eventually picked up by a crack-squad of Carmelites while wandering the streets and begging for scraps, a macabre shadow of my former self. Thus began the slow trek back to recovery. I was treated at a renowned clinic for formerly famous sex addicts. I am learning to take it one lay at a time.

Fame costs, gentle reader. And it cost me dear. And here we come to the meat of the matter.

It is with a melancholic sense of true resignation that I announce — yes — my resignation. My loves, my angels, the time has come. Even the best of friends must part. This is the Last of the Irish Males.

I know this will be hard for you to take. Dearly beloved companions, even as I pen these difficult words in my terrifyingly elegant study, I can almost see your quivering lower lips, and almost hear your pitiful bleats and almost touch your outstretched yearning hands, indeed almost smell your … Ah, stop, stop. What good is mere language to convey the poignancy? Even as I uncork another jeroboam of Bollinger, I can hear from every corner of our little land, nay, from every sod of this admirably spherical world whereupon the Irish Male has placed his sturdy brogue, the passionate chant as it begins: FOUR MORE YEARS! FOUR MORE YEARS! But no — alas, it is not to be. Ah, how I am reminded of that oh-so-truthful couplet of our arguably talented colleague, the late Mr Shakespeare:

Dum-dooby-do-dum-dum
Breakin up is hard to do.[2]

By now, no doubt, you will be going through all the traditional excuses for resignation. Ill health? No. The drink? Not at all. Wanted to make room for young blood? Yeah, right. Felt it was in the best interests of the Party and indeed the nation to end the damaging speculation and step aside? *Pas de tout*. Wanted to spend more time with his family? HA HA. Sacked for thieving? Would you get up the yard.

No, the reason is none of the above. Rather it is the knowledge, as the Scriptures tell us, that to all things (not just football) there is a season. A time to be born and a time to die. A time to sow and a time to reap. A time to Noel and a time to Liam. A time to surf and a time to wax your board. If you know what I mean. And I think you do.

Thespians among you will already know there are a number of ways to make an impressive exit. (1) Close the door quietly, possibly followed by a single gunshot offstage. (2) Give each of the minor characters in turn a terrifying glare. Murmur 'You've not seen the last of *me*, you poor fools' — and off. (3) As above, but accompanied by flash of lightning. (4) Stagger to your feet and begin a slow, painful limp upstage, brushing off the offer of help from the girl who scorned your love (the dignity of the vanquished). (5) Pick up tennis racket and bound through French windows with a nonchalant laugh. (6) Peer about interior of thatched cottage recently departed by emigrating son. Raise trembling hands to face, while the single spotlight slowly fades. (7) '*Yes, dammit Inspector, I KILLED him!*' (then swoon to the floor in heart-rending tears). But you wouldn't expect the Irish Male to

---

[2] *Othello*, act III, sc.4; Ed. Prof. N. Sedaka.

employ these cheap gimmicks. Instead I shall maintain my dignity in a manly manner as the single violin starts wailing in the pit and you take out the free souvenir tissue that came with this book to dab your moistening spaniel-like eyes and other body parts. (If you didn't get the free tissue, please apply in writing to the publisher, enclosing a cheque for £3.20 made out to Cayman Island Books 'Tissue of Lies' special offer.)

To all those who took the trouble to write in concerning some matter in Book One (the Old Testament) or Book Two (the Second Coming), particularly those who used joinedy-up writing, may I say a sincere 'Get a life'. Sorry — I mean 'Thank you'. Yes, even to those who wrote in to lambaste me for being vulgar, might I now reach out in a spirit of love and reconciliation and say just one brief word especially to you? Swivel.

A small number of people need to be thanked. Christ knows I wouldn't do it if they didn't need it. The wonderful Edwin Higel and the marvellous Dermot Bolger spawned — I think that is the correct verb — the Irish Male series, way back in the Roaring Nineties. As we boldly march on through the Naughty Noughties, I can pay these comrades no higher compliment than to state that I think of myself as their scandalous love child. The practically divine Ms Anne-Marie Casey provided spiritual nourishment and emotional solace. The sensational Anthony Glavin, peace be upon him, edited these tomes with much scrupulousness, professionalism, and attention to detail, not to mention jimson weed. Like the above-named excellent gentlefolk of letters, the outstanding Ms Ciara Considine was as a lighthouse in the storm, a ray of hope when all was obscurity. And my Goddess of an agent, Carole Blake at Blake Friedmann (122 Arlington Road, London NW1 7HP, not that I'm desperate for work) was a true friend and advisor on many difficult occasions. I am not, as yet, able to repay the bail money. But when I die, I have arranged for her to receive fifteen per cent of my ashes.

So now, I leave you with these last thoughts on the Irish Male, and may they guide you on the path through this rough-and-tumble world. And as I bring my heartbreaking valediction to a shuddering climax, might I dare to pass on one last brief story, which captures the very essence of my personal philosophy?

No?

Tough. I'm going to anyway.

Picture if you will the tiny village in Connemara, where a competition is planned to ascertain who is the greatest fiddler (stringed-variety) in Ireland. The time of the epic contest arrives; it is a cold, stormy night of the folkloristic class. See them, dear reader, the simple-hearted Gaelic villagers as they leave their humble homes and crowd into the village inn (Fisty Flanagans: Two Free Drinks For Ladies). Observe the tense looks, the gnawing on fingernails, as they anxiously await what is coming.

Plack-plock goes the grandfather clock. Outside in the night the tempest is wailing. Just before ten, the sound of hooves is heard. (No no — we are not in Finglas.) A moment later the door is flung open. A faint whiff of sulphur seems to colour the air, as in from the swirling snow stalks the first contestant. The cruelly handsome stranger is wearing a beautiful tuxedo, hand-tailored shoes, a cloak of raven black. Out of a case finished in finest calfskin, he gently lifts his magnificent instrument. A rare Stradivarius. Look at the sheen. But alas! — when he plays it, he is utterly shite.

Just as the clock is striking eleven, onto the premises strides competitor number two. Swathed in robes of ermine is this prince of the gypsies; perfumed with rare spices from the mystic east (Ballinasloe). Inside the expensive and neatly pressed trousers, the very nads are bedusted with talc, like little globes of Turkish delight. And as for his fiddle? Would you stop and don't be talking. His fiddle is the most beautiful instrument *ever seen in this world*, hewn from the wood of the One True Cross, encrusted with diamonds and glittering rubies. But oh! — when he plays it, he too is shite.

Now hark! The clock announceth midnight. Will no man come to claim this prize? As the final stroke is dolefully tolled, the last contender staggers half-dead from the blizzard. His pitiful rags are sodden and torn. His miserable arse is hanging out of his drawers, powerfully reminiscent of two eggs in a hanky; his poor broken excuse for a fiddle held together with Sellotape and bits of twine. And yet — when he takes up the bent old bow and commences to play, a truly extraordinary realization dawns.

Unearthly silence descends on the crowd. The villagers gape in utter astonishment.

Because he's a lot more shite than the first two were.

Go safely, with blessings and benedictions. May your mail always come early. (But not your Male.)

Now where's the door? I'm outta here.

Naughty Noughties:
The Irish Male in the 2000s

In Ireland the inevitable never happens.
Sir John Pentland Mahaffy

Especially under a Fianna Fail government
Anonymous Irish Male

ARE **YOU** AN IRISH MALE?

What a piece of work is a man! How noble in reason! How infinite in faculty! In form, in moving, how express and admirable. In action how like an angel! In apprehension how like a God! The beauty of the world! The paragon of animals!

William Shakespeare *Hamlet*

Animals is right.

Anonymous Irish Woman

You know, people often stop me and say: 'Hey, you! Get away from my clothes-line!' And I do. Because I can't afford the fines any more. But sometimes on my way home I am also stopped by total strangers who recognise my finely chiseled features from the literary supplements, not to mention the Wanted posters, and who need to know if they too are Irish Males. You can usually tell the answer merely by looking at the questioner. If, for example, he is wearing the jacket from one suit and the trousers from another, and if both garments look like they've been recently washed in a washing machine, then the chances are probably fair to middling.

But tell me this. Are *you* an Irish Male? Do you believe a woman's place is in the home? That real men don't eat quiche? That boys don't cry? Do you pine for the dear old dirty days, when men were men and babes were birds? Here then is a simple questionnaire which will help you calculate your IQ (Irishmale Quotient). Simply select and tick the relevant answer; then, at the end, add up your points. (If you can't actually add, ask your Mammy to do it for you. God knows, she does everything *else* for you.)

1) Your idea of a good night out is:

a) fifteen pints of snakebite and a doner kebab with the boys.

b) a romantic dinner for two with your girlfriend.

c) a romantic dinner for two with someone else's girlfriend.

2) Competitive sport is:

a) a barely veiled form of fascism.

b) a pleasant-enough diversion but not to be taken too seriously.

c) *Come on, United! STUFF the lousy bastards!!*

3) Given the choice of thirty seconds of fellatio from Britney Spears or a long happy life of monogamy and fatherhood, you would choose:

a) the latter.

b) the former, but absolutely hate yourself for it later.

c) … er … is this a trick question? *WHERE DO I SIGN?*

4) If your mother-in-law saw a sign saying WET PAINT:

a) she'd be alarmed.

b) she'd be confused.

c) she would.

5) You wash your hair:

a) once a year when you bathe.

b) every day when you shower.

c) never, but you truly believe that if you don't wash it at all, it washes itself after a couple of weeks.

6) Aerosol Deodorant is:

a) for girls.

b) not really acceptable to those who are concerned about the environment.

c) a midfield player with Dynamo Kiev.

7) A friend is getting married and has asked you to organise his stag-night. Your ideal image of such an evening is:

a) a few beers, a curry and a bit of a chat.

b) the world première of the new Brian Friel play.

a) going to an abattoir to shoot cows.

8) You like to discuss your feelings in an open, direct manner:

a) very frequently.

b) very rarely.

c) … huh?

9) The last time you actually cried was when:

a) one of your parents died.

b) Ireland so narrowly failed to qualify for Euro 2000.

c) you caught your pubic hair in your zipper.

10) Physical contact with another male is acceptable:

a) at any time.

b) in a boxing ring/rugby scrum/car-park fight.

c) when he is giving you the Last Rites — and even then there should be witnesses present.

11) The dishwasher is:

a) a useful domestic machine.

b) a strange box-shaped object in the corner of the kitchen, the function of which you have never been able to work out.

c) your pet name for the wife.

12) The tumble-drier is:

a) a machine for drying laundered clothes.

b) a 1920s' dance craze.

c) a sexual position.

13) Sometimes you break down:

a) in tears of happiness.

b) in tears of sadness.

c) in your Hiace van on the Naas dual carriageway.

14) Irony is:

a) the humourous or mildly sarcastic use of words to imply the opposite of what they actually mean.

b) a powerful dramatic convention developed by the ancient Greeks.

c) the art of ironing well (as practised by the Mammy).

15) Sex without love is:

a) a meaningless experience.

b) morally wrong.

c) the perfect end to the perfect night.

16) You want to get most women you meet into:

a) intelligent conversation.

b) bed.

c) a phone-booth.

17) Your idea of helping out with domestic chores is:

a) dividing them up fairly and happily doing your share.

b) opening your own bottles of beer.

c) not flicking cigarette ash on the carpet.

18) How often do you clean the toilet in your house?

a) very often.

b) not quite as often as you know you should.

c) never, but then again you pee in the sink, so why should you?

19) Scruples is:

a) a subject that is worth thinking long and hard about.

b) a question of knowing right from wrong.

c) the name of a night-club in Mullingar.

20) You would cheerfully enter your family's poodle:

a) in a beauty pageant for canines.

b) in a Talented Pets contest.

c) if nobody else was available at the time.

21) Marriage is:

a) the bedrock of society.

b) a word.

c) a whole bloody SENTENCE.

22) The cornerstone of a successful marriage is:

a) good communication and a sense of humour.

b) not getting caught and vigorously denying it if you do.

c) apathy.

23) Your partner seizes you passionately and says 'Take me now!' Do you:

a) strip down to your posing pouch and uncap the massage oil.

b) laugh so loud that a ball of snot rockets from your nose and adheres to her glasses.

c) say 'Where do you want me to take you to? Bray?'

24) Most of your previous girlfriends were:

a) sometimes difficult to understand.

b) very nice people but it just didn't work out.

c) inflatable.

25) Your ideal woman is:

a) your Mammy.

b) Saint Bernadette.

c) Jackie Healy-Rae in a dress.

26) The Clitoral Orgasm is:

a) a complete myth.

b) often the subject of articles in *Cosmopolitan*.

c) an important river in Central Bulgaria.

27) Since you were fired for fraud, finances are a little tight. Your seven-month pregnant partner suggests a part-time job might be the answer. Do you:

a) agree and immediately start applying for interviews.

b) resist and say you're not feeling well.

c) say 'Ah, Jayzus, love, I couldn't ask you to do that.'

28) Cunnilingus is:

a) an intimate and exciting form of foreplay.

b) a mortal sin that makes the Virgin Mary cry.

c) a subdivision of Ireland's national airline.

29) Your favourite sexual position is:

a) y'know … the usual one.

b) the other one.

c) either of the above, but with your socks still on.

30) What do you do immediately after sex?

a) hold your partner tenderly and whisper soft words of love.

b) roll over and go to sleep.

c) ask for the loan of your bus-fare home.

31) You wouldn't describe your mother-in-law as ugly:

a) although you wouldn't describe her as a supermodel either.

b) because you don't believe offensive labels should be applied to human beings.

c) but when she was born, the *midwife* needed gas.

32) Children are:

a) a blessing in a marriage.

b) sometimes demanding, but ultimately a source of wonderful joy.

c) the reason you can't lie in bed scratching your arse until lunchtime any more.

33) Lesbianism is:

a) a perfectly valid lifestyle choice.

b) morally repugnant and deeply sinful.

c) well-worth paying to see performed live.

Now add up your points and consult the following table:

Q1 (a)2 (b)0 (c)1	**Q18** (a)1 (b)0 (c)2
Q2 (a)0 (b)1 (c)2	**Q19** (a)1 (b)0 (c)2
Q3 (a)0 (b)1 (c)2	**Q20** (a)1 (b)0 (c)2
Q4 (a)1 (b)1 (c)2	**Q21** (a)0 (b)1 (c)2
Q5 (a)1 (b)0 (c)2	**Q22** (a)0 (b)1 (c)2
Q6 (a)1 (b)0 (c)2	**Q23** (a)1 (b)0 (c)2
Q7 (a)1 (b)0 (c) 2	**Q24** (a)2 (b)2 (c)2
Q8 (a)0 (b)1 (c)2	**Q25** (a)1 (b)0 (c)2
Q9 (a)0 (b)2 (c)1	**Q26** (a)0 (b)1 (c)2
Q10 (a)0 (b)1 (c)2	**Q27** (a)0 (b)2 (c)1
Q11 (a)0 (b)2 (c)1	**Q28** (a)1 (b)1 (c)1
Q12 (a)0 (b)0 (c)0	**Q29** (a)0 (b)1 (c)2
Q13 (a)1 (b)0 (c)2	**Q30** (a)1 (b)0 (c)2
Q14 (a)0 (b)1 (c)2	**Q31** (a)1 (b)0 (c)2
Q15 (a)1 (b)0 (c)2	**Q32** (a)0 (b)1 (c)2
Q16 (a)0 (b)2 (c)1	**Q33** (a)0 (b)0 (c)5
Q17 (a)0 (b)1 (c)2	

More than 40 points: You are so Irish Male that you should probably seek immediate counselling or apply for a sex-change operation. The chances of you ever forming a stable relationship — and by that I don't mean 'with a horse' — are really very slim indeed unless you mend your ways immediately. You suffer from low self-esteem, and correctly so. You have all the attractiveness of a tapeworm in Doc Martens and your intelligence is on a par with that of mayonnaise. Have you ever considered living in a cave? You probably should. If the bats and dung-beetles would let you in.

Between 20 and 39 points: You seem to be a reasonably well-adjusted fellow. Yes, you have your moments of drunkenness, sloth and goatish lechery, but in general you are calm, charming, in touch with your feelings, polite, restrained and frequently, if not comprehensively, washed. With a little effort you could have a career in politics.

Between 10 and 19 points: A New Man such as yourself is so rare that you should be in a glass-case (or behind bars) in the National Museum. Several of my sisters would like to meet you.

Less than 10 points: You *are* actually a man, are you?

Friends, Romans, Countrymen —
Lend Me Your Beers!

*He knows nothing and he thinks he knows everything. That
points clearly to a political career*

George Bernard Shaw *Major Barbara*

Political life in Ireland is an interesting thing when you have
played as central a role as I have myself. Yes, I don't like to
talk about it much — indeed, the Official Secrets Act prevents
me from so doing — but perceptive readers must surely have
discerned by now that I have obviously walked in the halls of
power, have pored long and deep over the sacred text of the
Constitution, have studied the cadences of the great Irish
orators: Parnell. Larkin. Bertie Ahern. Happy Bertie, as I call
him.

Ah, sweet memory. The smoke-filled rooms of Party
headquarters, the committee chambers, the private bar and
massage parlour in the attic of Government Buildings, these
were once as familiar to me as my own home. Once upon a
time there were even invitations — call them pleadings — to
put myself before the people and allow the sham that I wasn't
running the country to be ended. But I demurred. The Cabinet
table held no attraction for me (though there *was* one night of
lazy love thereupon with a Junior Minister, now retired). A
seat in the Senate was gently refused, the lofty bench of the
Supreme Court likewise declined. I am by nature a backroom
boy. I find I can grip the reins of power more tightly if nobody
can see exactly which donkey I'm riding.

No, my role was to help with what is called presentation.
Packaging, if you want. Or 'spin-doctoring', as the black art is
sometimes known by those on the outside of the Golden Circle
which I, in former days, so excitingly penetrated.

Naming no names, but many's the *bon-mot* penned by your modest scribe has ended up peppering the speeches of the good, bad and cuddly of Ireland's political elite. Indeed, many's the night close to a Party conference and I'd be about to lep aboard the four-poster waterbed with the Mahatma, a great nosebag of chips and finest venison deep inside me, the remains of a presumptuous Mouton Rothschild atop the bedside locker, when the majestic clang of the doorbell would sound loud and long through the Killiney night and moments later the butler would come knocking on the boudoir door. 'It's happened again, Sire,' Henri would softly say. 'I think you had better follow me.'

Down in the snooker room would be You-Know-Who, the rain sleekly dribbling down the bri-nylon anorak. Usually accompanied by one of his henchmen. A pillowcase of cash clutched in one mitt, a bottle of single malt in the other. The dazzling headlights of the state Mercedes beaming in through the Graham Knuttall stained-glass windows like the eyes of some vengeful and terrible God.

'We need yeh,' he'd say. 'I'm stuck wit de speech. Would y'ever givus a birrof a digout?'

Neither did such approaches only come from the Republican Party, oh no. Blueshirts, Reds, Pinkos and Greens were often seen trudging up my vulgar driveway, the mastiffs snapping about their heels, the overhead seagulls delivering terrible retribution. Certain Ministers of Justice were by no means at all the rarest visitors. Taoisigh, Tanaistí? Don't be talking. Chief Whips and Attorney Generals? Like swallows in summer. Sure back in the days of the distant past, even Kinsealy's proud eagle Himself would sometimes roost beneath my humble and undeserving slates. Though that was usually to ask me for money — which I, of course, was happy to give. A finer man never seduced my wife.

But anyway. Those happier days are now lost and gone,

and will return with the late Mr Poe's raven, *viz*, nevermore.

Meantime here is my simple multiple-choice blueprint for the all-purpose Irish political speech. It has served many of our elected rulers well over the years and now I pass it on to you. Simply go through and tick off the options which suit you best, and you will have the mob cheering you from the rafters and singing hallelujahs. (With a little adaptation it is also suitable for weddings, First Communions and funeral orations.)

Colleagues Friends/*A chairde Gael*,

As I stand before you here today, my modest (a) *heart* (b) *ego* (c) *bank balance* actually swells with the thought of being (a) *your leader* (b) *your candidate* (c) *recently released from prison*. It is an honour (a) *bestowed on many greater men than myself in the past* (b) *that I truly don't deserve* (c) *for which I paid in hard cash*.

As many of you know, I did not seek this honour. No, at first I was reluctant, I would even say unworthy. As you will all be deeply aware, I am a great believer in Family Values. And in (a) *making this decision* (b) *accepting this burden*, most of all I put my family's interests first — all four of my families and also the twin au pairs, Mitsy and Melanie. But finally I was persuaded by the numerous (a) *pleas* (b) *threats* (c) *brown envelopes full of money* I received to put my deep reservations to one side and allow my name to go forward. In the end — after much reflection, fasting and prayer — I saw that the call to serve my Party and country in whatever modest way I could was far more important than merely personal considerations such as a massive salary, a chauffeur-driven limousine and the kind of untrammeled power that would give a dead man the horn.

Of course, my family has a long tradition of public service. My father, from whom I inherited my seat, proudly served (a) *his constituents for many decades* (b) *the cause of national freedom and independence* (c) *four years for indecent assault on a goat.*

He was, as many of you will recall, a fantastic lover. Of the national language. Often he would address me in the beautiful and ancient tongue which our ancestors spoke. But other times he would speak to me in Irish. And I find myself thinking of those words of wisdom today.

(Here utter a few meaningless platitudes in Irish, then finish by wiping a small tear from your eye. This will keep the Aran-Knickers Brigade happy. Or content, at any rate. They tend not to be actually happy unless they're miserable.)

Colleagues, partners, brothers and sisters, this is certainly a (a) *historic building* (b) *marvellous edifice* (c) *magnificent erection*, and being, all of us, gathered here today provides a welcome opportunity for (a) *renewing old acquaintance* (b) *coming together in a spirit of true comradeship* (c) *getting rat-faced drunk and back-stabbing each other.*

Looking around this noble hall wherein we find ourselves begathered I see many (a) *crooked property developers* (b) *bastards who owe me one, so keep schtum or else* (c) *old and trusted friends who kept faith with this great Party when fainter hearts fell away.*

And with deep and absolute certainty I can now say I know (a) *that the painful divisions of the past are well behind us* (b) *that I have your loyalty* (c) *where the bodies are buried.*

I would also like to welcome our friends in the

press (a) *who do so much to keep our democracy healthy* (b) *whose sterling work in exposing corruption is so sincerely valued by us in this Party* (c) *the nosey interfering swine, may they die roaring with their legs in the air.*

Lord knows, ourselves and the ladies and gentlemen of the Fourth Estate do not ALWAYS see eye to eye (*pause for sycophantic laughter and all around thigh-slapping*) but I would count many of them among my (a) *close personal friends* (b) *heroes and role models* (c) *potential recipients of damaging leaks about colleagues.*

Lastly I would like to extend a special welcome to our oldest delegate (a) *Mickey Joe 'The Stiffer' Mulligan* (b) *Bridie 'Big Guns' Brannigan* (c) *Maeliosa Óg Mac An Sassanachbasher* from Tralee in the kingdom of Kerry. You would not think it to look at *him/her/it* but *Mickey Joe/Bridie/Maeliosa Óg*, a founder member of the Party, was actually one-hundred-and-forty-seven years young last Tuesday and looks, if I may so (a) *the picture of rude good health* (b) *twice that age* (c) *like something the cat dragged in and nibbled to death.*

(Pause for thunderous ovation, during which Mickey Joe/Bridie/Maeliosa Óg wakes up, pisses in slippers and punches nurse.)

Yes, we in *Fianna Fail/Fine Gael* are the Party of the old AND the young, the rich AND the poor, the blind AND the lame, the rhythm AND the blues. Of the East, the West, the South and — let us say it unashamedly — the North! (*Cries of 'Up, yeh good ting'.)* I do not presume to question the patriotism of any citizen of this Republic. That, as you know, is not my style. But we in *Fianna Fail/Fine Gael* BELIEVE in Ireland. WE will never do this country down. WE will never cause Old Mother Erin to weep piteously and proclaim that nobody loves her and she'd be better off dead for all anyone would care and no wonder she has to take Prozac. Not like those no-good dirty TRAITORS in *Fianna Fail/Fine Gael* who would BURN THE TRICOLOUR FOR A FEE OF TWO QUID!

(Pause to acknowledge ROAR of applause.)

Yes, we in this Party have certain core values. Values that have STOOD THE TEST OF TIME. Values that have SEEN US THROUGH THICK AND THIN — as the young people of today like to call Donald Beckham and his wife Baby Spice. (*Wild, manic, helpless laughter.*) Decent values. Honest values. LASTING values. Maybe it isn't so 'fashionable' to have values these days. Maybe it's not 'trendy' to KNOW WHERE YOU STAND. Well, if people in this so-called age of progress don't like the values on which this great Party was FOUNDED? Well that's just FINE. We'll change them immediately.

We in this Party believe in JUSTICE (*administer thump to rostrum*). In PEACE (*another thump*). In peace WITH justice (*BATTER the rostrum*). In justice with TRUTH. In truth and COMPASSION and LOVE and FORGIVENESS with a side order of French fries, hold the lettuce, extra ketchup.

You know, some people these days say all politicians are the same. (*Hysterical chortles.*) They say we are inadequates and frauds who are all on the make. (*Awkward silence and rustling of envelopes.*) But it is the distinctive and totally unique POLICIES of this Party which mark us out sharply from our evil opponents. We are AGAINST unemployment, inflation and burglary. We are FOR economic success, worldwide peace and nice weather. As for the problem of drugs which have ravaged so many young lives — let me spell out OUR policy in no uncertain terms: SOMETHING DEFINITELY NEEDS TO BE DONE. And we will DO IT. Make no mistake.

Winning policies. Winning ways.

Yes, we will yield to NOBODY in our love for Ireland. We love it. We do. We can't get enough of it. We love Ireland in an almost FRIGHTENING sense. When I think of Ireland my resolve actually STIFF-ENS. Yes indeed, when I consider the ancient glory of our noble, proud and wise people who suffered centuries of famine, oppression and folk-singing I actually get a lump (a) *in my throat* (b) *in my under-pants*. And I know you do too. And so does my wife.

But make no mistake, we are not complacent. In this Party we are not afraid (a) *to ask the difficult questions* (b) *to think the unthinkable* (c) *to challenge outmoded perceptions and pieties*. In this Party we profoundly believe (a) *that policies, not personalities, are the important thing* (b) *in the ultimate soundness of our economic strategy* (c) *that in the final Star Wars movie Luke Skywalker will triumph and The Force will win*.

The Irish people are no fools. There is NO POINT in spouting clichés at them, as I wish our pig-ignorant opponents would finally realize. So I say THIS to the Irish people: Be assured, we are determined to keep our (a) *shoulders to the wheel* (b) *noses to the grindstone* (c) *backs to the wall*. We have our (a) *feet on the ground* (b) *heads in the clouds* (c) *fingers in the till*. You can lead a horse to water. But a stitch in time saves nine. And as for too many cooks? Well you CAN'T make them drink.

As we stand (a) *at the start of a new millennium* (b) *at a crossroads in the history of this great nation* (c) *with our foreheads drunkenly resting on the surface of the bar*, it behoves us all to think about our Young People *(put on baseball cap here)*. Because we ABOVE ALL ELSE are the Party of Young People *(turn baseball cap back-to-front)*. They are truly (a) *our greatest asset* (b) *our proudest hope* (c) *not as bloody gullible as we'd like them to be.* They are (a) *eager to succeed in a changing new world* (b) *impatient with the jaded slogans of the past* (c) *trying to crash a rave night off the South Circular Road by saying 'Hugo' sent them and they've brought many drugs.* We must reach out. We must 'get hip'. We must be the Party that parties on down. We must say there is a groovy home for you here in *Fianna Fail/Fine Gael*, the Party that will put the funk back in your face, the Party that wants to shake its bootie, the Party that wants to boogie-oogie-woogie till it just can't boogie no more, as U2 said. Because we owe the Young People of this proud and thrusting nation (a) *our very best efforts* (b) *a meaningful future in a prosperous dynamic Ireland* (c) *a good hard kicking* … AND WE WILL GIVE IT TO THEM!

(Hearty applause. Cries of 'Hear, hear'.)

People sometimes say that our policies are vague. So I want to take a moment to spell them out in careful detail.

Yes, we live in a changing country. In a changing world. In a changing solar system. Life, like politics, is a funny old game. A game of two halves. A game of chance. One day you're up. Next day you're down. For every step forward? A step back. For every swing — if you will — a roundabout. As that great supporter of our Party, William Butler Yeats, once put it (a) *All changed, changed utterly, a terrible beauty is born* (b) *All change at Limerick Junction* (c) *If you vote for me, I'll get your drains fixed.*

But let me say something about what change really MEANS for Ireland. Because we ABOVE ALL ELSE are the Party of Change. *(At this point, simply rearrange the following words in any order you like, making sure to string them together using short quotations from The Cranberries.)* Internet. E-mail. E-commerce. E-volution. Fast-track along the Inform- ation Superhighway. Microchip. New technology. Computer. Mobile telephone. Website. Dazzling mod- ern age. Embracing future. Boldness required. No room for complacency. Imagination. Skills. Training. Modem. Whole world at touch of a button. Celtic Tiger economy. Keyboard. Mousepad. Microsoft Word. www.bigbuzzumbas.com.

Many young people these days are deeply concerned about the environment. And I say to all three of them — come and join us. For we ABOVE ALL ELSE are the Party of the Environment. We have put the mental BACK into environmental. When it comes to the great questions which confront not just my constituency but less importantly the planet, we must think of our children. And our children's children. And even our children's children's children.

(Cue patriotic music.)

You know, my friends, when I walk the hills and meadows of this beautiful nation for which our forefathers laid down their very wives; when I hear the soft calling of birds and other small furry creatures, I

37

think of a wise old Gaelic saying which my grand-father would often quote before trying to French-kiss me: "We can never *own* the land, lad. We only hold it in trust. An offshore trust in the Cayman Islands."

Yes, as we march into the Brave New Future, there *will* be problems along the way. But we don't see them as problems. We see them as exciting CHALLENGES.

Let me say a word about the exciting challenge of refugees and asylum-seekers. I am often accused by my enemies of giving 'mixed signals' on the matter, even — astonishingly — of outright Racism. (*Cries of 'Shame' and 'West-Brit bastards'.*) How ridiculous. And how very sad.

How many of our own ancestors took the long, lonely journey across the seas? THEIR lot was not the cosy job in *The Irish Times* from which to look down on the hard-working people of Ireland and pontificate about Racism. No, it was the coffin ship, the Brooklyn slum. In America, in Australia, in Canada they prospered, these non-Negroid Catholic home-grown Gaels who wore proper rags and not animal pelts like the SCALPING REDSKIN SAVAGES. What were THEY, if not economic migrants? What were THEY, if not refugees? Admittedly, THEY were not skivers, thieves and spongers like this shower we have pouring in today to steal our jobs, murder our children and seduce our women with their strange gypsy ways. But this is not a Party of Racism. Racism will NEVER find a home in this Party! Intolerance, especially, will NEVER be tolerated!

Let me say this in plain ENGLISH that even our enemies will understand. (*Grip the lectern here.*) As long as I have a single breath left in my Caucasian, Irish, non-Pagan body, foreigners will ALWAYS be more than welcome here. Particularly Jersey bankers and wealthy Arab autocrats who want to invest in the brother-in-law's donkey-breeding business down the country.

FAR from being cold or unwelcoming — FAR from issuing 'mixed messages' — I say to ALL darkies, dagos, towel-heads, gyppos, fuzzie-wuzzies, sun-worshippers, Bosnian layabouts and other idle robbing scum — welcome, *welcome* to Ireland of the Welcomes. We will not lock you up in 'flotels'. We will lock you up in secure aquatic reception facilities where your children may go hungry but not without a nice view of this great Republic through the porthole. I ask you, friends, what could be fairer than that?

Of course, constructive criticism and free speech in these matters is VITAL. Thank God our Party treasures its proud democratic traditions of banning people we don't like from the airwaves and tapping journalists' telephones. In that noble spirit of openness, of generosity, of *tolerance*, I say to those of my fellow citizens that take a different view to my own that they can shag off back to their wife-swapping vegetarian dinner parties in Dalkey and snort cocaine off each other's thighs if they want to, but WE KNOW WHERE YOU LIVE, YOU DIRTY LESBIAN TROTS!

In conclusion, we have a vision. We have a dream. A dream of a vision. A vision of a dream. We dream of the past but remember the future. We imagine the present and anticipate the pluperfect. We boldly wrap our arms around History and slide our hand up the back of Destiny herself, trying to unclip her bra-strap without her noticing. As Seamus Heaney has written so beautifully *(get advisor to insert wildly out-of-context but evocative quotation here*). And I think that puts it very well.

Goodnight. Thank you. And GOD BLESS IRELAND!

Flatley Will Get You Nowhere

There are many kinds of dances, but all those requiring the participation of the two sexes have two characteristics in common; they are conspicuously innocent, and warmly loved by the vicious.

Ambrose Bierce *The Devil's Dictionary*

Lady readers will find this difficult to believe, but it used to be thought that the Irish Male was not good at dancing. Yes, I know, it is almost impossible to credit, and yet, believe me, that was the case. The muscular coordination and sheer physical grace he employed to such devastating effect upon the hurling pitch or handball alley seemed to desert him inside the night-club. Nor was the happy agility he displayed when scuttling up a mountainside after a lost sheep ever observable on premises licensed for the jitterbug, jive or boogaloo. God moved in mysterious ways, and so did His finest creation — the Irish Male.

Perhaps the strobe-lights put him off. (I mean the Irish Male, not God.) Perhaps he was exhausted from his hard day struggling with the silage. Perhaps it was what happened when he found the sheep that wore him out and sapped his vitality. (For in certain parts of rural Ireland the truth of the Good Book is often quoted: *The one sheep that was lost hath now been found. PARTY TIME!)*

Many theories were formerly advanced to explain the Irishman's strange ungraciousness.[1] Whatever the cause, the

---

[1] See Sprocklemann, Travolta and Coogan, 'The Irish Male: Two Left Feet?' in the *Yale Review of Boogie*, Fall 1986; though Hinkleheim and Foster offer a perceptive revisionist critique in their *Funking Barstewards: De Valera and Disco*, Oxford University Press, £19.89.

effect was not good. An Irishman dancing was like a rhinoceros doing yoga. Ungainly, unnatural — yet horribly compelling to look at.

Understandably the Irish Male was written-off as a non-dancer. Lacking the swerve of the Italian or the strut of the Frenchman, out of step with the civilized world, Pat was doomed to a life of cruel mockery, dismissed by hoofers everywhere as choreographically illiterate. But then, a few years ago, anthropologists began to re-examine the evidence, in particular the intricate patterns of Irish Male night-club behaviour. Dusty textbooks were scrutinized, experts consulted. Field-trips were undertaken to the Irish Midlands, that region known in academia as 'Darwin's Waiting Room'. And so it came to pass that the scholars discovered an absolutely astounding fact about the nocturnal activities of *homo erectus Hibernicus*.

He was dancing all along — *but in his own unique way!*

Yes, he was dancing to a different drum. Not for him the Twist, the Watusi or the Mashed Potato. He scoffed at the Pogo, the Tango and Mambo, he barred the Beguine, the Bolero and Body-Pop. These were ugly shufflings, hideous foreign gyrations, unchristian lurchings designed to corrupt. The Irish Male had devised his own wholesome dances, and today we are happy to share those with you.

(1) The Bar-Prop

This strangely beautiful form of Irish Male dance is usually performed by a herd of younger specimens, but is sometimes attempted individually. The male enters the night-club and hauntingly staggers for the bar. There, in a movement as swift as it is subtle, he leans quickly forward, rests his elbows on the woodwork, and pertly sticks his bottom out, often to rapturous and prolonged applause. Observe him, reader. Dundalk's Dhiagelev. Poignantly he raises his eyes to the television screen. There they remain for the rest of the night. This is a tremendously difficult position to maintain (particularly while drinking heavily) but a really well-trained ballerino can keep it up for days at a time, even while making regular overtures to the bar-person.

(2) The Lep With The Lads

A large rowdy circle of young native Irish Males performs this ancient tribal dance, which is part mating-display, part initiation ceremony and part fully fledged football riot. Details of costume are vitally important here. Each brave will know the ritual's intricacies, having learnt them as a nipper on his grandfather's knee. Neckties are removed and affixed about the head. The jumper is whipped off, the arms knotted loincloth-style around the waist. (In extreme cases, the trousers may go too.) The shirt is opened right down to the navel, revealing the obligatory grey string vest given by the Mammy last Christmas. Then it's on with the Quo and away we go!

> DOWN DOWN, DEEPER AND DOWN
> DOWN DOWN, DEEPER AND DOWN
> GET DOWN, DEEPER AND DOWN
> DOWN DOWN, DEEPER AND DOWN

Ah, the Yeatsian delicacy of the lyrics.

The main feature of the dance is that the feet do not actually leave the ground, but remain firmly planted while the body jigs rhythmically up and down, enabling the blubber to slap the ribcage in time with the music. Grunts, barks and ululations are optional. The head rocks vigorously back and forth, filling the air with a blizzard of dandruff. As for the more detailed upper-body movements — the arms are used either to clutch the most adjacent Irish Male or thrash one's invisible Stratocaster.

Brief respectful invocations of each other's tribal ancestors are often chanted, for example 'Hey, Leppo, yer granny's a fookin ride.'

(3)   The Lunge of Love

This is an exquisite and enchanting form of Irish courtship *pas-de-deux*, performed by an Irish Male and Female who have only just met. The two partners modestly slow-dance for a time, all the while making polite chat about such light-hearted matters as the affairs of the nation, their musical tastes and whether frequent attendance at these premises has become customary — 'So tell us, love, jeh cum here often?' The initial stage being properly completed, the male delicately approaches; the female retreats with maidenly modesty. The man shimmies forward again, the movement courtly and elegant. His hands respectfully move southwards and clench her buttocks. Firmly she removes them. The moment has come. He LUNGES forward and deftly inserts his slab-like tongue in her mouth, wiggling, waggling, probing, poking. The movement is completed with the traditional knee in the balls and that ancient ceremony known as the Calling of the Guards.

(4)   The One-Handed Celtic Urinal Shimmy

This is the Irish Male equivalent of 'The Dying Swan', a poignant and desperately moving hymn to existential suffering. Though it may just as easily be attempted in the privacy of the home — indeed it often is in mine — the usual venue for this deeply affecting dance is the male public lavatory of the average Irish night-club. Enter quietly any weekend evening around midnight and you will see it in all its pitiful glory.

There he is, the Irish Male, swaying at the urinal, much the worse for strong drink. One hand is firmly clamped to the wall in front of him, fingers splayed in an attempt to gain purchase; the forehead may also rest against the tiles and the tongue may hang out a bit and drool. The body is slowly rocked from side to side; the knees sag, the shoulders slump. Soft groans of distress add to the profound sense of tragedy. The performance even has a religious dimension — 'Jayzus Mary and Jozeph,' he moans devoutly, 'I'll never fookin dhrink aghain, I swear.' He begins to swallow hard, his abject face turning forty shades of green, until — '*Bwaaaaaaawwwghgh-ghgghhghgh*!' With that piteous mantra, full catharsis is achieved (all down his shirt and tie).

(5) The Space-Cadet

This is another piece for the soloist, possibly related to the 'Sundance' ritual of many Native American tribes, though it is mentioned in the annals of ancient Ireland and was often performed by Cuchullain himself.[2]

All these centuries later the mystical dance is still performed. The young Irish Commanche, having smoked perhaps too deeply from the pipe of peace, totters to the very centre of the dance floor and begins rotating in ever-decreasing circles, waving his arms like a windmill gone mad and crying gaily at the top of his voice 'Fatboy Slim! Fatboy Slim!' until the security staff are called to put him out.

(6) The Father of the Bride

This dance, an essential part of the Irish nuptial ceremony, is exclusively reserved for weddings. In it, the bride's father performs a holy rite of abject self-humiliation as a sign of his

---

[2] See ref. in Trinity College Dublin Early Manuscripts collection, *'Boogí an Domhain'*, folia 47/a/XX1, p. 4032: *'He slew false Ferdia with the sacred spear of Harney, yea, even unto his heart. Then didst the Hound of Ulster, scourge of the foe and glory of the Gael, get on up and do it like a sex machine.'*

undying love for his daughter. The dance traditionally commences with a courteous cry from the singer/drum-machine-operator of the wedding band: 'Hey, baldy, get up there now and give us a twirl.'

At this point the poor man struggles to his feet, as the wedding band — 'Boogie Knights' or 'Hi-Way Star' — strikes up the opening recitative of that beloved Irish traditional tune *Amhrán na n-Éan* ('The Birdie Song'). The important thing is for the dancer to possess absolutely no sense of rhythm whatsoever, rather to display all the grace of an octopus on dry land as he disco-dances with one of the hefty bridesmaids. From time to time he clicks his fingers in the air, gestures which bear no relation at all to the beat of the music. Sometimes he shakes his bottom from side to side, inducing loud mirthful roars from the assembled guests. Elements of flamenco are often in evidence, particularly in the playing of invisible castanets. Occasionally the bride's father also attempts to incorporate 'the twist', which was all the rage back when he was young in the late 1400s. The dance concludes with violent jeering, gratuitous flash photography and bottle-throwing.

(7) The Walls of Limerick

This fine old dance brings together the *corps-de-ballet* of Irish Males for a rousing finale to any evening. In deceptively simple formation they totter to a wall and in unison graciously urinate up and down the side of it, while singing a lusty chorus of 'The Fields of Athenry'.

Now you know how to dance like an Irish Male. So git on up! (I know I do.)

Socks, Pox And Two Smoking Saucepans: The Irish-Male Guide To Good Housekeeping

Cleanliness is next to Godliness.

Queen Victoria

Not in MY dictionary.

Anonymous Irish Male

Let's face it, the traditional Irish Male has not had a good press. People say his ten worst features are that he is lazy, undomesticated, slobbish, rude, dishonest, sarcastic, stubborn, mean, drunk, hypochondriacal and sexually unimaginative. But that is not the whole picture by any means. (He is also not very good at mathematics.)

Yet it is perhaps in the area of domestic life where the Irish Male most abjectly fails to score big points. A recent survey of Irish females found that 85 per cent of their partners thought the phrase 'pre-wash cycle' as found in washing machine instructions meant riding your bike before rinsing your armpits. (The other 15 per cent never bother rinsing their armpits.)

The same questionnaire asked the ladies to guess what their partners would consider the greatest innovation in human history: (a) the printing press (b) preventative medicine, or (c) the internal combustion engine. Almost all the respondents crossed out the above three answers, scribbling instead 'the beer-mat'.

The statistics do not make for happy reading. A separate survey of younger Irish Males found that in nine cases out of ten the simple phrase 'food processor' was thought to be an affectionate synonym for 'Mother'.

Yes, at first glance it does not look at all promising, especially when you consider our Continental counterparts. The new men of Europe apparently can't wait to get scrubbing, cooking, scouring and sweeping. *Monsieur* merrily mops up around *le maison*, and *Mein Herr* helps Helga about *das haus*. Give any self-respecting Dutchman a pair of rubber gloves and a sink-plunger and he knows exactly what to do with them. But this is not an article about hardcore pornography, so never mind that.

Irish brothers, it is truly time that we changed. Our habits. Our thinking. Our socks once a fortnight. We have nothing to fear but fear itself! Fear itself and 'Match of the Day' being cancelled.

Here is my own personal guide to the domestic niceties, the little things that turn a house into a home — or, at very least, an acceptable shag-pad.

LAUNDRY AND PERSONAL HYGIENE

Thus were they stained with their own works; and went a whoring with their own inventions.
Psalm 106, verse 38

Many Irish Males have little or no idea of laundry, having been raised by their Mammies to sincerely believe that once a week Santa Claus creeps into their rooms while they are sleeping and replaces all their dirty clothes with bright, clean, fresh ones. This, of course, is total nonsense. It is the Laundry Leprechaun who does that.

But sadly there are times in adult life when the Laundry Leprechaun goes running back to her mother taking the kids with her, and consequently you have to take care of your own laundering needs. There is no need to panic. With a little concentration the crisis can be managed.

The time-honoured way to decide whether intimate garments are in need of laundering is, of course, to throw them against the bedroom wall and see if they stick. If that happens, here's what to do: scrape them off the wall, go into the bathroom and wait for the offending articles to walk in after you. Pick them up and throw them onto the floor of the shower. Next sprinkle them liberally with washing powder — you will find this aromatic granular substance in a cardboard box under the sink, just beside where your partner hides the Children's Allowance book — and run the hot water over them for a good long time. When the water is hot enough to kill all known germs, step in and trample your smalls for a while, taking care to remove your Tellytubby pyjamas first.

There is no point in being half-hearted about it. Don't be afraid to give them a good hard stomping. It sometimes helps to picture yourself as a French grape-treader while you're doing this, although a proficiency at Irish traditional dancing is even more useful here. (*See chapter 4 for details*.) 'Dance away the heartache,' as Brian Ferry once advised. But dance away the dirt as well.

Since you're in there anyway, you may as well attend to your personal cleanliness. (There is no point in wasting hot water, after all.) However, you probably shouldn't use the Daz or Aerial for washing *yourself*, not unless you want to end up whiter-than-white, or, even more alarmingly, 'with a dazzling blue whiteness'. A special chemical substance called 'soap' has recently been developed for the specific purpose of personal ablutions. It usually comes in a small hard block. A few small bites and you will be clean again. It may also be smoked, sniffed or inserted.

Some Irish Males find the details of personal hygiene embarrassing to discuss, but there is no need at all for such shyness any more. The human body is nothing to be ashamed about, not even yours and Christ knows that's saying something. Simply make sure to thoroughly wash you-know-where and then, y'know, there and there. And all around there. And under. And around. Carefully. Both of them. And across a bit. And don't forget the area below your waistline either.

While your clothes are marinading you should get out of the shower and take a little time to clean your teeth and fingernails. It is advisable not to use the same brush for both but if you must, at least remember to rinse it afterwards.

By now your clothes will be thoroughly clean. Hose off the suds, scoop them out of the shower and bring the laundered garments downstairs to the kitchen, then switch on the oven at 200 degrees (gas mark 4). Place your clothes inside and close the door. Do please remember that you have turned the dryer on, however. And don't leave them in there too long. Nothing can ruin an enjoyable evening like the abject realization that you are wearing toasted underpants.

Ironing should only be attempted when absolutely necessary; for example when you've run out of money to buy new clothes. But do remember, in these ecologically aware times, that is always good to conserve energy. There is no need at all to iron an entire shirt. Simply iron the front (which is all people actually see) and then make sure you leave your jacket on for the night. Should you find yourself in circumstances where you have to take it off, you're doing well enough for her not to mind your lack of ironing skills. I mean, why would she mind? You're paying her, aren't you?

CLEANING THE BEDROOM

It doesn't matter what you do in the bedroom as long as you don't do it in the street and frighten the horses.
Mrs Patrick Campbell, a female impersonator.

As an Irish Male your bedroom is tremendously important, since you will be spending a lot of time alone in there.

The British conceptual artist Tracy Emin recently exhibited a work called 'My Bed' complete with grubby undergarments, used contraceptives, vodka bottles and overflowing ashtrays all strewn around like snuff at a wake. The installation aroused a good deal of controversy in the British tabloid press, which is of course a bastion of taste in matters artistic: (PHWOARRR!! TOPLESS TEENAGE DEBBIE ON PAGE 3 INSIDE! WOOF!)

Yet when I visited the Tate Gallery to view the contentious piece, frankly I found it pretty tame. In fact, Ms Emin's scratcher made my own look like something out of a horror film, encouraging me to apply to the British Arts Council for an almost offensively large grant.

One important thing to remember about bedroom maintenance is that sheets are not entirely necessary for the traditional Irish Male. But if he can afford them, they do come in handy for when he wants to blow his nose in the night. (Although blankets, being that bit more absorbent, are even better suited for that, indeed for bodily evacuations generally.) If you do have sheets, they should be changed before they become so crispy you might actually cut yourself on them.

It is also important to make a little effort with the marital bed itself, since that is where you will be celebrating one of the most sacred rituals of life, that magical, beautiful, spiritual activity without which none of us would even be here.

That's right. Eating.

A wide variety of healthy and nourishing foods may easily be enjoyed in the Irish Male's bed, such as toast, peanuts, bacon sandwiches, jelly and ice-cream. But it is important not to be slobbish about it: a couple of pillows make an acceptable table, and your wife's nightdress will do as a serviette. The space between the headboard and the wall is the ideal place for refuse disposal, though under the bed itself will also suffice. Meanwhile the best way to deal with crumby sheets is to turn them over repeatedly so that the maggots eat through from both sides, giving a not unattractive 'lace' effect which would cost you a lot of money in an up-market store. Finally, smoking in bed is a disgusting habit. It should be completely avoided unless you use a convenient glass or shoe as an ashtray.

Always remember that it is just as easy to keep your bedroom tidy as it is to have it a horrible mess. That may sound unbelievable — in fact, it is — but with just a little effort it can be done.

Little things are important here. The chest of drawers is a handy place for storing beer cans, while your wife's wardrobe may be used as a comfortable home for your golf-bag, snooker cue, fishing rods or mistress. The dressing table is another useful piece of furniture, provided you take the time to drape clothes, newspapers and football banners over it, adding a lively splash of colour to what would otherwise be aesthetically dull. Use your imagination! Be all you can be!

But the best way to keep the bedroom neat is to make a regular time for that purpose, at least once a week, and then stick to it. (The plan, I mean.) Bring a sweeping brush or vacuum cleaner into the bedroom. Open your wardrobe and shoo away the bats. Then pick up all your clothes from the floor and stuff them into the wardrobe, rolled into a neat ball. Next, wedge the wardrobe door closed with the sweeping brush or vacuum cleaner extension and exit the room as quickly as possible.

You see? It's easy when you try.

CLEANING THE BATHROOM OF AN IRISH MALE

This passage has been removed by order of the County Court, under the provisions of the Offenses Against Common Decency (Toilet Humour, Puerile) Act, 1922, His Honour Chief Justice McPayola presiding, ipso facto, a priori *and* inter-milan.

CLEANING THE REST OF THE HOUSE

The first question is, should you really bother? Why not just go out a lot? And if you must come home, why not sleep in your garden? Or in a builder's skip at the end of the road?

I know people believe domestic hygiene is important, but then people once believed all sorts of patently absurd things, such as the world was flat, there were monsters in the sea and the Labour Party was capable of transforming Irish society along broadly socialist lines. Let us look at the actual facts of the matter.

Dusting is a completely pointless activity as it merely moves particles of dust from one surface to another, thereby making them angry. And an angry piece of dust is a dangerous piece of dust. Just leave it alone and it won't hurt you.

Polishing, window-cleaning, floor-scrubbing and carpet-beating are all bourgeois fripperies which should be avoided. They can make you weak, blind or mad. Excessive indulgence can even give you warts on the palms of your hands.

As for dirt, please bear in mind that you would have to eat a mound of it before it would do you any real harm.

Believe me. I know.

My drinking companion, the late Quentin Crisp, never in thirty years cleaned the Manhattan apartment in which he lived and in which I so often rested my own weary ego. He used to say that if you leave dirt alone for a period of four years it doesn't really get any worse. But I think he was wrong. I think it actually gets better.

There is a sound scientific basis for this theory, but the mainstream media is too scared to report it. In the bachelor flat of the traditional Irish Male, little Irish filth-microbes are born every day, in the carpets, in the cushions, in the bed and the sink. And what do they eat? That's right. *Big* filth-microbes that are too fat and ungainly to run away. Logical isn't it? So allowing your dwelling to be remain in a state of perpetual putrescence means that nothing gets the chance to grow *too* dangerous, while simultaneously you support an ecologically valuable life-system. An admirable policy in these green times.

Yes, the best thing to do with dirt is not to worry about it very much. It is a completely natural product which contains much that is probably quite good for you; if you had to buy it, it would cost you a packet, and if you think nobody would ever buy actual dirt, look at the millions of people who buy records by S-Club 7.

Stop worrying and learn to love the dirt. I know I did. And I've never looked back.

GRIME AND PUNISHMENT

If you can't stand the heat, get out of the kitchen.

Harry S Truman, 28 April 1952 (to an eskimo).

May terrors lurk in the Irish Male's kitchen, not all of them actual quadrupeds.

Let us begin by considering the sink. You can successfully avoid having to wash dishes at all by eating only takeaway food, which comes these days in many tasty varieties not all of which will give you Mad Cow Disease or Botulism. Another popular dining option with the typical Irish Male is the pre-cooked snack. These may be purchased in many health-food outlets such as late-night petrol stations on the nearby dual-carriageway. They come in a variety of exciting flavours and taste-sensations including monosodium glutamate, Kreutzvelt Jacob Syndrome and barbecued listeria with genetically modified sauce.

There are three basic criteria for purchasing a nourishing pre-cooked snack (a) it should come in a plastic tray (b) it should be capable of preparation by merely adding hot water

— from the tap if you can't be bothered to fill the kettle (c) the container must be capable of being used as an ashtray.

If you must do your own home cooking — and I would strongly advise against it — do remember that if you buy *tinned* foods you don't actually have to use pots or pans at all. Simply jemmy open the can and sit it in the gas flame. Bingo! An eye-watering meal in minutes.

A good rule-of-thumb is to clean the kitchen whenever you think there is something actually living in the plumbing, or at the first signs of light fungal growth on the linoleum. 'Scuttling' sounds from under the floorboards are not always mice, but often quite harmless poltergeists which will only make your property more valuable, particularly to the burgeoning Irish film industry. Many's the home of an Irish Male has been made happy by the patter of tiny feet.

The fridge is an area that can cause great difficulty. Who knows what unspeakable terrors lurk behind that white door? Well, *you* don't, you fool; you haven't opened it for weeks. What are the tell-tell signs that you should? Well, if you notice that buzzards have been landing in the front garden and trying to peck their way through the windows, it is a safe bet that the fridge really does need to be emptied. Get an industrial flame-thrower, open the fridge door and stand well back. If nothing jumps out and savages you, begin clearing out your fridge, being careful not to inhale too deeply. If something is trying to chew its way out of a milk carton, please proceed with GREAT CAUTION.

When planning to give the rest of your kitchen a spring-clean, it is best to form a systematic plan and stick to it rigidly. Proceed in calm, logical steps. For example:

a) Put some very loud punk-rock on the stereo.

b) Firmly grasp the vacuum cleaner, sweeping brush or mop.

c) Using the vacuum cleaner, sweeping brush or mop as a

microphone stand, pretend that you are Johnny Rotten.

d) Do this repeatedly, until you are quite tired.

e) Get back into bed with a bottle of gin.

f) Pull the covers over your head.

g) Next day put your house on the market.

AT THE SUPERMARKET

*What peaches and what penumbras! Whole families shopping
at night! Aisles full of husbands! Wives in the avocados,
babies in the tomatoes! — and you, Garcia Lorca what were
you doing down by the watermelons?*

Alan Ginsberg *A Supermarket in California*

Many Irish Males find the supermarket an extremely
frightening challenge, but with a little counselling and
coaching their fears can be overcome.

The main thing to remember is this: women tend to make a
lot of unnecessary fuss about grocery shopping, allowing
themselves to become neurotically fixated on the search for
completely unnecessary things such as protein, nutrients,
essential minerals and vitamins. The old-fashioned belief that
such luxuries were needed for healthy development has
recently been discredited by the results of important new
research.

All major foodstuffs can be broken into four basic
categories, each of which is vital for the traditional Irish Male
to enjoy a truly balanced diet. Here they are:

Crisps.

Pizza.

Beer.

Cigarettes.

Each of these health-giving items may be found in the local
supermarket at a fraction of the amount it would cost in your

usual provisions-shopping place, *viz*, a night-club.

Another dimension to supermarket shopping must be briefly considered. People say the supermarket is a good place to meet and have interesting encounters with young professional women. In my own case that has often turned out to be true. (But more and more store-detectives are men these days.)

The supermarket is also a very good place to keep yourself informed about contemporary events. Here at the checkout counter you can find fascinating publications like *The National Enquirer* with many important stories that the mainstream media is totally afraid to cover such as FIVE-TON WOMAN ATE MY VOLKSWAGEN, FACE OF MOTHER TERESA APPEARED IN MY CORNFLAKES and KURT COBAIN FOUND ALIVE ON JUPITER. (The last is from the *Daily Express*.)

And finally, a little joke. Why is a shopping trolley unlike an Irish Male? Because a shopping trolley has a mind of its own. Ho ho ho.

COOKING

Heaven sends us good meat, but the Devil sends cooks.

David Garrick *On Doctor Goldsmith*

Food preparation is another activity which is all too frequently mythologised. Honest to God, from the way people like so-called TV superchef Jamie Oliver go on about it, you would swear there was more to cooking than opening a tin, incinerating the contents and using an old screwdriver to scrape them off the pan. And no, I am NOT jealous of Jamie Oliver just because all the women fancy him.

I have travelled the world and consulted with many of the leading international chefs — i.e. NOT Jamie Oliver — and my researches have led me to an inescapable conclusion: they don't know a bloody THING about horse-racing.

But all would concur on the following point: the one important secret of really great cooking is to actively seek out:

(a) tasty, nourishing and above all FRESH ingredients.

or

(b) a girlfriend.

So if *(b)* is not a viable option, and let us not be foolishly optimistic, here is a simple recipe of my own devising:

Irish Male Stew

(Bourginon de l'homme Irlandaise)

serves one

1. Buy a selection of tasty, nourishing and above all FRESH ingredients.
2. Place them in a pot of boiling water (i.e., water that bubbles).
3. Season lightly to taste.
4. Return to boil and simmer.
5. While mixture is cooking under a high flame, switch on television and watch snooker/'Robot Wars'/old episode of 'Baywatch,' while consuming half-bottle of Scotch (ice cubes optional).
6. Wait for smoke to start billowing from kitchen.
7. Tug semi-molten pot off gas-ring to which it has adhered.
8. Throw whole ghastly mess over garden wall.
9. Open packet of crisps.
10. Serve with garnish of chilled beer and freshly lit cigarette.

Et voila!

Tasty, nourishing and not at all expensive. Jamie Oliver, eat my shorts.

But seriously, it is important that we Irish Males try to become a little more health-conscious these days. So do remember that frying your food in rancid lard is a highly effective way of killing harmful germs. Excessive grilling is another healthy technique. Incidentally, please also remember *never* to wash your grill. Congealed fat and solidified grease add a not unpleasant aftertaste to many dishes and have the added benefit of providing a protective coating which dangerous microbes find difficult to penetrate. Another extra advantage of the rigorously uncleaned grill is the constant possibility of being treated to that glory of the Irish Male kitchen, the spontaneous *flambée*. WHOOOOOOSHHHH!!!!! Nothing can get your dinner parties, not to mention your eyebrows, going like that one!

Light stir-frying is best avoided. It tends to leave vegetables a bit raw — or *al dente* as it is known in the trade (after Alfonse D'Entée, the inventor of Hard Cheese; also Cowardy-Cowardy Custard). Raw food of any description is highly toxic to the Irish Male. His stomach secretes a unique enzyme called alphasider which enables him only to process vegetation that has been boiled down to a watery pulp just like the Mammy used to make with the turnips of a Sunday.

Try to keep an eye on the booze. Nobody wants to be a bore about this, and hey, we all make mistakes sometimes. We're only human, after all, and it's easy to fall into bad habits. But when dealing with a powerful stimulant like alcohol which works by attacking the central nervous system and inducing a spurious feeling of well-being, do try to act like a responsible grown-up and BUY YOUR BLOODY ROUND!

Always remember, if you have eight beers the size of your brain actually shrinks. That's the bad news. The good news is that it makes Jamie Oliver seem somehow attractive. (Not that I am jealous in ANY way.)

Mineral water is a lot more pure than the vile chemical-filled stuff which gushes from the taps. Use Evian or Ballygowan in the ice-cubes for your favourite methylated-spirits cocktail or home-produced moonshine.

Fresh fruit, pulses and dairy products should be avoided; as should anything unprocessed, unpreserved, unsweetened or lacking in unsaturated fats. Take it from me — you just can't trust 'em.

If in doubt, the simple rule is: never eat anything that didn't once have a face.

Root crops, tomatoes and other nourishing vegetables should be eaten only when you have run out of jelly, and even then only after vigorous frying. By the way, a handy way to avoid that nasty 'stinging eye' sensation when peeling onions is always to peel them under water. But do remember your sub-aqua equipment.

Finally a serious word of warning. It is a well-known fact that muesli is particularly bad for you. In a recent experiment at the Higher University of Mannheim, Germany, human subjects who ate a strict diet of muesli and other rabbit food all developed such disturbing features as red eyes, hopping around and wanting to fuck a lot.

Your average engineering student, basically.

SOME TOP TIPS FOR THE GARDEN

Such was that happy garden-state
While man there walked without a mate.

Andrew Marvell *The Garden*

It is lovely to have a well-kept and restful garden.
But you don't.
And you never bloody will.

It is probably best just to try and accept this. I don't mean to be defeatist, but come on, let's face it — gardens simply weren't *meant* for people like you. People like you don't even have *window boxes*.

Get a grip on yourself, man. Are you losing it or something? God invented gardens for people who are creative, thoughtful, sensitive and profound. People who enjoy the heady aromas of nature. People who enjoy feeding tiny little birdies. That just ISN'T YOU. I mean *dream on, bud*.

You are a man in whom shallowness runs deep. The only time you've ever fed tiny little birdies was when you were feeding them to your pet python Lemmy. You have better things to be doing than gardening, such as nothing. So go on, sod off back inside the house.

Oh, and by the way — don't bother cutting the grass. It'll only grow again when your back is turned.

PAYING THE DOMESTIC BILLS

A man doubtful of his dinner or trembling at a creditor is not much disposed to abstracted meditation.

Samuel Johnson *Lives of the English Poets*

There are two simple rules to remember when it comes to household finance.

a) Everything will always cost more than you thought.

b) Your income will always be less than you deserve.

But do try to bear in mind that bills are not always a bad thing. 'One must have some sort of occupation nowadays,' wrote Oscar Wilde. 'If I hadn't my debts I shouldn't have anything to think about.'

Yes, it must be conceded that bills are an inescapable part of life. And it is good to act like a responsible grown-up. So ALWAYS query EVERY bill. This is both good mental training and an agreeable leisure activity. Write back to the grasping meanies saying that you weren't in the country, that you have lost your mind, that you actually died two years ago and were cremated abroad. It won't always work — though it sometimes will — but it is usually a good delaying tactic.

Remember when dealing with people like bankers: if you owe them a grand, you are in trouble. If you owe them four million, *they* are in trouble. Try telling them you are a former Irish Prime Minister. After they write off your debt in full, they will offer you even more of their customers' money for those little necessities like refurbishing your yacht!

If all else fails, and it probably will, I am pleased to recommend the bill-paying method pioneered by the late journalist, Claud Cockburn. Put all your bills into a plastic bag as they arrive. Then, once every three months or so, sit down at your desk and reach lucky-dip style into the bag. Pull out one bill at random and pay that. Dame Fate has an uncanny way of identifying the most urgent priorities, and your child probably doesn't need that expensive ear operation anyway. You don't want to spoil her, after all. This way you are definitely making an effort to honour your debts and nobody can accuse you of being irresponsible.

If the Bank Manager/Credit Card Company/Debt Collection Agency sends you a snotty letter, simply write back explaining the above system. Sign off by saying 'That is the way I pay my bills and if you ever again dare to write me a rude letter, then you, my good man, WILL BE OUT OF THE GAME!'

ENTERTAINING AT HOME

A bishop then must be blameless, the husband of one wife, vigilant, sober, of good behaviour, and given to hospitality.

I Timothy, Chapter 3, Verse 2.

One nice thing about having your own home is inviting your friends around. If you have any friends. Which you probably don't if you are reading this book.

Ah yes, what could be more pleasant than a night spent around the glowing hearth, conversing with a small assortment of trusted old pals? That's right. A lot of things. But those are illegal.

You may feel you acquired some experience at home-entertainment back in the days when you were a student. But a packet of peanuts, ten flagons of shoplifted cider, a violent argument about who is truly more socialist than whom and a drunken punch-up as the dawn rises over Belfield is not everyone's idea of a tasteful soirée.

A little effort will reap rich rewards. Think about your guest list thoroughly. Do not invite:

- anyone you have ever dumped.
- anyone who has ever dumped *you*.
- either of their husbands.

Try also to remember to invite someone of a shy disposition who will volunteer to wash up rather than having to converse.

Use the handy cleaning techniques described above to get your home into reasonable shape. If the rats are actually visible a lot of the time, either kill them (by trapping, poisoning or simply stomping) or try negotiating with them to leave, at least on a temporary basis. They may very well be glad of the break.

Minor vermin such as cockroaches, spiders, flying ants, bluebottles, silverfish and former members of The Eagles are best simply ignored.

Prepare your home for a pleasant evening. Why not steal some flowers from a neighbour's garden and arrange them nicely around the rooms? Your local church will be a good source of candles. Remember — Our Lord helps those who help themselves!

The general ambience of your home is important to get right. Many cleaning and disinfecting products are cheaply available these days — buy some and leave them lying in a prominent place. Your guests will assume you have been cleaning all day in preparation for their visit, particularly if they are drunkards, addicts or rampant egomaniacs.

If you absolutely must, spray a couple of cans of air-freshener around the living room. There is nothing quite like the noxious stink of factory-produced pine to damp down the whiff of rotting carpet or leaking pipes.

Make sure there are fresh towels in the bathroom. Make sure that the toilet is flushing correctly, that there is plenty of hot water, that your pet guppy Ronald has been removed from the bidet. Music can add to the atmosphere of a pleasant, relaxed evening, so do tell everyone to bring along their banjos.

As your guests arrive, take their coats and put them in the bedroom. (The coats, that is. Not the guests.) This simple, hospitable touch will put your visitors at ease while giving you an excellent opportunity to rifle through their pockets, wallets, etc.

A brief word about nibbles — any old stuff you found in the fridge may be used as *hors-d'oeuvres*. Simply scrape, smear or coax it onto crackers, smother the lot with mayonnaise or cottage cheese and serve quickly at room temperature and arm's length. In the unlikely event that anyone eats them, they will be too polite to actually chunder in your presence. Even if they do, console yourself with the happy thought that you have put the hospital back into hospitality.

As host, it is your job to keep the conversation going. Try to remember to ask a lot of questions. If nothing else, this is a good way to stop people asking them of *you*.

And finally — sex at the dinner table should always be avoided. It is terribly rude to talk with your mouth full.

The Irish Male — A User's Manual

*All tragedies are finished by a death; All comedies are ended
by a marriage; The future states of both are left to faith.*

George Gordon *The Byronic Man*[1]

It was the great Leo Nikolayevich Tolstoy who wrote: 'All
Irish Males can be a pain in the ass; but each Irish Male can be
a pain in the ass *in his own way.*'

Women readers will sadly concur. They will know that
living with an Irish Male is on very rare occasions not the
blissful paradise it customarily is. He is by nature a solitary
beast — really he lives inside his own shell. If the Italian is a
stallion, the Irishman is a tortoise. (Witness his remarkable
fondness for hibernation, especially on mornings when the
bins must be taken out.) Not that there is anything wrong with
that either, for as devotees of the fabulous Aesop can attest,
even the tortoise may gain in the end. Mainly by cheating and
lying, but that's another story.

But yes, the Irish Male finds it hard to converse in an open
fashion. Compared to him, a brick is eloquent. Thus he finds
sharing his thoughts and emotions almost impossible. This
reticence came home to me forcefully a short time ago when a
close friend I have known since my difficult childhood
confessed that he had fallen passionately in love with me. 'But
you can't be gay,' I said in amazement. 'We used to go out to
night-clubs together looking for girls.'

'Jesus,' he said. 'I thought we were dating.'

You see what I mean? The Irish Male does not notice silent
signals. His social antennae are not finely tuned. Misunderstanding is the sea through which he haplessly paddles, with

---

[1] As famously played by Lee Majors in the 1970s' TV show.

only his bafflement and incomprehension for armbands.

If confusion and lack of empathy were his only real crimes, the Irish Male might reasonably ask for the benefit of the emotional probation-act. But alas, there are several more additions to the charge-sheet. When it comes to the business of courtship, for example, the Irish Male has a lot to learn. It isn't that he is unromantic, as such. It is just that your average Irishman, when pursuing a woman, is a bit like a dog chasing after a car. He wouldn't really know what to do if she stopped. (Perhaps sink away in dejection and pee against a lamp-post.) Yes, as they age, they gain a bit of experience. It is a well-known fact that older Irishmen can keep matters going for longer in bed. But then again, when you really think about it, who wants to shag an old man for a long time?

So, Ladies, if you must live with an Irish Male — and please do ask yourself whether there are not real alternatives, such as emigration, lesbian separatism or entering a convent — there are a few points which are well worth remembering.

Being an Irish Male myself, I forget them all. But here are some I made up earlier.

1) The Irish Male Is Always Right

It is a surprising but well-established biological fact that the part of an Irish Male's brain which admits to making mistakes (the *cortex maximus apologeticus*) actually shrinks during early adolescence, finally disappearing around the age of fifteen. How this happens we don't quite know — and obviously if we did we wouldn't tell YOU — but by his mid-teens the cortex has been entirely replaced by the frontal rationalization lobe and the cranial utter-denial node (*cerebellia non mea culpa, honestus*). Parents can tell this has begun to happen to their teenage sons when they start saying things like 'It wasn't my fault I burned down the school' or 'I know I tattooed the baby, but she was asking for it'.

As the Irish Male achieves what is euphemistically called maturity, a new sponge-like tissue called the evasionary gland develops (*glandus irresponsibilius et molto stupidissima*) until it fills almost half the cranial cavity by the late-twenties. (Its growth seems to become much more pronounced immediately after mating.) Again, there are a number of tell-tale verbal signs, e.g. 'Look, I don't see what we're doing as *going out* together, as such. We're just having a large number of consecutive one-night stands.' Or 'All right, so I slept with your mother and showed the photographs to my friends, but I only did it twice and it didn't mean anything.'

For an Irish Male at this stage of development to admit he might be wrong is to concede that the world is fundamentally flawed, that God is dead and life is pointless. It would be a statement of existential failure. It is something that simply *cannot* happen. For him to fess up to even a minor error, such as stealing your wages or selling your underwear to perverts over the Internet, would mean this goodly frame we call the earth would spin off its axis and out into interstellar space. Yes, by now he is a believer in the wise maxim first coined by the great novelist Eric Segal (brother of Jonathan Livingstone Segal) — 'Love means never admitting you're sorry.' Or something like that.

As the years roll on, the evasionary gland swells even further. By the time the Irish Male is thirty, it will have expanded to fill his whole head, resulting in his widely noted inability to listen. It's not that he doesn't *want* to listen, it's just that his ears are under severe pressure. By now he is biologically programmed. for utter pomposity and self-righteousness and may even have embarked on a career in the church or literary criticism. Once this happens there is really no cure, although a stake through the heart at a crossroads at midnight may be worth an attempt.

So now you women can see why we Irishmen have a

problem admitting we're wrong. That's right. It's not our fault. In fact it's probably yours. So really, you should show a bit more understanding. We Irish Males are victims of our own biology. And it isn't as though we're not making an effort. Take myself, for example. I often point out to my wife that whenever I *am* wrong I immediately admit it. It is just that I am never wrong. But even if I were, I would be *right* to be wrong. And she would be wrong for questioning that. And I would be right to point that out. And she would be wrong if she didn't agree. And we find this approach works quite well for us. At least we did, until she divorced me.

2) The Irish Male Is Fond Of Cursing

OK, OK, you have a point here. If they took the four-letter words out of the English language most Irishmen would be f**king speechless. But this love of effing and beeing shouldn't be taken too seriously. It is only a form of affectionate punctuation.

I remember once being in a pub in Dublin — all the other times I don't remember at all — where I witnessed an extraordinary scene. A man was sitting alone at the bar, deep in mystical contemplation of his pint, when the door opened and another fellow, bedecked from head to toe in black, entered the premises unobserved by the former. The new arrival crept up to My Nabs at the bar and quickly tapped him thrice on the shoulder. The philosopher turned, a smile of surprise and delight playing about his lips.

'Would yeh FOOK OFF, yeh fat fooker-yeh,' he happily cried. 'I haven't seen yeh in BLAYDIN AGES!'

Only in Ireland do men greet each other thus. Although even making allowances for local cultural idiosyncrasies, I thought it was a bit much to talk to an Archbishop like that.

3) You Will Never *Ever* Compete With His Mammy

Look at her, the fossilised old reptile. You hate her, don't you? With a pure, clean, WHITE-HOT kind of hatred. Look at her thoughtfully stroking her beard. Making little comments about the dinner you've cooked. Sitting there in her Christmas party hat. Frightening the children. Frightening the *dog*.

Hallelujah.

Behold — His Mother.

God in heaven, look at the state of it. Face like a bag of rusting spanners. You wouldn't say she was ugly exactly but last time you saw her she had potato-sacks over two of her heads.

And it's *ALL HER FAULT*, what you have to put up with. It was she who raised your so-called husband to be the incapable dweeb he is. She's as bonkers as he is anyway. Bloody madwoman. Treacherous COW! When she finally dies, there'll be one minute's violence. Smile at her. Offer her some gravy. That's right, have some more, you vile ugly hippo. Oh? You think it's a bit lumpy, do you? Dear, oh dear. How very sad.

You hope it bloody CHOKES her, the vicious troglodyte.

Remember the second time you went out with him? What did he say when you asked him back for coffee? That's right.

'Oh … urm … The Mammy wouldn't like it.'

'I wasn't asking your Mammy,' you pointed out.

That was your first-ever row, wasn't it?

Look at her, the evil conniving baggage. Pretending she 'doesn't really drink' when she'd get down on all fours and suck the amontillado out of the shag-pile if you spilled a drop. Remember how she ruined your wedding day? Had to be the centre of attention, didn't she? Had to have everything her own way, despite the fact that *you* paid! Because he — her useless, brainless GOM of a son — spent all his wedding savings on *gravelling her driveway*.

You know she gives out about you behind your back, don't you? When he's driving her home, when he's taking her shopping, when he's painting her house, when he's mowing her lawn. She doesn't like how you bring up the kids. Doesn't like the shirts you buy him. Doesn't like the fact that you work. Doesn't like ANYTHING, EVER.

And you know what's coming next, right? Oh yes you do, come on, don't pretend. *He wants her to come and live with you!* Yes, he's been building up to it, bit by bit. You know that sneaky way he goes on, the low coward. Can't bear to say it out like a man, just tries the occasional pluck on your heartstrings. How she 'isn't that bad when you get to know her'. How you'd 'have to laugh at the way she goes on'. How lonely she feels now his father is gone, kicking around by herself in that house full of memories. (Not that his father's *dead* or anything. He's just bloody GONE. And who could blame him?)

Well she can get a bloody tenant in, because she's not coming here. No WAY. Over your dead body. You'll even help her put the ad in the paper. You've thought up the wording already. ROOM MATE WANTED — MUST BE HEAVY SLEEPER WITH POOR SENSE OF SMELL.

Oh? Surprise, surprise. She doesn't like the way you've done the parsnips. Go on. Pick up the turkey and *brain* her with it. The judge will understand. You'll get time off for good behaviour. Go on. Right in the kisser. You know you want to. Yes. Do it now. *DRUMSTICK THE WITCH!!*

4) The Irish Male Believes He Is Good At DIY

You know the story. You have seen it unfold.

Normally your adult Irish Male cannot be roused to vacate the sofa, except if the house is actually on fire. If he gets off his backside to dander down the end of the garden, he nearly sends you a postcard saying WISH YOU WERE HERE.

But once in a while, a strange thing happens to him — do not argue, it is the call of the wild. There is nothing you can do, this is something quite primal. (It is often brought on by the vernal equinox.) He will start expressing a frightening desire to repair or refurbish things around the house. If that occurs, and it almost certainly will, you should move children or pets off the property immediately.

Yes, you are confused, and you are right to be. He knows nothing at all about manual labour and precious little about labour of any kind. The phrase 'Good With His Hands' was not coined for this man. (Not in *any* sense, if you know what I mean.) But all of a sudden he is rummaging around in the garage for a hammer, borrowing a bricklayer's hod from a chap across the road, speaking with the authoritativeness of Isambard Kingdom Brunel about joists and flanges and lengths of four-by-two.

You point out that you only need that dodgy bookshelf in the living room straightened. Really you can do it yourself. But look at him, the monster, as he reaches for his spirit level. Observe the patronisingly understanding smile. 'If a job is worth doing, dear, it's worth doing properly. So off you toddle and make me a sandwich. And don't be worrying your pretty little head. This' — he brandishes his tool — 'is MEN'S WORK.'

Away to the kitchen you retreat with the children. You try to distract them but the poor wains are crying. The terrible thudding, the whine of the drill, the shrieks, imprecations and dark Satanic oaths — it keeps them awake for several nights; you would swear he was building the ark in there. Finally, a week later, he flings open the door. Bruised, bleeding, bog-eyed with exhaustion, his arm in a tourniquet improvised from a cushion-cover, he looks like he has undergone ten rounds with Mike Tyson.

'Woe-man,' he grunts. 'Must come. See my work. Ungh.'

You enter what used to be your living room. There is a large star-shaped hole in the gable wall. The ceiling has collapsed and the carpet is in shreds. A drumlin of rubble has obliterated the sofa. The floorboards have been ripped up to serve as scaffolding. Water is gushing down the chimney. You have bribed the children not to cry, but when they see the devastation they just can't hold back. By now he is standing beside the bookshelf, fingering his spanners and screwdrivers and pliers. He raises the drill and coolly blows on the bit-end — the gunslinger who drove Wild Bill from the town.

'That's a nice piece of work if I say so myself,' he avers. 'And when you think of all the money we've saved.' He runs his fingertips lightly along the shelf. It immediately collapses, sending the Waterford Glass bowl you inherited from your grandmother into a spin across the room, where it shatters into a thousand shards, one of which takes an eye out of the cat.

'Of course,' he continues, 'the drill was defective. And anyway, Tiddles had it fucking coming.'

5) The Irish Male Knows All About Packing

This is the source of many a domestic altercation, but in fairness the Irish Male can't be blamed for it all. His female companion is equally guilty, if not more so. *(See Section 1 — He Is Never Wrong.)*

When presented with the prospect of vacational travel, she feels she must pack every single item of clothing she possesses. It does not matter that you two are going to Majorca in the middle of July. She *needs* those woolen long-johns and tea-cosy hats. And even if she doesn't, *YOU NEVER KNOW*.

Her suitcase is stuffed to bulging point. For even a one-night stay at a wedding down the country the following items will be *sine-qua-non* for the Irish Female: Sandals, dresses, eiderdowns, hats, lotions, potions, mixed emotions, fifteen pairs of shoes, hot-water bottle, make-up, lipstick, tights, socks, intimate garments, sun cream, moisturizer, mosquito repellant, mosquito attractant, diarrhoea pills, cough bottle, whalebone corset, photographs of chidden, hair of the dog, rub of the relic, complete and unabridged works of my good friend Marian Keyes.

The Irish Male, on the other hand, tends towards the opposite extreme. He is by nature a light traveller. On a four-year expedition up the Amazon he would take along a change of socks and a copy of *The Racing Post*. And he mightn't even bother with the change of socks.

Here, as in all things, compromise is the solution. Simply agree never to go on holiday. It is far too stressful and not worth the money.

6) The Irish Male Will Not Communicate Openly

Even his stoutest defenders will concede that communication of deep emotion is something at which the Irish Male does not excel (except about beer). He is a person of many strengths and qualities — although just at this moment I can't think of any of them — but in the great Eurovision of emotional openness the Irish Male tends to score *nul points*.

Here is an all-too-typical scenario. The Irish Male will come in from the pub, sit down and immediately switch on the television. For him, the television has replaced the traditional hearth of his infancy. Note how he actually holds his hands out towards it and rubs them together.

His unfortunate wife glances across from her book and says 'Well, Dear, how was the pub tonight?' But by now he has found a tremendously important football match (Falkland Islands vs. Chad Reserves) and is engrossed in it. 'Grand,' he mutters. She looks at him and tries again. 'Any of the usual crowd in?' she enquires brightly.

'Hmm?' he responds, his eyes focused intensely on the

screen, as though he would actually burst into flame were he even to blink.

'I asked who was there? Anyone interesting?'

'… Where?'

'In the pub of course.'

'Oh … Mickser Mulligan.'

'Oh great. How's the bould Mickser these days?'

'Grand.'

'He's out of the Mental Hospital then?'

'Yeah.'

'And he's in good form?'

'He's grand.'

'He's not too upset? About his father?'

'Hmm?'

'You know, about his father becoming a transvestite? Going around the shopping centre in a ballgown and telling everyone to call him Victoria Beckham?'

'He's grand.'

'That was all he said for the whole night, was it?'

'Hmm?'

'That he's grand?'

'Basically.'

'But you were out for six hours. He must have said something more than that surely?'

'Not really. [*burp*] But he's … [*shrug*] … y'know … .he's grand.'

You try to read another page of your novel. Really you should just let matters lie, but you find yourself determined not to be defeated this time. You look up at him again — the father of your children. He has his paw thrust down the front of his trousers, thoughtfully scratching his flute as he ogles the screen.

'How's that wooden leg he had to have fitted after the accident?'

'Hmm?'

'You know. When the psychopathic crocodile attacked him.'

'Oh. It's grand.'

'Is that really all you have to say to me?'

'Hmm?'

'That everything's grand.'

'Well … everything *is* grand though … isn't it?'

'Don't you ever feel like opening up?'

'Opening up what, pet?'

'I mean, you know … sharing your needs? Your inner desires?'

'Whoah, *FANTASTIC* save! Ah, come ON, ref, are yeh bleedinwell BLIND?'

'Because I really feel we don't talk enough any more. In fact, I've been thinking about filing for a divorce. And you may as well know I've been sleeping with Mr Delaney from the butcher's shop for six months and he says he want to move to Bermuda with me and the kids.'

'Mmm … Any chance of a cuppa there, love?'

Women can get upset about this kind of thing. But then women are biologically programmed to see slights where none are intended. They simply don't understand the basic facts about men. For example, there is really no point in asking an Irish Male to share his feelings with you because a lot of the time he doesn't have any. Frankly put, he couldn't be arsed. Like a small confused semi-extinct woodland creature he is quite content just to mullock along, unencumbered by any emotion that does not involve his belly or adjacent areas. Feelings would only get in the way of his happiness. He doesn't need them. He can't afford the luxury.

In his ground-breaking study 'Towards A Psychology of Being' (1962) the great psychologist Abraham Maslow expounded his theory of 'the hierarchy of prepotency' as a means of explaining human motivations. Observing that 'man is a wanting animal' he argued that 'one desire is no sooner satisfied than another takes its place'. To give his theory graphic force, he famously represented human needs as a pyramid. At the broad bottom of the triangle he placed absolutely essential physical requirements such as shelter, food, water and warmth. Higher up the narrowing pyramid he represented the higher yearnings, such as love of beauty, appreciation of the arts, spiritual awareness and so forth, leading finally to the apex — complete self-actualization. But Maslow ran into trouble when attempting to apply his theories to the Irish Male. Indeed, as he wrote to a renowned colleague, Dr Rollo May, on 9 June, 1948: … 'even my "Human Pyramid" itself becomes totally inadequate to explain the basic components which the Irish Male requires for a fulfilled existence. I believe, old friend, that I shall have to construct another diagram, especially for him.'

Sadly Maslow died before he could publish his research on Irishmen. But here, for the first time, is his previously unknown representation of Irish Male needs, which the great scholar labelled 'The Irishman's Christmas Tree':

Beer.

The lads. The Mammy.

Sandwiches. Sky Sports. Occasional ride.

Pub football team. Clean pair of drawers of a Monday.

Old re-runs of Starksy and Hutch. Acute and frequent hypochondria.

Porn stash under the floorboards.

The budgie

The dog

The kids

Navel fluff

Oh yeah … the wife [1]

---

[1] Reproduced by kind permission from the forthcoming *Towards A Psychology of Being an Irish Male*, Harvard University Press, Emeritus Professor Carl Jung (at heart), Ed.

(7) The Irish Male Can Be Sarcastic.
OK, I admit it.

But I like people who are sarcastic. I don't know why. Yes, sarcasm is the lowest form of wit, but if you think about it, the individuals who tell you this so confidently usually don't possess *any* form of wit. The people who tell you this usually think that politicians who are rabidly opposed to asylum seekers 'have a point really, when you think about it' and worse, that 'at least they're stimulating debate'. Stimulating bloody debate! As though *that* excuses anything. Good God. If Hitler had only thought to say he invaded Poland 'to stimulate debate' his face would be on the Euro now.

But anyway. As the Third Epistle of Saint Michael to the Jaggeraguans tells us, 'You can't always get what you want. But if you try sometimes, you can get what you need.' So it is with humour. Some kinds are better than others. Yes, a brilliantly Wildean epigram incorporating a series of multilingual puns and several allusions to Greek mythology is what we must aim for at all times. But no power in the world has quite the devastating force of a simple 'Oh yeah, really' delivered at just the right moment and with just the right degree of sceptical detachment.

Think about it. For example, when His Holiness, Pope John Paul II, told us young people of Ireland that he loved us, if we had all chanted back in one great big sarcastic roar 'OH YEAH, *SURE* YOU DO' instead of bursting into a spontaneous chorus of 'He's Got The Whole World In His Hands', the course of modern Irish history would have been radically changed. (Those were more innocent days, of course, when the whole world was *all* we suspected leading churchmen had in their hands.)

I remember, when I was much younger, going out with a girl who was never sarcastic. It was great. Well, no it wasn't, I'm being sarcastic. We would enter some dubious pub where the glasses had not been cleaned in several centuries, where the clientele was so cheesy it could have been melted down and spread on toast, where the malodorous barman looked like he shaved regularly with a piece of sandpaper — in fact there was more toilet paper hanging from his chin than there was in the men's jacks. I would say, 'Wow, this is a bit of a palace, isn't it?' And she would say, 'God, really? You reckon? I think it's pretty disgusting actually.'

For a while I think I must have found this charming. Sometimes when we fall in love, what we are attracted to is the seemingly artless public display of qualities we could never dream of acquiring ourselves. Perhaps I was still in that phase of retarded adolescence where the dream of being, y'know, a complete person, still held some kind of spurious validity. I was attracted to this woman because she 'believed' in things I didn't. Like 'nature'. We would be strolling down the street and she would start going on about flowers, leaves, little birdies, dogshit, the planet, etcetera. I would start going on, sarcastically I must admit, about how little birdies should be hollowed out and turned into carpet slippers. And she would laugh. And I would be more sarcastic. And that was how we related to each other.

After a time, though, her innocent sincerity, her total lack of sarcasm, started to drive me screaming mad. We would be sitting there skulling into a take-away vindaloo and watching 'George and Mildred' on the telly (yes, I know how to show a gal a good time). Then said dismal sitcom would end and I'd say 'Bleedin *hilarious*, huh?' to which she would smile sweetly and respond 'I didn't think it was funny at all really'. And at that point I would start chewing the nearest light-bulb.

The poor girl. We would sit up late at night discussing 'God', a fictional character whose many exploits she was fond of relating. At this stage I had honed my sarcasm to the point where I could dismiss millennia-old belief systems with a scarcely discernible raising of one eyebrow. I told myself I looked like Jeremy Paxman, but, actually, I must have looked like a fat Alvin Stardust.

In the end I decided to deal with my sarcasm by being more open about my emotions. I confronted her, saying 'Listen, I know I'm sarcastic sometimes, but really you mean an awful lot to me'. She smiled and said she was breaking it off with me anyway, to take up with some Aran-wearing ornithologist geek she'd met at a born-again Christian prayer meeting. A charismatic, she said. Reader, let me tell you candidly, I had thought hurling was a Gaelic sport until that moment. I mean, you should have MET this guy. How anyone could use the adjective 'charismatic' about him is still, after all these years, a mystery which for me is right up there with the Blessed Trinity. But anyway. There I go being sarcastic again. One of these days I better try to give it up.

Yeah. Right. Sure I will.

The Irish-Male Companion to Great Sex

*I have made love to ten thousand women since I was thirteen-
and-a-half. But it wasn't a vice. I needed to communicate.*

George Simenon

Ten Top Tips for Meeting Girls

Throughout my long years of unstinting public service I have received many letters from concerned disciples about the burning questions of our time. What is the actual point of existence? Why is there only one Monopolies Commission? Why do people send flowers to a funeral? (Well what did you expect? *FRUIT?*)

But the contents of my mailbag — when you removed the envelopes stuffed with death threats — were usually concerned with one important subject.

Girls.

How do you meet them? How do you understand them? How do you cope with their funny little ways? Why do they go to the bathroom in large groups? Are men from Mars? Are women from Venus? If so, where is the artist formerly known as Prince from?

Well, one doesn't mean to blow one's own tuba, but I have had my fair share of success when courting the ladies. (Not for nothing was my nickname 'the *supreme* court'.) And in the dance of romance I have learned something vital: when dealing with women, it is a great thing to get on with them. But getting off with them is another matter.

If the latter is what you want to do, here is some sound advice:

1) Use Intelligent, Non-Sexist Chat-Up Lines.

The Irish Male can sometimes let himself down by his failure to master the skills of verbal seduction. Gone are the days when 'I have a farm and most of my teeth' was enough to make women want to gratefully marry you. In the modern world a little sophistication is required, but a very small investment will pay rich dividends.

Here are some of my own road-tested favourite chat-up

lines, each an absolute sure-fire winner, particularly when delivered with a rakish leer:

(a) Hello there. May I buy you a drink or would you rather just have the money?

(b) Listen, I don't actually dance myself, but would it be OK if I held on for a few minutes while *you* do?

(c) Hi, I don't believe we've met. I'm Mr Right.

(d) God, I'm relieved that you don't recognize me. It's so nice just to be liked for myself for a change.

(e) If a really cute puppy's life was at stake, would you be willing to spend the night with a man you didn't know?

2) Forget About Physical Beauty.

You should always remember in dating situations that physical beauty is not the most important thing. Strictly speaking it does not actually matter if you have all the appeal of a dog turd in a tank-top. The modern woman will be looking for more valuable things, such as personality, charm, reliability, a good sense of humour, a kind heart and a Mercedes Benz 380SL convertible (with optional CD player).

3) Where To Go On the First Date.

The Irish Male would do well to note that the race-track, snooker hall, bookie's shop or alleyway are not venues conducive to the flowering of love. On this important subject I tend towards the traditional. Take her out for a romantic meal. And make a little effort with the choice of venue. As the great lover Giovanni Casanova (1725-98) reflects in his infamous *Mémoires*: '*Elle n'etait pas tres content si vouz l'invitez pommes frites.*'[1]

If you can possibly afford it, invite her to a really chic restaurant. Here the waiter will greet you with an impressively

---

[1] Literally, 'She will not feel too chipper if you take her to a chipper'.

snide attitude, as though the seam of his bollocks was hand-stitched by Dior. When you sit down you will notice that there is enough cutlery on the table to perform a triple heart by-pass operation. Don't be intimidated. Always remember about knives and forks — these, like seduction, should be approached from the outside, slowly working in.

Order some wine. Take a little time to read the menu carefully. Again, don't panic if you find it confusing. What should you do if it offers such heady delights as 'slivers of blackened wild octopus slowly flailed to death by the commis chef, served on a desiccated bed of arugula and kumquat, drizzled with a reduced *jus* of boar's blood and ostrich tears?'

Order the hamburger.

If you have selected a seafood restaurant, the menu may offer carp, cod, and flounder, not to mention several other fishy verbs so deeply beloved and often embodied by our politicians. If brill is featured, don't have it. I always feel terribly sorry for brill. It must be awful having to live up to a name like that.

When the *sommelier* brings the wine, don't slug it, belch, dribble or spit it out. Take a small delicate sip, roll it around your cheeks for a bit and then say, 'It's an amusing little bastard with obstreperous hints of fruit but I think you'll find its cynicism challenging.'

If your date is still here, give her a smile. Look around. Enjoy the ambience. Don't be put off if the place looks more like an aquarium than a restaurant. This is a sign that you have chosen the venue well. Very elegant people like to see their potential dinner demonstrate its physical prowess by breast-stroking up and down a slime-filled tank. All aspiring sophisticates should get to know the drill. Serge or Gaston reaches a mitt into the murky depths, seizes a wriggling pelagic monster or calloused crustacean and waggles it before your eyes, from which vantage point it promptly grits its teeth and widdles all over you. If it's cashing in its chips anyway, it reckons, it's bloody well going to make a nuisance of itself on the way out.

You, the customer, take a good long decko at the incontinent aquatic beastie, sizing it up, assessing its attractiveness and judging its candidacy for peristalsis. Does it have all the qualities you want in a dinner? A nice even coating of scales, for example? The requisite number of pincers? You lick your lips, and then, if you are very lucky, the lips of the person you are dining with and then — KERTHUNK — dinner is executed.

Some people feel all this carry-on is disgustingly decadent, but not me. I feel the approach should be extended to other food types. You want potatoes? Here's a sack of them; pick your faves. You would like some wine? Here's a pound of grapes; peel off your socks, bud, and get stomping. You order the roast beef? A cow is led in on a piece of string and briskly shot in front of you.

One last note concerning the menu: if it offers sweetbreads, don't order them. I am not going to go into what sweetbreads actually are, because you may be reading this early in the morning. Suffice it to say, the late Teutonic Chancellor, Herr Hitler, is popularly reputed to have been singularly challenged in the sweetbread department.

Other delights of the expensive modern restaurant include blood pudding, chicken livers and tripe. If your date asks what you think of the menu, simply smile and reply, 'It's offal'. (Ho ho.)

By now, you will be feeling more relaxed and confident. Try ordering in French. This will impress the waiter enormously. Unless it's an Italian restaurant, of course.

4) Making Conversation.

As you talk over dinner, pay your date compliments. Flatter

her a little. Don't believe all that garbage about beauty only being skin-deep. What does she want, a cute *set of intestines*?

5) Who Pays On The First Date?

I tend to be a bit of a liberal on this. In my view, society should pay.

6) Driving Her Home.

When stopped by the police, be polite at all times. If asked to blow into the bag, do so immediately, WITHOUT then trying to twist it into a Chihuahua shape.

7) Kissing.

Remember, whatever else you do, that it takes a heck of a lot of practise for a person to kiss like a total beginner. A light labial contact is sufficient to start with. Swapping spit should not happen until the second date, and even then, only sparingly. Certainly do not kiss as though you are trying to remove a fishbone caught in your partner's throat.

8) Approaching the Second Date.

The first date passed off successfully and did not result in actual criminal charges. You have now progressed to the second date. A night at the pictures.

When selecting the film, use your intelligence (if you have any). You might do well not to suggest *Naughty Schoolgirl Classroom Romps*, *Bludgeon Seven: Return of the Zombie Slasher* or *Alien Space-Nymphs Suck Out Earthlings' Eyeballs*. Women tend to prefer 'romantic comedies'. You will know these because they are neither truly romantic nor by any stretch of the imagination comedic. Rather they are works of an almost frighteningly high degree of implausibility, usually featuring Meg Ryan or Hugh Grant, and predicated on the laughably absurd notion that anyone in their right mind would ever want to have sex with Hugh Grant, except if they lost a bet.

9) The Third Date.

Astonishingly she has invited you around to her house for dinner. Tonight may be the big night.

You have licked your plate clean and are on the dessert course. Strong drink has been taken, the lights are low. The romantic music is softly playing as you reach out and gently take her hand. She glances up from her trough of jelly and gives a lovely tender smile. 'So,' she says, 'what would you like to do after dinner?' The *correct* answer is: 'The washing-up, darling,' *not* 'Get ourselves naked and fuck like bunnies.'

10) The Morning After.

Don't be afraid to show your emotions. Be gentle, soft — even sentimental. Don't just ask for a lock of her hair as your keepsake. Go ahead, ask for the whole damn wig.

Oh, The Tangled Web We Weave:
The Irish Male Penetrates Cyberspace

Man is born free, but he is everywhere in chains.
Jean Jacques Rousseau *Du Contrat Social*.

As you know by now, I will do anything for my readers. When I say 'anything', I mean anything legal. Like I probably wouldn't break into a house for you, for example. Well, OK, I might do that if the money was right, but I *definitely* wouldn't forge a cheque for you. Not unless it was absolutely necessary. And when it comes to stealing you a high-quality sports-car that has hardly *ever* been used and is usually parked just down the street from where I live, I … .excuse me, my dears. I got carried away.

The simple point is: readers, I love you. My love has been primal, occasionally ferocious. Yes, perhaps I have even loved too much. My constant search for material that will entertain and enlighten you has ruined my health, destroyed several marriages, and made me a veritable nervous wreck. Little enough have I asked in return and that is exactly what I have received (especially since my bastard stockbroker ran off with my royalties). No turn has been left unstoned in my quest to bring you sweetness and light. I have gone to every corner of the civilized world for you (also Portarlington). I have detailed many of this these wanderings in this very volume, a book about what made me the man I am today. And no, smart-ass, it *isn't* a cookbook. But there comes a time when the world is not enough, when fresh pastures must be bravely explored. And so, purely for the benefit of yourselves, my darlings, one night recently when the wife was out I hitched up my pony and rode off into cyberspace.

If you are even an occasional devotee of the Internet you

will know that it contains some highly unpleasant and offensive material which might well influence young impressionable minds. But you will only be exposed to that tawdry rubbish if you go at all regularly to www.progressivedemocrats.com. (You can protect your child from stuff like this by installing a programme called NetmichaeldhigginsTD.) No, what I was in search of was low smut and FILTH of a sexual nature; vile SLEAZE intended to deprave; lustful cyberpits of OOZING sweaty carnality designed by none other than SATAN HIMSELF. But it seems you need a credit card for most of those sites.

So instead I logged on to a site which I shall not name here, but which specializes in 'adult conversation'. By that description is not meant dialectical chatter about property values and the role of the artist in contemporary society. Like the adjective 'democratic' as used by a Stalinist, 'adult' is one of those words that frequently means its opposite.

The site's homepage formed on my screen. It featured photos of a number of healthy-looking young people who were helpfully removing each other's clothing and behaving in a remarkably friendly manner. They were either engaged in sex or all-in wrestling, I could not be absolutely sure which. There followed a few brief introductory notes. Newcomers — or 'newcummers,' as it was amusingly rendered — were advised to fill out a profile. 'Be accurate and honest,' the guidelines suggested. 'This will make your cybersex experience even more erotic for all concerned.'

I wasn't too sure about that *all concerned*, but nothing if not game, I followed the advice. I tapped in a brief and honest description of myself — 'chain-smoking, overweight Irish writer who has a hard time relaxing. Difficult childhood but all own hair' — after which I entered a chatroom charmingly called 'The Hump House'.

Several hundred guests were already chatting, some quite

openly and a few in private. Some had quite intriguing names, such as 9ANDAHALFINCHDONG, 48DD, STROKEMEHARDER and INADEQUATEBASTARD.UK. My own name — 'J' — was perhaps so modest as to be actually off-putting, the Internet equivalent of sauntering into a full-scale orgy with a mitre on your head and a pair of secateurs in your hand.

The conversation I could see on the screen was of a type which in real life is usually confined to adolescence, or at least the Hollywood version thereof. There was a bit of general boasting about the dimensions of one's extremities, their general desirability and shape and consistency, not to mention their degree of tumescence. Enquiries about erotic experiences were frequently made. French maids, air hostesses, policewomen and nurses featured prominently, as did hotel rooms, train carriages, cockpits and desert islands. If one were to believe even a fraction of the reminiscences which were being so cheerfully shared, I am one of the very few men on the planet who has never been smeared with ice-cream by a pair of lesbian public service workers and efficiently fellated by those ladies to within an inch of my life — or even the nine-and-a-half inches thereof.

For some reason I found that my profile, admirably honest as I had tried to make it, was failing to attract me any chat partners at all. I did try typing 'hello' to a couple of my fellow inmates but no response whatsoever was forthcoming. By now, I confess, I was feeling uneasy. Nobody likes to be ignored in a social situation, even one where people are conversing about their genitalia.

To pass the time I decided to look up some of the other profiles. SHYJANE had described herself as 'a shy, quiet, vixen-cum-fox, who can put my feet behind my own ears'. BALDBALLS had indicated an enthusiastic fondness for 'getting down and very dirty with much larger ladies'. SCREWMESIDEWAYS had indicated that she was 'a profesionel woman from New York. Business manger wit a lot of powr in my job. This is true. I am a POWRFUL woman, lookin to conect with SIMILUR for erotac conversating. Pichures avalable.'

Hmm. This was all a little odd. Call me a devastating genius if you like, but let's just say that when you possess the combined insights of a detective and a literary critic it doesn't take you too long to discern that perhaps not ALL of these women were actually women. (I know, I know. I am deeply perceptive.) As for why they were pretending to be female, only God knows. (Also, perhaps, a psychiatrist or two.) Maybe it was simply to increase demand for themselves as prospective chat partners. Real women, after all, were about as rare in the Hump House as quarterbacks in a convent. The most ancient rule of the marketplace is seemingly unchanged by technology. If you've got it, flaunt it. And if you haven't, pretend you have.

In any case, it became quickly apparent that honesty was not the best policy, after all. It certainly hadn't opened too many doors for myself. I hung around The Hump House for almost ten minutes, but nobody gave me so much as a cyber-smile.

By now I could see that radical action might be required. So I decided to allow myself one small lie. And here on the Internet, just like in real life, if you really must tell a porky-pie you better make it a bloody good one.

So I became 'Wanda, 19, cheerleader, lingerie model and bisexual nympho', which saw my sexual stock-price soar, along with my self-esteem. Suddenly I was wanted, needed, *appreciated*, the centre of attention, the new girl in town. Total strangers were pleading to buy me cyberdrinks. Well-endowed individuals were offering to display their equipment for no other reason than my own delectation. Someone even asked what kind of panties I was wearing. ('Dunnes Stores' was the best I could manage. For a lingerie model, I was somewhat ignorant of the full range.) Another guest — HUNGLIKEADONKEY — politely enquired as to the size of my breasts. I had resolved not to lie any further if possible, so I answered with scrupulously Jesuitical truthfulness that while I was not what you might call a large girl, I was nevertheless happy with what God had given me.

'You wanna screw me, baby?' was the very next question. I said that while I was tremendously grateful for the offer, I would probably have to think about it first. Well come *on*, for Jesus's sake. A laugh is a laugh. But I just wasn't that kind of girl.

I think I was expecting to be taken out for a cybermeal, maybe a cybermovie, then driven home in my date's cybercar and walked in a gentlemanly manner to my cyberdoor, where we might — repeat might — exchange a chaste cyberkiss on the cybercheek, before we got around to arranging our next *several* cyberdates, *after* which we MIGHT, if we discovered we had hopes and dreams in common, get around to the actual cyberscrewing and then I would bring him home and introduce him to my cybermother who would ask him if his cyberintentions towards me were honourable, whereupon she and I could embark on destroying his life. I explained all this, as best I could.

'You're a very unusual girl to find in here,' HUNGLIKEADONKEY typed.

That was probably correct, I conceded.

'It's nice to find an old-fashioned girl,' he continued. 'Some of them in here are very crude.'

This from a guy whose *second question* had been to enquire whether I would derive enjoyment from his penetration.

'You're nice,' he said. 'You really got … how can I put it? … like this little something extra that girls don't often have.'

Little did he know just how true that was.

'You want I should describe myself to you?' he asked.

I replied that really it was up to him. (Well sometimes in the subtle minuet of courtship it doesn't pay to appear over-interested.)

HUNGLIKEADONKEY was from Columbus, Ohio, where he very believably claimed to be working 'as a lifeguard, gigolo and professional basketball player'. He described himself as having 'nice eyes and a swimmer's build'. Big deal, I thought. So does a walrus.

I know it will astound you to hear that he was 'six-foot four, with blond hair, good muscle-tone, a sixpack stomach and firm butt'. Indeed it was amazing that so many of the men at the site were also potential fashion models. Not to mention how almost all of the 'women' had sea-blue eyes, 38-inch breasts ('with erect nipples') and a waist you could wrap a watchstrap around. It was as though a master-race of overexcited Nordic Aryans had taken over the world and exterminated the rest of us.

It was the great Monsieur Sartre who said we choose what we are, whether or not we are aware of the choice. I guess that is what The Hump House allows for. If it does, then each to his own say I. But I did find myself wondering if the men who were imagining these pneumatic female bodies for themselves had a difficult time concentrating at work. Would they be cruising along the highway in their articulated trucks thinking '*Yes!* — tonight I'll be a petite brunette with a pert bottom and one of those navel piercings'. Would they drift off into daydream during the management conference and think '*I* am Mrs de Winter now'. Would BUSTYBABS have risen early that very morning and trudged down to the lower meadow to milk his cows, consoling himself with the happy thought that in only a few hours he would be 'wearing my favourite leather bikini and running my fingers through my long golden ringlets'?

'You got a boyfriend?' HUNGLIKEADONKEY asked me.

'Well … not just at the moment,' I answered truthfully.

'You like boys?'

'Some of my best friends are boys,' I confirmed.

'I bet. You like girls too?'

'Oh certainly.'

'You ever fooled around with a girl, babe?'

'Not quite as often as I'd like,' I replied.

'But you have sometimes?'

'I have sometimes,' I agreed.

'*Wow,*' he typed. 'That is the MAX.'

'Have you had much real-life sexual experience yourself, HUNGLIKEADONKEY?'

'Oh yeah,' he assured me fervently. 'Lots and lots. Really a LOT. Ain't nothin' I like better than BANGIN BEAVER.'

Jesus Christ! What was I dealing with? Should I log off and immediately ring the ISPCA?

But then again, I told myself, it was not for me to be judge and strict jury (although some of the guests would probably have liked that).

'So you wanna get sociable?' was the next question he put.

'How do you mean?' I quickly answered.

'Why don't you tell me about your pussy?'

'What do you want to know about it?' I asked.

'Well … You do have one, right?'

'As a matter of fact I do.' (Well I do.)

'What's it look like?'

'It's a tabby,' I typed, with total honesty.

There was a tremendously long moment of cybersilence. And then:

'*Tabby?* What the fuck colour's that?'

'Well I believe the dictionary definition is brownish, tawny or grey, marked with darker parallel stripes or streaks.'

'Wow,' he typed. 'Far OUT.'

'Thank you very much, HUNGLIKEADONKEY.'

'I never seen one like THAT before.'

'You should try and get out more often,' I advised.

'You like it? Having one like that?'

'Sure,' I said. 'I talk to it sometimes. I find it good company when the house is empty.'

Again there was a silence, even longer than the last. And then: 'You … talk to it?'

'Well why not?' I said. 'Sometimes it even appears to talk back.'

This time the cybersilence seemed to last an eternity. I wondered if HUNGLIKEADONKEY and I had lost that lovin' feelin'. (In the early stages of a romantic relationship things can go wrong so terribly easily.) But no, finally he addressed me again:

'Let me understand this? You feel … it *talks* to you?'

'Well, obviously not in the literal sense.'

'OK. I'm relieved to hear it. Cos I certainly never talk to my cock.'

And he typed that little sideways cybersmile thing. :-)

'My grandfather was very proud of his own cock,' I said truthfully.

'… He was?'

'Certainly he was. It even won prizes.'

'They got PRIZES for that kinda stuff where you live??'

'Oh yes. My grandfather's cock was widely admired. People said it was the most fabulous cock in the whole of Ireland.'

'You're … shitting me, right?'

'No no. They came from miles around to see it.'

'For REAL?'

Certainly. But then it got squashed by a bus one night.'

'*Your grandfather's cock got squashed by a BUS??*'

'Yes.'

'Jesus CHRIST. How'd THAT happen?'

'I don't really know. But one thing I can tell you — he was never the same afterwards.'

'Aw, gag me with a SPOON. The poor guy.'

'I know, it was awful,' I fervently agreed.

'Wow, I can imagine.'

:-(I said.

'Exactly,' he agreed. 'Bummer.com.'

'Totally,' I said.

'I bet your Grandmother was pretty upset too, huh?'

'Yes,' I responded. 'But she keeps a photograph of it on top of the television. For old times sake.'

This time the silence went on for a full minute before being broken.

'A PHOTOGRAPH? Of your grandfather's COCK?'

'Well yes,' I answered. 'With a couple of his favourite chicks.'

'They obviously had a pretty far-out marriage,' he finally opined.

'Oh yes,' I concurred. 'They certainly did.'

'Can I tell you something kinda personal?' he requested.

'Sure.'

'You won't be offended?'

'I'll try not to be.'

'Sometimes … I think about shaving my cock,' he revealed.

'Gosh,' I said. 'Wouldn't that ruin its feathers?'

It was at that point he logged off. *Typical* bloody men, huh? They're only after the one thing, and if they don't get it, they walk out of your life. What on earth is a girl to do?

I had gained some enlightenment from our brief exchange but I wasn't too sorry to see HUNGLIKEADONKEY go. We probably didn't have much of a future, I felt. And he definitely wouldn't respect me in the morning.

I left The Hump House and wandered around for a while, through the Porking Palace, the Oral Office, the Bonkathon Basement, the Kinky Kitchen, the Leatherwear Lounge and the Sub's Saloon (nothing *at all* to do with sport, I assure you), before strolling quickly down Mammary Lane and finally entering the Livingroom of Lust. Here the conversation was a good deal more explicit. People were having cybersex with each other.

Like most forms of pornographic activity, cybersex is arresting for about four minutes and numbingly wearisome after that. Basically, you type what you would be doing if you were having real-life sex, although I must point out that nobody actually typed 'eyeing the Munster Hurling Final on the TV in the corner' or 'silently reciting the Glorious Mystery in gratitude'. The thing I found oddest about the process was that in the attempt to keep the thing as realistic as possible people were taking the time and trouble to compose typographical representations of sexual noises.

'Oooooooooh,' said BIGBREASTS.

'Ahhhhh *yeahhhhhhhh*,' replied BLACKSTALLION.

'Groaannnnn,' said BI-GIRL.

'Unggggggggggggg,' grunted FUCK-IT-FROM-NANTUCKET.

'FaaaAAAaasterrr,' pleaded FIRMTHIGHS.

'Lowerrrr,' moaned CLEAVAGE.

'Eeeeeeeeeeeeeeee,' sighed STUDBOY.

'Woargggggghhhhhhhhhhhh,' groaned HIS-MOST-ROYAL-HIGHNESS-THE-PRINCE-OF-PERVERSION.

Not wanting to let the side down I did my best to join in — but 'Janey mac' was the best I could manage under pressure.

Cybersex is probably the ideal form of sex for the more traditional Irish Male, since it doesn't involve any emotional entanglement and you can have it while enjoying a beer and a cigarette. One doesn't want to be too crude, but if people were truly enjoying themselves as much as they claimed, it is hard to see precisely how they kept up the chatting — unless they were skilled at one-handed keyboard manipulation, or perhaps typing with their left foot like the late Christy Browne.

Suddenly a sentence was addressed to me privately.

'Wanna go for the burn?' asked SATAN-FROM-DAYTON, adding for effect an excited little } :>

I told him I couldn't help him, since I myself was an

O:-)

'Woh yeah,' he typed 'I'm nearly there.'

'Nearly where?' I asked.

But too late. My screen filled up with climactic vowels.

Now I don't know about you, but 'AAAAAAAAAAAA-AAAAAAAAAAAAAAAAAAAAAAAAAAAAAAAAAAAAAA AAAAAAAAAAAAAAAAAAAAAAAAAAAAAAAAAAAAAA AAAAAAAAAAAAAAAAAAAAAAAAAAAAAAAAAAAAAA AAAAAAAAAAAAAAAAAAAAAAAAAAAAAAAAAAAAAA' is not actually the sound I make at such a moment. Or at *any* moment, if it comes to that.

'Well I hope you're happy now,' I tapped out, feeling the lack of a typeface for irony.

'ZZZZZZZZZZZZ,' the brute replied.

And that's cybersex for you.

A to Z in twelve-and-a-half minutes.

Not at *all* like the real thing, huh?

*-)

TONIGHT — or at least in the quite near future, possibly. And that is ABSOLUTELY GUARANTEED!

Mr B Ahern of Dublin wrote 'Dear Idiot, How can I EVER thank you for helping me find love at last'. Garda Sergeant Boris Ossory (retired) of Co Laois joked 'Tears of happiness are trickling down my cheeks — *and* my new wife's!' Dr JP Magillycuddy of The Reeks, Listowel, said 'On my knees I BEG you to accept my life-savings in appreciation for all you have done in brightening the boreen of my existence with the headlamps of love.' These are extracts from GENUINE LETTERS not made up by our receptionist Bridie during her lunch-hour. (Names have been changed for reasons of honesty.) And we have THOUSANDS MORE too humourless to mention.

As soon as we receive your remittance we will waste no time in IMMEDIATELY ~~spending it on drink~~ rushing you a carefully selected list of fascinating single women any one of whom would be a privilege to know. If you are not LITERALLY ONE HUNDRED AND TEN PER CENT HAPPY with our service we will refund your money WITHOUT DELAY, IN TOTAL, NO QUESTIONS ASKED.***

AT IDIOT© WE CARE. SO YOU DON'T HAVE TO!

So go on. Take a few moments to change your life. Because hey, Mister — you know you deserve it.

(Send cash only. Cheques and butter vouchers will NOT be accepted.)

***

*** *some terms and conditions may apply*

YOUR DETAILS

Mr _____

Address _____

Age (mental and physical) _____

Prisoner Number _____

I am SERIOUSLY interested in changing my life and finding true and everlasting love with an Idiot©.

☐ yes

☐ no

(Tick appropriate box)

I understand that in the interests of finding REAL LOVE, I am hereby waiving all the legal rights to which I am entitled under the Protection of Consumers Act, 1971.

☐ yes

☐ no thank you, I wish to remain unloved and lonely

MARITAL STATUS

☐ Single

☐ Widowed

☐ Divorced

☐ Christian Brother

EDUCATION

☐ Primary

☐ Secondary

☐ University

☐ None — but vague feeling of superiority anyway

BUILD

☐ Scrawny

☐ Boringly average

☐ Fat

☐ Gargantuan

EYES

Please indicate number ___

☐ Green

☐ Blue

☐ Red

☐ Glass

YOUR DEGREE OF ATTRACTIVENESS

☐ Preternaturally hideous

☐ Plain

☐ Barely presentable

☐ A fecking lash

YOUR LOGICAL REASONING SKILLS

(A) The opposite of 'happiness' is:

☐ Woe

☐ Misery

☐ Despair

☐ United losing

(B) The opposite of 'woe' is:

☐ Happiness

☐ Joy

☐ Delight

☐ Giddy-up

YOUR PERSONALITY

If you **have** a personality, tick which traits closely describe you. If you don't have one, you needn't worry; our Director-General has multiple personalities and we'll loan you one he isn't using.

☐ Conventional

☐ Eerie

☐ Intense

☐ Groping
☐ Catatonic
☐ Rampant
☐ Self-destructive
☐ Dishonest

YOUR INTERESTS

Please tick for a liking, cross for a dislike, or leave blank for no preference:

☐ Wining and Dining
☐ Whining and Pining
☐ Strangling small woodland creatures
☐ Cinema
☐ Nose picking
☐ Politics/History
☐ Pets
☐ Farmyard animals (please state if you have a conviction)
☐ Mixing with friends (if any)
☐ Current affairs
☐ Extramarital affairs
☐ Biting your toenails
☐ Gardening
☐ Music
☐ Pleasant conversation
☐ Unpleasant conversation
☐ Other

YOUR ATTITUDES

Tick for yes, cross for no or leave blank if you don't feel strongly:

☐ I am looking for an old-fashioned girl
☐ I am looking for a sophisticated modern woman
☐ Anything in a skirt would do me just fine (except a Scotsman)

☐ Even a Scotsman might be all right
☐ I just haven't met the right girl yet
☐ I met the right girl but she happened to be a nun
☐ I am ready for a serious, committed relationship
☐ All my friends are married so I may as well be too
☐ No way am I desperate, absolutely NOT
☐ OK, OK, I'll take the bloody Scotsman

YOUR IDEAL PARTNER

☐ Nymphomaniac recently released from solitary
   confinement
☐ High priestess of Babelonia
☐ Lollipop lady
☐ Student nurse, masseuse and part-time Wonderbra girl
☐ Lash-wielding Mistress of Utter Submission (Limerick
   only)
☐ Daily communicant
☐ Andrea Corr
☐ All of the Corrs simultaneously (Jim optional)
☐ Six-pack of Heineken and twenty fags

Please send your completed survey and cash to: IDIOT, New Bribeland Books (Offshore Account) Ltd, c/o Ansbacher Holdings, 71 Rue Traynor, Jersey 417 NQA. (No questions asked. And none answered either.)

Across the Water:
The Irish Male Does England

*England resembles a family, a rather stuffy Victorian family,
with not many black sheep in it but with all its cupboards
bursting with skeletons.*

George Orwell, *The Lion and the Unicorn*

Faking Friends with the Irish

Picture the scene.

You are in a pub where the barman is called Seamus. You are enjoying a plate of corned beef and cabbage, washed down with Bushmills, Murphy's or Guinness. The antique jukebox is playing 'Danny Boy'. On the wall behind the bar is a framed photograph of John F Kennedy; another of Michael Collins, a third of Samuel Beckett. Where on earth are you?

That's right. North London.

You have entered 'an Irish pub' for a good night out. You are tired of The Duke and The Cock and Feathers. The Prince of Wales has no appeal. Fecky Flanagans is what you want now. Down the street from Murder Mulligans. Across the way from The Emerald Oil.

You know the kind of place I mean. Sepia-tinted photographs of thatched cottages beside lakes. Posters of Georgian doors in Dublin. Tables made out of redundant agricultural machinery. Begorrah! *Bejayzus!* How very Irish it all is. Why, even the condoms in the vending machines are green. And as for the tampon-dispensing unit in the ladies loo? Oh no, *those* aren't tampons. Those are banshees' fags.

These stupefyingly vile places bespeckle the whole world now. The Irish bar in all its quasi-Hibernian horror. From Hamburg to Paris, from Bangkok to Rome — wherever you go stands one little corner of a foreign field that will always be Irish, no matter how ridiculous that might be. Hansi or Luigi or Lee Ho Hung will be ripping it up to the sound of the fiddle. But England has more 'traditional' Irish hostelries than anywhere else on the face of the planet — certainly many more than we have in Ireland, or ever did have, if it comes to that. And as for London, to judge from its pubs, the city has turned into Oirland-on-Thames.

This dreadful proliferation of the Irish pub, this

excruciating epidemic of ersatz Eire. Is there any way we can all band together and stop it? What can it mean? How do we explain it?

Bored with trying to understand the Irish — and who could possibly blame them for that? — the English have lately decided to imitate us. They want to be Irish *too*, bless their hearts. And why shouldn't they? Often I think they are remarkably good at it. To be honest I think they are much better at being Irish than *we* are. Whenever I see English people enjoying themselves in a London-Irish pub I realize that history means nothing at all. 'Feck!' they shout. 'Are you having the craic? … er … Top o' the mornin. *Diddly-deee*!'

Irish readers will know all too well that up until recently a *truly* authentic Irish pub was usually a filth-encrusted, draughty, malodorous hovel with a leaky roof, corrugated iron walls and a hole in the ground down an alley as a toilet. That is not what you find in Camden and Islington but in Ireland not too long ago that would have been common enough. When I think of the Dublin bars I frequented in my student days my heart begins to pump and sputter. There was no fine menu featuring Yeatsburgers or Baked Behans, no autographed portrait of Shane McGowan, no selection of potent cocktails named after characters in James Joyce's novels. A packet of nuts was all the food you could ask for and the regular punters would laugh if you did.

The glass-collectors were not smiling russet-headed colleens, but grim-faced viragos with blackened teeth, or sullen pimply teenagers saving up for emigration. The walls were adorned with jolly Irish notices saying DON'T ASK FOR CREDIT AS A TRUNCHEON IN THE KISSER MIGHT OFFEND. The furnishings weren't distressed but the customers were. The barman was not an Aidan Quinn lookalike with a lovely little song perpetually on his lips about his wee grey-haired mammy in the County Donegal. More often than not he was an outright bollocks who would gnaw his own leg off for a tenpenny piece.

Oh, how we pined for the bars of London, those of us who knew we would soon take the emigrant boat. Buxom barmaids! Dartboards and pork scratchings! Skittles! Warm bitter! Watney's Red Barrel! Dot Cotton in the corner sharing a sherry with Doctor Legg. Bunting out the front on Coronation Day and a bunk-up out the back on Christmas Night, followed by a punch-up with Big Grant Mitchell and a roll in the cellar with Wellard the pub dog. How could any self-respecting Irishman want more?

But no. Alas. It wasn't to be. The fashion for 'Irish pubs' took off just as soon as we stepped from the mailboat. London bars began to fall in love with faked Irishry. It was as though our horrible past was stalking us.

Back home in Ireland people soon came to realize that business opportunities were presenting themselves across the Irish sea. The mighty English, we soon realized, were the only people in the whole world who really *would* give you money for old rope — provided the old rope had once been in a Dublin alehouse. Attics were ransacked, old buildings stripped. We emptied our skips, threw open the museums and sent the dusty contents across the water to be nailed and hammered to the walls of *faux*-Irish speakeasies.

This exporting of crap was good for Ireland. It really helped to clean out the country. Other European nations have wine lakes or butter mountains. In Ireland we had a Tat Pyrenees. But soon we were recycling whole mountains of old junk, selling them to the ancient enemy to put in his pub. Lord in Heaven, what sweet revenge.

But the Irish pubs of England wanted more and more. Soon the demand reached crisis proportions. Slowly, inexorably, Ireland was sucked dry of drek as every last little piece of it was exported to England's inns. For a brief period in the mid-

1990s there was actually a serious Irish junk-drought, an epidemic of craplessness.

Grot was rationed by the Irish government, tat and garbage strictly limited. Mothers with young children were allowed small weekly supplies of Val Doonican album covers; a granny with good connections could sometimes get her hands on a battered old harp or a plastic leprechaun. But still the Irish pubs of Britain demanded more. *Give us postcards of donkeys! Faded icons of Saint Patrick! BUSTS OF BOB GELDOF CARVED OUT OF TURF!* In no time they became completely insatiable. But we had no more bits of old junk to sell. We soon realized there was nothing else for it. We started *manufacturing* bits of old junk.

Thus it is that deep in the peaceful Irish countryside there are now many large and successful factories churning out broken spinning wheels, battered ancient books with their jackets ripped off, rolls of atmospheric spider-web to be sold by the yard to the Irish pub market. Once a poor and backward country, these days Ireland has the healthiest economy in Europe. Now you know why. It's all down to you.

So remember tonight, as you sink your pint, in Buggery Boylans or the Shamrock Shebeen — authenticity is absolutely everything. If you can fake that, bejayzus, you've got it made. Big time. In spades. With shillelaghs to go. Cheers now. Pass the credit card. *O Danny Boy …*

The Beautiful Norf

I have an Irish friend who used to live in an attic in Finsbury Park. It was in a grim tenement with a red door, near the Tube Station. The only functional toilet in the entire building was down in the dark and echoing basement, and the space between said vile subterranean latrine and his lofty gaff comprised five pitch-black landings inhabited by cockroaches the size of tractors. I don't know why he didn't just pee out the windows when caught short in the night. But he says he honestly never did.

If he had, he would have been peeing on one of the most interesting parts of North London. Fabulous, funtastic Finsbury Park, a place for which I have a tremendously soft spot. (No, not a bog in County Wicklow.)

One reason I like this fine quarter is that it used to contain the legendary Sir George Robey pub, now the Powerhaus. When I first came to London, in the 1980s, I would go to 'the Robey' to see new bands, the lyrics of whose songs seemed to be exclusively made up of the words 'Thatcher, fight, miner, fascist, bastard, kick, struggle, bludgeon, stab, gouge and Mandela' rearranged in more or less random sequences. Ah, those glorious days of the Eighties benefit gig! As John O'Farrell tells us in his marvellously amusing memoir *Things Can Only Get Better*, 'Sometimes it was Billy Bragg supporting Hank Wangford but other times it was Hank Wangford supporting Billy Bragg.'

A short trot — no, I don't mean Billy Bragg — down the street, at 129 Seven Sisters Road, is the Red Rose Club, traditional haven of North London lefties. The hallowed walls have witnessed many an ideological dust-up over the years. Once, in my youth, I went there to attend a meeting of the North London Revolutionary Pacifist Front. Forget parliamentary politics, all three of us were told, the masses were ripe for revolutionary pacifism. (That's where you storm the gates of Buckingham Palace but offer to pay for any damage afterwards.) It was here in the Red Rose Comedy Club that I first saw young, hungry comics like Ben Elton, Julian Clary and Jo Brand. Not actually *them*, you understand. They were merely *like* them.

Yes, Finsbury Park has absolutely everything the heart could desire. A pub, a comedy venue and three revolutionary pacifists. But these days the main thing it is famous for is the Finsbury Park Fleadh.

'Fleadh', as Irish readers will know, is an Irish word. When properly pronounced it rhymes with the noise a sheep makes. (I mean 'baa'.) The meaning of the word is a little difficult to define, but depending on which ancient Gaelic text you consult it is either (a) 'a conference of wise elders' (b) 'the soft piece of skin under a leprechaun's armpit' or (c) 'an annual congregation in a north London field for purposes of drinking and dancing around like eejits until Van Morrison comes on and you sit on the wet grass and wave a cigarette lighter in the air and ask the inebriate in front of you not to let his girlfriend perch on his shoulders like that because you didn't pay good money to see her big fat arse, though heaven knows on another occasion you might.'

June 1990 saw the first Finsbury Park Fleadh. In the grand tradition of the outdoor rock festival, there was fantastic live music, ferocious drinking, a paucity of toilets and an awful lot of mud. Somewhere mouldering in the bottom of a suitcase in my attic I still have the Pogues T-shirt I was wearing that day. It was clean when I left my flat that morning. By the time I got home, it could have been used to grow potatoes.

Since then, the Fleadh has become an annual event, and, not unlike Van Morrison actually, has expanded in quite a magnificent manner as the years have rolled by. By now Finsbury Park has truly earned its place in any list of the sacred pilgrimage sites of alfresco rock and roll. Glastonbury! Altamont! Woodstock! ... er ... Finsbury Park!

Despite its smooth organisation and mesmerising line-ups, it is sometimes hard to understand just why this annual celebration of Irishness, and specifically London-Irishness, has become quite so wildly popular. But it has. Perhaps it's because these days in Britain being Irish is groovy. People with accents on which you cut yourself will happily tell you that they are ectually Arish.

But we in Ireland don't mind people doing this. In fact we like it. We claim everyone we can as one of our own. A man in Dublin once honestly tried to convince me that Elvis was from Tipperary 'on his mother's side'. (Elvis Presley, I mean. Elvis Costello *is* Irish.) Like sad Hibernian versions of the gay stereotype, some of us sit in front of our televisions at night going '*He's* Irish, you know ... So's he ... And *he's* as Irish as you or me ... And I mean, look at *HER*, she's practically banging a bodhrán' (Her Royal Highness, Princess Michael of Kent).

No other ethnic group in Britain indulges in this odd behaviour. You don't find black Londoners looking at, say, Tony Blair and going 'See him? ... You know he's black of course? ... No he *is*, honest.' Obviously that would be ridiculous. Because Tony Blair is *Irish*. Seriously. On his mother's side. (HE IS!)

Sometimes this can get out of hand. Occasionally you will find a London-Irish person who will insist that everything of any merit at all in the last twenty-five years of English culture is actually Irish. But clearly this is laughable. I mean, yes, admittedly, just off the top of my head there's Roy Keane, John Lydon, Father Ted, Martin McDonagh, Denis Irwin, The Smiths, Tom Paulin, Pauline McLynn, Philip Tracey, George Best, Shane McGowan, Ronnie O'Sullivan, Oasis, Orla Guerin, Fiona Shaw, Steve Coogan, Caroline Aherne, Frank

Skinner, Feargal Keane, Graham Norton, Patrick Kielty, Owen O'Neill, Sean Hughes and The Divine Comedy. But it's nothing to write home about really. Not when you remember that the English produced Mr Blobby.

Still, on the day of the Fleadh, *everybody* is Irish. The event provided a fine opportunity for getting down and getting jiggy, for reeling and rocking, for romping and riverdancing. Although would-be Michael Flatleys should be advised that it takes many many years of selfless dedication to make Irish dancing quite as hideous as Michael does. Fleadhgoers, please do take note: the trick to traditional Irish dancing is to keep your hands by your sides no matter what else is happening. (This is the trick to traditional Irish sex also.)

There is a certain variety of Irish music fan who insists that enjoyable Irish music isn't merely music, but that it somehow, y'know, embodies the soul of Celtic yearning, the mystical hunger for spiritual transcendence, the poetic struggle to reconcile the conflicting demands of heart and mind. It is vitally important to remember this when you are listening to The Corrs.

'What Can I Do To Make You Love Me?'

Oh Andrea. *There's* a question.

In years gone by, Irish traditional musicians could sometimes be a bit parochial. ('People who sing through their nose by heart,' my father used to call them.) If you weren't a beret-wearing, pipe-smoking sheep farmer you weren't considered exactly kosher. But these days the organisers of the Fleadh cast an admirably wide net. You're as likely to see George Thorogood and the Delaware Destroyers as the Dubliners, De Dannan or Davey Spillane.

So if some July you find yourself in North London, you could do a lot worse than pop along to the Finsbury Park Fleadh. Have a dance and a drink, discover your inner Irishperson. But on your way home, if you find yourself on a road near the Tube Station, outside a grim five-storey house with a red front door, just take my advice. Don't stand under the windows.

Dating Dames Along The Thames:
The Irish Male Guide To London

'When a man is tired of London, he is tired of life,' said Mississippi blues legend Doctor Samuel Johnson. 'For there is in London all that life can afford.' With remarks like that, I don't know what he was a doctor of, but it must have been something like pitch-and-putt.

People sometimes say that Britain is an unfriendly, xenophobic society where outsiders or the underprivileged are made to feel unwanted. But this is very far from the truth. In fact the English have a tremendously deep affection for such groups as ethnic minorities, sexual misfits and the chronically unemployed — i.e. the Royal Family.

One great argument in favour of the Royal Family is that they do a lot for British tourism. Of course, the French Royal Family do a lot for French tourism too, despite all having their heads chopped off back in the Revolution, but never mind that, there are begrudgers everywhere and that is simply the price of success.

Prince Andrew, Prince Charles and Princess Anne are all deeply involved in charity work, as is Her Majesty The Queen, to give Prince Edward his correct title. Yes, taken together the Royal Family is probably Britain's most successful charity, netting a cool hundred million a year for itself, and almost all of it completely tax-free! '*Honi Soit Qui Mal Y Pense*' is the proud and ancient motto of the House of Windsor, which may be roughly translated as 'Show Me the Money'.

These days, of course, the Royal Family is working hard to adapt to the times, not to mention The Sun and The News of the World. Change is very much the order of the day. Queen Elizabeth recently embarked on a number of well-planned spontaneous meetings with her subjects in ordinary places such as supermarkets, dole offices and car parks. The event in the supermarket was only slightly spoiled when it became clear she hadn't a clue what a bar-code was.

His Highness Prince Charles (the Grand Old Duke of Dork) has given a number of high-profile speeches on matters like animal rights, wildlife preservation and how there's nothing he likes better than gunning down a deer. And his redoubtable father, the Duke of Earl and Edinburgh, recently garnered some useful publicity when he waded into a river to save a drowning tramp. (And I never even knew that Fergie *liked* swimming.) So you can't say they're not making an effort.

Prince Edward works in the television industry and has made a number of exciting programmes for the American market such as 'My Granny, The Queen Mother', 'Ancient Treasures of England: Buckingham Palace' and 'What It's Like Being A Prince'. No shortage of imaginative ideas there, but that didn't stop the whingers of the media mocking their betters. He recently got into trouble with the British tabloid press when it was revealed he'd said, in an interview in America, that the British people envy entrepreneurial spirit and creative success. But I thought that was a very brave thing for him to say, especially when you consider he's had sod-all of either.

MAKING CONVERSATION IN ENGLAND

The weather is the most frequent topic of conversation among the natives, so it is wise to have a few appropriately meteorological remarks prepared. England is a land of sweet moderation, so as always when considering engaging the locals in chat, it is best not to say anything too extreme. Something like 'Turned out not too bad again' is probably better than 'That bastard rain makes me want to SLASH someone'.

By the way, never ask an English person for directions. They are too polite to tell you if they don't know the way, and will send you somewhere else instead — usually Wales.

SOME USEFUL ENGLISH PHRASES

*Gladstone spent his declining years trying to guess the answer
to the Irish Question; unfortunately whenever he was getting
warm, the Irish secretly changed the question.*

WC Sellar and RJ Yeatman, *1066 and All That*

One of the many myths about the relationship between the
Irish and the English is that both nationalities speak the same
language. This is simply not the case. We use the same words
and phrases, admittedly, but only rarely do they mean the
same things. If you doubt the truth of my theory, try asking an
Englishman if a ride would be out of the question. He will
offer you the loan of his polo-pony. And take it from me, you
probably *shouldn't* ride it. Conversely, if you refer to the
pony's sister as a damned attractive filly upon whom you
wouldn't mind having a vigorous jump, he will look upon you
as an unashamed pervert and immediately invite you to join
the Conservative Party.

Even the very words 'Irish' and 'English' mean profoundly
different things depending on who is using them. To most
English people over the age of fifty, 'a bit Irish' means
feckless, lazy or stupid. 'Wonderfully Irish' means 'amusing
by virtue of being illogical'. 'Irish' is also the adjective that is
used to describe anyone at all from the island of Ireland.
'Anglo-Irish' or 'Northern Irish' mean absolutely nothing to
your average Limey. To a Londoner or Mancunian, Ian
Paisley and Gerry Adams are basically the same —
troublesome Paddies who talk too much.

Yes, English-English and Irish-English are two different
languages. So the young Irish Male in London may well find
himself linguistically adrift. But if he simply commits to
memory the following key phrases and translations, they

should get bring him smiling through most everyday challenges. The English-English expression appears in bold on the left, the Irish-English translation alongside. Tally ho!

Too clever by half[1]: Of roughly average intelligence.

Mustn't grumble: My life is totally shit.

No, thank you, I don't like dancing: Feck off or I will call the police.

Come around for supper: Come around for dinner.

Come around for early lunch: Come around for late breakfast.

You really *must* come around some time: I never want to see you again.

Weather turned out nice again, eh?: I really can't think of anything to say.

Public school: Private school.

Airing cupboard: Hot Press.

***New Musical Express*:** *Hot Press*.

Woman who does: Cleaning lady.

Woman who doesn't: Nun.

Lady I visit once a week: Psychotherapist/hooker.

Dipstick: Eeejit.

Plonker: Gobshite.

Cripes: Jayzus.

Jacksy: Arse.

Jiminy Cricket: Cricket played by midgets.

Dick Van Dyke: A pre-operative transexual.

Fraud Fiesta: The Conservative Party Conference.

---

[1] NB: Be *very* careful indeed about saying this to anyone English. It is the most insulting phrase in their entire language.

Blow me: Exclamation of surprise (N.B. *Not* a chat-up line).

Trafalgar Square: An unfashionable person.

Letsby Avenue: What a policeman says while making an arrest.

Millwall supporter: Gurrier.

Glaswegian: Gouger.

Chippy: Oversensitive/a carpenter.

Chippy Chippy: An oversensitive carpenter.

Chippy Chippy Bang Bang: An orgy/gunfight of oversensitive carpenters.

Lippy: Lipstick.

Nippy: Sub-zero temperatures.

So **pleased to meet you:** You bore me to death.

Let's meet for a drink: Let's meet for *a* drink.

Let's get totally rat-faced drunk: Let's have two pints.

German: Humourless.

French: Smelly/conniving.

Italian: Cowardly.

American: Stupid/vulgar.

Scottish: Mean.

English: Perfect in every way.

England: Largely unsuccessful football team.

Rule Britannia: What Tony Blair does.

Selling Britain down the drain: Participating meaningfully in Europe.

Paki: Former Celtic and Ireland goalie.

Whacky Backy: Marijuana.

Dotty: A bit eccentric.

Tottie: Posh term for an attractive lady.

Dotty Tottie: The Duchess of York.[2]

Could we ... you know ... that is to say: I desire you sexually.

Did you ... urm ... you know ... was it?: Did you achieve orgasm?

Steady as she blows: English idea of foreplay.

I say!: Oh wow, I'm *coming!*

Todger: A penis.

Old thing/Old bean/Old scout: Terms of affection for the todger.

The mutt's nuts: The dog's bollocks.

United fan: Manchester term for a person not from Manchester.

Glasgow kiss: Head-butt.

Scouser's wages: Social security.

Kipper Tie: A cup of tea in Birmingham.

Air Hair Lair: How to greet the Queen.

HOW TO SPEAK COCKNEY

True Cockneys are a tightly-knit community, with their own habits, customs and social mores. Often they don the brightly coloured outfits of the Pearly King or Pearly Queen, though other traditional costumes frequently worn by Cockneys include suits with arrows on them and also balls-and-chains.

Cockneys have their own repertoire of delightful indigenous folksong, including 'My Old Man's a Dustman, He Wears A Dustman's Hat', 'My Old Man Said Follow the Van' and 'My Old Man Was A Slasher for the Kray Twins (And He Didn't Dilly-Dally On The Way)'.

For the Cockney, a real Londoner must be born within the

---

[2] So-called because she too 'had ten-thousand men'.

sound of Bow Bells. This is a little difficult these days, as Bow Bells were stolen and melted down by the locals some years back. But the point remains — these people can be insular. Outsiders may be regarded with suspicion and unease. If you are stopped in the street and asked for your name, answer 'Dick Whittington' or 'The Artful Dodger'.

The East End language, Cockney Rhyming Slang, is famous all over the civilized world for its juiciness, colour and total incomprehensibility. *Boat-race* is the word for *face*; *tin-of-fruit* is the translation of *suit*, *Sigmund Freuds* means *hemorrhoids* and so on. Where it becomes difficult is when the slang is edited or abbreviated. *Plates* is short for *plates-of-meat*, therefore *feet;* the affectionate phrase *my old china* is derived from *china plate* or *mate.* The insulting epithet *berk* is actually an abbreviation of *Berkshire Hunt*, which shouldn't need much further elucidation, particularly to a clever Barclay's Banker like yourself.

When Cockneys flip into full-abbreviation mode it is almost impossible to know what they are on, let alone mind what they are on *about*. It is probably best just to grin and nod. I remember a native of Stepney saying to me once: 'Well, stone me pink and twoddle me parsnips, but the berk comes up with a boat like Abbyssinia and I rogered him up the Old Kent Road.'

You might be surprised that a vicar would talk like that. Particularly when 'I now pronounce you man and wife' would have done just as well. But that's the East End for you. Very expressive.

SHOPPING

London has all the commerce the heart could desire, with many fine stores adorning each High Street in between the mini-cab offices, kebab shops and derelict office-blocks.

You will have heard of the great popularity of the annual

sales in the larger stores of Chelsea and the West End. People queue up well in advance to avail of the massive reductions and special offers. In fact if you pass by the doorway of a London shop any night of the week there will usually be a number of bargain-hunters sleeping in it, wrapped in their handy cardboard boxes or newspaper blankets. Clearly they shopped till they dropped! It is a quaint custom of modern British life that these eccentric but hardy consumers are simply ignored by everyone else. Take a moment to stand and watch as the socialist theatre-goers step over them to get back into their limousines!

The city is the hindquarters of the international fashion industry, with its amusing and clever slogans such as 'Black is the new brown', 'Up is the new down' and 'Staying in is the new going out'. People sometimes think that designer clothes are expensive, but even in the exclusive couturiers of Covent Garden it is still possible to buy a suit for only *slightly* more than you would pay for a new car — though you will have to search carefully and buy off the rack.

A fun alternative to the official premises of Gucci, Paul Smith and Hugo Boss is the thriving culture of London outdoor-trading, as practised on many street corners and in Tube Stations. Cynical observers sometimes wonder how the absolutely authentic designer goods offered here are so unbelievably cheap. The simple truth is that by buying their stock in very large numbers the traders are able to pass on considerable savings to their customers. If you are as street-wise as I am you can sometimes find incredible bargains. In fact I once bought a silk tuxedo personally hand-made by Gianni Versace for only two hundred pounds, with a bottle of totally genuine Givenchy perfume thrown in, from a very nice man called Pentonville Ronnie who had some fascinating tattoos across his forehead.

Yes, street-trading is great crack! And when dealing with

the merry merchants of the sidewalk, there is none of that unpleasant harassment to buy something else which you frequently find in actual shops. Indeed, as soon as you hand over your money to a trader, he actually seems to disappear! (Particularly if a policeman is coming.)

London can be an expensive city. But through careful scrutiny of the payment system used in the smarter of her stores, I have developed a cunning little technique that can make your shopping a lot cheaper, or even earn you a tidy profit. Try it out! Go into a store and buy something for, say, fifty pounds, paying with your credit card. When the assistant asks if you 'Want any cash back' simply say 'Yes, please, forty pounds' and smile nicely as she hands it over. That way you'll only have spent ten pounds in total! It is only a matter of time before the English cotton onto this scam, so act quickly and without mercy and FILL YOUR BOOTS!

I have a number of similar financial ploys, full details of which are available in my latest brochure *One Hundred Ways To Make Money Without Working* — price £147.50 from New Island (Cooked) Books. Stocks strictly limited so do order NOW.

ENGLISH NEWSPAPERS

You cannot hope to bribe or twist,
Thank God! the British journalist.
But, seeing what the man will do
Unbribed, there's no occasion to.

Humbert Wolfe, *Over The Fire*

The English press is the glory of the world, a model of balance, integrity and fair play. Examples of this may be seen in daily headlines such as KEN LIVINGSTONE IS A NUN-MURDERING FREAK, GERMAN FOOTBALLERS A PACK OF NAZI POOFTERS, OFFICIAL! and LABOUR

ROCKED BY CONSERVATIVE POLL SURGE OF ONE PER CENT — IT'S THE END ADMITS EVIL TONY.

And then there are the tabloids.

These fine publications occasionally get a bit of criticism, but who else can supply millions of everyday readers with the news, comment and topless sixteen-year-old girls which are the lifeblood of any healthy democracy? For what did the thousands of British servicemen who died with their faces buried in Flanders mud give their lives, if not free speech and ads for telephone sex lines? But I do sometimes think it is a pity that the tabloids are quite so obsessed with soap-opera stars and pop celebrities. If they took out all those features about talentless, unintelligent, overpaid scroungers, it would leave more room for articles about the Royal Family.

ENGLISH FOOD

Once upon a time Londoners ate very strange things, such as jellied eels, spam, sago dumplings and humble pie. But in recent years London has become a great culinary capital, offering all that is best in traditional patriotic English food — the curry, the doner kebab and the Chinese take-away.

London is also the home of fish 'n' chips which as everyone knows is the perfectly balanced meal, featuring just the correct blend of grease 'n' fats.

ENGLISH POLITICS

Britain is the home of elective democracy and Westminster, of course, has always been known as the Motherfucker of all Parliaments. The Strangers' Gallery (named after Mrs Thatcher, who got stranger and stranger) is open to the public on every single one of the eighty days a year on which the hardworking parliamentarians bother turning up to debate anything. Here you may see all the Honorable Members — and I do mean members — shouting abuse at each other, throwing things around and making long speeches about how appallingly behaved young people are these days.

It is always good to visit during Prime Minister's Question Time. Now a regular thrice-weekly event, it has taken place in some form for over a century, and is an absolute cornerstone of the British democratic way. Question Time provides an opportunity for ordinary MPs to call the Prime Minister himself to account, and he must answer completely off-the-cuff with only his large team of researchers, speech-writers and make-up artists to help him. Often it gets incredibly dramatic. You can see even the *government's own MPs* putting fearlessly demanding questions which might jeopardise their chances of promotion, such as 'Excuse me Tony, but how do you manage to be such a dead-on guy?' (Younger Labour members are colloquially known as 'Blair's Babes'. This is because many of them are still only learning to crawl.)

Yes, 'New' Labour forms the present government, ruling with a mixture of aromatherapy and Stalinism. Other parties currently represented at Westminster include the Conservatives, Liberal Democrats and Democratic Unionists, the latter led by Apprentice-Boy Slim, the Reverend Ian Paisley.

The House of Lords is another ancient seat of accountability. Here you can observe all the unelected Lords and Ladies wafting about in their pretty robes and making sharp contributions to debate, such as falling asleep or daydreaming about their favourite racehorse. Admittedly most of the Lords and Ladies are only here because *(a)* they are so far up the government's bottom they are peeping out through Mr Blair's eyeballs *(b)* pending legalization of euthanasia, nobody can think of anything else to do with them, or *(c)* one of their ancestors blew the king. But that doesn't mean they don't have talent. And just because nobody voted for them and most of the electorate thinks it should be abolished doesn't mean the chamber isn't democratic. Oh no.

It is sometimes said by cynics that the House of Lords is a sad anachronism, desperately out of touch with the modern world. But personally I feel that any legislative assembly *without* footmen in tights has nothing to offer the twenty-first century.

THE INDIGENOUS PEOPLES

Visitors to London often seem to feel that the natives aren't as welcoming as they might be. But in my experience Londoners are in fact very friendly. So friendly that many of them leave their telephone numbers in public phone-booths, inviting you to ring them up any time you are feeling lonely and come around to their discreet apartments for a spot of vigorous social intercourse. Some of them walk right up to you in the street — or more usually the alleyway — and ask in a pleasant manner if you are 'looking for any business tonight'.

Make a little effort and it will be well-rewarded. With a vigorous thrashing from the Vice Squad, and a social disease.

EXPLORING THE CITY

The traffic in London can be a little trying at times, but it is best to consider total and utter gridlock an opportunity for reflection. How many other modern cities actually give you three or four hours per day to sit in your car, listen to drive-time radio and breathe very deeply to avoid getting a heart attack? If you do get caught in a traffic jam, my advice would be — look around and enjoy the scenery! You will notice the citizens calling out cheerful greetings to you, making friendly hand gestures at each other and sharing a little gentle joshing which shouldn't be taken seriously unless actual weapons are produced. Do not return fire unless seriously provoked.

The Tube is an excellent way to get around the city. Some

of the stations are architectural marvels, not to say glorified public toilets where you can be bludgeoned if you're not careful. Yes, it is overpriced, the elevators rarely work, the ticket machines are broken and the trains are frequently late, but you can always kill the boredom of waiting by observing the rats as they scuttle happily about the platforms. It isn't every city that boasts such active wildlife.

The Tube Station is a good place to witness that famous phenomenon, the good old British sense of humour. You will hear hilarious and obviously ironic announcements being made over the station's loudspeaker system, such as 'the train is delayed due to late arrival' or 'the train will be here in four hours, we promise'. Please don't take these seriously at all. British Rail announcers are actually recruited from the ranks of former stand-up comedians who have fallen on hard times.

The important thing to know about Tube travel is that it has its own customs, habits and traditions. The main one is — when on the Tube, never *ever* talk to anyone. This is hard for the younger Irish Male, suffering as he does from the weak desire to be friendly. It is admittedly very difficult not to talk when they are six hundred of you jammed into a carriage originally designed for forty-eight and the motion of the train combined with the friction of some chartered accountant's bottom is gradually bringing you to a shattering orgasm. But try to maintain your stiff upper lip. Really, silence is what is expected, although a soft cough at the moment of climax is acceptable, followed by a vigorous rustling of your *London Evening Standard*. Generally, however, follow the rule. Even if the man beside you spontaneously combusts, the best thing to do is say nothing at all. He is probably only looking for attention.

London is a fine city for walking around, but running is more advisable, particularly after dark. I am not saying the place is a den of thieves, villains, psychos and delinquents but the obvious precautions of city life should be observed at all times. Do not carry expensive camera equipment, flash expensive jewellery or have a shirt on your back. If, or rather *when* you are mugged, try not to take it too personally. Being mugged in London is rather like puberty — difficult and embarrassing, but it has to be gone through. Make an effort to see it as a rite of passage. Hey, you are a real Londoner now! Your outsider status has disappeared along with your watch.

Following your mugging there is probably not too much point in going to the police. Overworked and underpaid, the friendly London bobby has more than enough on his plate these days, without being bothered by *your* pathetic problems. The Metropolitan Police have come in for much criticism in recent years, most of it very unfair when you look at the bigger picture. Accepting bribes, getting fat and not catching racist hooligans are highly time-consuming activities. So go easy with Plod. Or don't go at all. Because when he hears you are Irish he might well beat you into confessing that you once bombed a pub!

Other pleasures of the city include the cheeky London taxi drivers with their merry banter, such as 'Sorry gov, I can't take you west, I'm on me way home' and 'Farking darkies coming over here stealing our jobs'. These jolly fellows are the salt of the earth, or one of the planets anyway (possibly Uranus). Every London taxi driver has to undergo an examination colloquially known as 'the knowledge'. This covers such absolute essentials of taxi-driving life as knowing every single street in London, taking you to your destination by the longest possible route and giving you hateful grimaces in the mirror if you interrupt his monologue on how crucifixion should be introduced for jaywalkers.

Unauthorized minicabs also proliferate. Though a good deal cheaper than the licensed black cabs, they can sometimes unsettle the unprepared traveller. To be honest the vehicles are not always what they should be, but when you are in a hurry to get home who needs actual brakes? Not having subjected himself to 'the knowledge', the minicab driver may not know where — or even who — he is. You may have to assist him by reading the map, asking for directions or gently prising his beer can out of his hand. Occasionally he may ask you to get out and help him push, but remember that pushing is a serious criminal offence, as is possession for that purpose.

THEATRE & CINEMA

London is the world capital of theatre. Here on the West End stage you can find many challenging works of contemporary drama such as 'Ooops, Vicar, Your Trousers Have Fallen Down' and 'Is That A Double Entendre In Your Pocket Or Is It Your Cock?' The pen is mightier than the sword, they say, but the penis is mightier still, apparently.

There are also several long-running and wildly successful musicals, not all of them about feline quadrupeds, alleged Messiahs or Argentine fascists' girlfriends.

The charming area of Soho also boasts a wide range of highly cathartic live performances, many of them involving ping-pong balls, cucumbers and actual donkeys. Another nice thing about Soho is its quaint little hotels. Twenty pounds per half-hour is really a most attractive rate and you will find the staff exceedingly hospitable, especially if you have a shower beforehand and remove your own socks.

Numerous works of contemporary cinema may be enjoyed in this area too, particularly those emanating from the Scandinavian countries. Simply settle back, ignore the aroma of disinfectant and relax! Sometimes you will hear a soft moaning sound from the darkness behind you, but that is nothing to worry about. British audiences are famously appreciative and when a film is particularly stimulating they do tend to come over all funny.

EXPLORING THE SUBURBS

Hampstead is another interesting area, very different in character in Soho. Many millionaires live around here, with the result that the place can be just a little snobbish. If a beggar approaches you in Hampstead High Street, he will likely ask if you can spare him three pounds fifty for a decaf cappuccino.

Notting Hill is my own favourite part of London. It was made famous by race riots, reggae bands, a spectacular annual Caribbean carnival and the noted film starring Hugh Grant in which black people do not feature. As ever it is nice to see the British movie industry doing its bit.

Greenwich down in Sarf-East London is where the English invented time. One day the breathtaking genius Sir Isaac Newton suddenly realized that time was there, and it was about time someone discovered it, and where would we all be now if he hadn't? That's right. A lot bloody happier, that's where. It has always seemed a little odd to me that wherever on the face of the planet you are, you measure time by your relative distance from Greenwich, a town that doesn't even have a disco. But I suppose anything is better than 'Limerick Mean Time'.

Greenwich is also the site of the controversial Millennium Dome which cost the British taxpayer seven hundred million pounds, or, to put it another way, one hundred million for each satisfied visitor. Much of the criticism of the Dome was deeply unfair, in my view. Incredibly spectacular performances were given there regularly, including 'Jimmy The Novelty Balloon Twister' and 'Mr Peterson's Puppet Show' (Tuesdays Only).

Another interesting part of South East London is Lewisham, which has given the world of popular entertainment such luminaries as Boy George, Jools Holland, Squeeze and Vic Reeves. Long ago the Beatles and David Bowie both played at the nearby Catford Odeon. For some terribly sad reason I also happen to know that the great Val Doonican got married in Lewisham Catholic Church. So all in all, Lewisham rocks! (It was also the birthplace of Albert Hall, after whom The Albert Hall is named.)

CLUBBING

If this happens to you, hand over your wallet and seek medical attention.

NIGHTCLUBBING

For those who like to boogie on down, London offers a plethora of excellent night-clubs. Many of these have strict admission criteria which will be explained to you by the helpful security staff. This tradition is known as 'enforcing the door policy', the main precept of which would seem to be 'If we don't like your face, we will enforce it through a door.'

When choosing which club you might like to attend, personal safety is very important. In certain establishments in South East London they search you on the way in for offensive weapons. If you don't have any, they advise you to go home immediately.

'Fetish' nights are currently all the rage in several London clubs. At these fun and relaxed events, people dress up in rubber, plastic and leather garments. This may be difficult for the Irish Male, whose leather garment of choice is often a scapular. But throw yourself in at the deep end and you may well be humiliated. Approach paying the bill with caution in these establishments. Suggesting a whip-around is not at all wise, nor may it turn out to be hygienic.

PARK LIFE

London offers many verdant open spaces, such as Clapham

Common, Regents Park, Primrose Hill and Hampstead Heath. These are wonderful locations for a relaxing walk, a brisk trot or a terrified gallop. Enjoy the fresh air, the charming wildlife, the Government ministers being set up in 'cruising' scandals by the tabloids.

Hyde Park is known as 'the lungs of London,' probably because it is often filthy and congested. The Rolling Stones played a legendary free concert here in July 1969, after which Mick remarked that while he couldn't get no satisfaction *per se*, he thought it had gone remarkably well. Speakers Corner (at the Marble Arch end of the park) is a famous oasis of free speech, not to mention outright lunacy. Here people gather on Sunday afternoons to listen to speakers of many diverse views and medication regimens explaining how Maoism/Fascism/Vegetarianism is the only answer to the problems of the world and how Our Lord is telling them to eat their own trousers. Do not make eye-contact with any of the speakers. And please do not attempt to feed them.

WIMBLEDON

The only thing you need know about this fantastic festival of world tennis is that the English players always get knocked out in the first round.

In that sense they are quite like most English boxers.

FOOTBALL IN LONDON

London is home to several exciting football teams, such as West Ham, Millwall, Tottenham Hotspur and Charlton Athletic (named after Jack and Sir Bobby Charlton-Athletic). Other London-based sides include Chelsea and Arsenal, two of the mightiest of all English clubs. Sometimes you will even see an English player on the pitch! (He will be the one missing the crucial penalty in the shoot-out.)

Other English cities also have truly great teams. For

example, Manchester (Manchester United), Sheffield (Sheffield Wednesday), Leeds (Leeds United) and of course Liverpool (Everton).

English football is going through a problematic phase at the moment. What with beating up their girlfriends and getting arrested in nightclubs, it is hard for some of the players to find the time to go on television and criticize the fans' loutish behaviour. But is vital to show a little understanding about this. When you are only being paid thirty grand a week, the pressure can really get to you.

Still, there is hope for a brighter future. Younger players have come up through the ranks, and the likes of David Beckham and Michael Owen may once again bring World Cup glory to England. (Don't laugh.) Though it is important to remember that a player as talented as Beckham comes with a lot of baggage — most of it Luis Vuitton.

For the visiting football fan a pilgrimage to Wembley, the spiritual home of soccer, is absolutely compulsory, especially because the government that gave England the Millennium Dome now wants to demolish the old Wembley Stadium so they can build in its place 'something people will like'. Walk the ruins of those historic terraces. Gaze down with love on the remains of that hallowed field. Who can forget the massed ranks of happy England supporters who thronged the stands for the legendary semi-final clash of Euro 96?

'Football's coming home,' they sang.

And it was.

To Germany.

A KNIGHT AT THE OPERA

My own introduction to the world of the English opera came about in a curious way. One evening several years ago, myself and a female companion to whom I wanted to give my whole heart and existence (at least twice a week) attended a performance, at the Royal Court Theatre, of Ms Marina Carr's excellent work *Portia Coughlan*. At a certain point in the proceedings the eponymous heroine expressed the view that sex was not worth having. It was nothing more than a vile concoction of sucking, poking, sweatiness and prodding, and it never led to anything good. 'Give me a good opera any day,' she said.

I turned to my date and hollowly laughed. 'Did you ever hear the like of it? Sex not worth having.' She peered at me in a way that made my blood freeze.

'Come on,' I said. 'Not as good as *opera*? A load of fat wallies poncing around in tights and warbling out of them about consumption? I'd rather bite off my own foot than *ever* waste money on such festering garbage. You're not really telling me that's better than sex? '

She nodded.

'Ah, but you haven't had sex with *me*,' I quipped. (In football parlance this is what is known as 'lobbing one in from the edge of the box'.)

'That's because you haven't brought me to the opera yet,' she replied.

So next day I booked tickets for the Glyndebourne Opera Festival.

The work was the late Herr Handel's opera *Theodora*, and cracking stuff it was too. Before long I was totally converted. If you like your classical music with extra helpings of violence, lust and revenge, then opera really is the thing for you. How it ever caught on with the toffs is beyond me, for opera is basically punk in a bodice. But the punters were even more entertaining than the show. Glyndebourne is the last place in England where you have to dress up formally to go to the opera, so monkey suits and posh frocks were *de rigueur*. Much jewellery was flashed, many a Rolex ostentatiously consulted. Looking at the faces of many of the audience, one couldn't help but get the feeling that the gene pool out of which the English aristocracy scuttled must have been a bit of a shallow puddle. Most of the women looked like dockers in drag and most of the men had either too many chins or none at all. I am sure I was the only person in the entire auditorium who didn't have an ancestor that got fucked by an Earl (except in the sense of being evicted by one).

Another interesting Glyndebourne tradition is the interval picnic. This proved to be a marvellous occasion for observing that extraordinary phenomenon, the English at play.

I cannot convey to you in mere language the utterly Pythonesque quaintness of the scene. Seated in the middle of a field in Sussex were sixty or eighty couples, all in formal attire, and all of them eating picnics out of hampers. Now, a picnic to you or me would be two slices of best batch with a triangle of Calvita wedged betwixt, the whole collation agreeably consumed on the beach at Bray or a sand dune at Brittas. But the English regard the humble picnic as a challenge. There were great big hampers and plastic wine coolers and folding seats and expandable barbecues and lobster salads and sides of roast beef. There were waiters trotting around with chilled champagne. There was a string quartet fiddling away under a tree. Very nice, you might well say. What is so odd and remarkable about that?

Well, what was so odd and remarkable about the proceedings was that they were taking place in the middle of the most violent thunderstorm I have ever seen in my life. Lighting was ripping the sky into fragments. The rain seemed to be coming down horizontally, in stinging sheets of ice-cold rage. Before long it had turned into fat smacking hailstones. The sky was black, as though stained with ink. Every time the thunder boomed I actually felt the earth shake beneath me. Soon the air was thick with falling leaves, while the ground had the consistency of lumpy porridge. Even the few people ⸖

who did have umbrellas were drenched and buffeted and windblown and battered.

But on they sat, the genteel English, exuding a kind of communal imperviousness, nibbling cucumber sandwiches and sipping *Cotes du Rhône*, princes of picnickery and all they surveyed. And on they played, the string quartet, though the tree that gave them shelter was actually rocking in the gale. And when it was time, the picnickers politely packed up their hampers and squelched back inside to watch the rest of the opera. There they sat, dripping and shivering, until the fat lady sang and the curtain came down, and then everyone got up and filed quietly out, the men holding the doors open for their sodden crumpled ladies, who laughed and smiled and gaily told each other they were glad that the weather hadn't been *too* bad this year.

And that's why the English used to run the world.

The Irish Male Goes Further Afield

To travel hopefully is a better thing than to arrive.

Robert Louis Stevenson

Especially because the airline will lose your luggage.

Anonymous Irish Male

Never Mind the Ballearics

Ah, Majorca! Fabled isle of lemon groves and brilliant sunshine, of olive groves and orangeries, of soft Mediterranean breezes and moonkissed golden beaches. Phooey. Balderdash. Ballearics.

I have had severely mixed feelings about this place ever since a family holiday in 1981 when I celebrated my first trip to a Continental resort by stripping down to my bathing attire and lying for eleven straight hours in the fiery rays that beat down on Palma Nova like a hammer. Without putting on any sun-screen.

You don't want to know the details. Let's just say that by the time the sun went down that night my chest and thighs were the colour of a London bus. So excruciatingly bad was the burning that even drawing a sheet over my naked, scalded body felt like being scraped to death with the cheese-grater from Satan's kitchen drawer.

As you can imagine, Palma Nova was a tremendously exciting place for a teenager with acute sunstroke. I spent three days in bed copiously vomiting. But after that, things improved a lot. I began to have hallucinations. I'd peer out the hotel room window at my beloved family besporting themselves in the kidney-shaped pool and marvel at how like aardvarks they seemed. The power of movement gradually came back. After only five days I could eat again. By the end of the first week I was actually allowed leave the hotel room, but only after sundown. Every night when my sisters and stepmother had retired, my father and I would venture down to the local bar and play the Space Invaders machine for four hours. Some nights he would control the left-right directional lever and I would be in charge of the firing. But other nights we would get bored with that and decide to push the boat out a bit. He would do the firing and I would operate the directional lever. By the end of the holiday we were really very good at Space Invaders. (My father is now a Jedi Knight.)

On the penultimate day of the trip I was finally allowed venture out into daylight again. Eyes blinking like a hibernating mole, I was somewhat crestfallen to note that the various teenagers I had befriended on the flight to Majorca had all been busy having fun, drinking sangria and wearing the faces off each other. Overcome with emotion, I spent the last night trying to get off with the tour guide, Valerie. I felt setting my sights high was the only way I could redeem the trip. But Valerie wasn't having any of it.

For some odd reason Valerie seemed to feel that restless young males on holiday were a bit of a professional hazard, that despite my declarations, I didn't really want a meaningful relationship but merely wanted to get her into bed. Nothing could have been further from my mind. Given the right circumstances, a broom cupboard would have sufficed.

In the eighteen years that have elapsed, I have learnt a thing or two about life. This time around I was determined to enjoy Majorca to the absolute limit. So I brought two vital accoutrements for holiday enjoyment with me; a large bottle of sunscreen and my first wife.

La Residencia in Deia is an expensive hotel. It is chic. It is classy. A place that reeks of unending choice. Two swimming pools, four lounges, an art gallery, a gymnasium, a massage centre, a beauty salon, three restaurants and a lovely bar on the sun-splashed terrace where you can order cocktails so strong they get you drunk in five minutes flat. And if you then want to sober yourself up in two, you just take a quick glance at the bill. So that's handy.

La Residencia (or 'La Rez', as it seems to be known to its admiring flock of largely English regulars) is also the home of 'El Olivo', the most expensive dining place on the entire island of Majorca, if not in all of Spain. As is usual in such joints all over the world, the staggering cost of eating turned out to be in inverse proportion to the efficiency of the service. *Mucha calma* is said to be the traditional motto of Majorcans, which roughly translates as 'Hey, relax,' or, perhaps more accurately 'Sod 'em, they can wait.' But I must record that the only place in Majorca we encountered this seeming indifference to our continued existence in the physical realm was at El Olivo. There it was allied to what seemed a kind of twattish condescension. We ate there twice, and it happened both times, and as Uncle Oscar said, twice begins to look like carelessness.

At any of the other fine restaurants in Deia village they don't exactly fall over themselves, but the nosh does at least arrive before you find yourself anxiously sucking the lemon wedge from the glass in which your aperitif came. Not at El Olivo. There when we asked whether there was any sign of our appetiser materialising that week, the waiter peered at us with a vaguely amused raising of one eyebrow. I am all in favour of a Latinly leisurely dining experience, but by the time the first course arrived we were taking it in turns to gnaw on the cutlery.

Around us the talk was of movie deals and modelling contracts, and the bougainvillaea-scented air rang with the buzzing and bleeping of mobile phones, as well as the thunderous rumbling of stomachs eagerly awaiting satiation. Indeed, a mobile phone would seem to be as compulsory at La Residencia as a thong bikini and a set of orthodontically perfect choppers. You would wonder, really, why some of these people go on holiday at all, so keen do they seem to keep in touch with the office.

But that is La Residencia for you. A tremendously lovely and unique place, there is no doubt, but it attracts, shall we say, a certain type. Perhaps it gives some indication of the predominant socio-economic profile of the clientele to say that the most disturbing sound I heard all week was the plaintive cry from the swimming pool, 'Mummy, Mummy! Caspar's got a varuka!'

And I shall never forget the sight of all those suntanned faces peering up in shock from behind their *Vogues* and *Wall Street Journals* when, another day, a couple of exhausted-looking Australian backpackers had the temerity to wander in off the street and dangle their proletarian tootsies in the deep end. I honestly thought one guest was going to summon a waiter and ask for a twelve-bore.

The surrounding village of Deia, and the pleasant nearby towns of Andratz and Soller, have all the commerce the heart could desire, but, unlike in the sprawling tourist resorts in the south of the island, nothing here hits you across the face. There are nice little restaurants, galleries and bars, *pensiones* and *bodegas* catering for all budgets; you get that rarest of feelings here, the sense of a region functioning in more or less easy relationship with the tourism that keeps it alive.

But scratch the surface and you find things are more troubled. In recent years, house prices in the area have soared, as foreigners have briskly bought up everything in sight. (It is a telling fact that Deia is simultaneously the richest town on the island and the one with by far the lowest rate of continuous home occupancy.) Geography, economics and almost baroque levels of governmental ineptitude have conspired to bring about a situation where it is impossible for a Majorcan to afford a house in the region any more. One night in a local bar I overheard a conversation so emblematic of the problem and so toe-curlingly embarrassing that I could barely walk home afterwards. (At least that's my excuse.) The friendly barman was explaining how his fiancée and himself were extremely worried about where they would live after their marriage. Each of them had been born and raised in Deia but they simply could not afford to buy a home there, there was no point in even fantasizing about it. 'Exactly, exactly,' a sloshed London yuppie was fervently agreeing. 'I really know how you feel. Every time we come here we try to buy a house. But it's seventy mill pesetas for a total bloody dump, and I mean, you don't even get *a parking space* for that!'

Poor, well-meaning Robert Graves probably had a hand in all this. He fell in love with this gorgeous place, lived and wrote here for many years but is no longer to be seen due to the highly technical business of interment. His affectingly simple tomb — 'Robert Graves, Poeta' — is in a quiet corner of Deia's little churchyard which looks down from a steep hill over the kind of vista you only see in dreams or television commercials. The azure sea, the broad, irregular stone terraces snaking up hills which rise from gentle, sloping pastures to pine-covered mountains, speckled with battered olive trees growing at every possible angle to the ground except the strictly vertical. The sheer tropical lushness of the vegetation, the trickle of water over the rocks, the great swathes of myrtles and caper bushes, woodbine and asphodel, lemon and orange groves everywhere you look, that extraordinarily pervasive aroma of citrus and honeysuckle sweetening the hot air late at night. You can see why this is the kind of place people have wanted to write poetry about.

Long before Graves' time, the surrounding region had become something of a haven for poets, musicians, novelists and arty types. The centre of it all used to be Valldemossa, a thriving market town twenty-five kilometres north of Palma, nestled neatly around a former Carthusian monastery which is now a vast souvenir shop with a small museum attached. The great Chopin himself lived here for a while, with a girl whose name was George. (It was the first recorded instance in Majorcan cultural history of real life imitating a Famous Five novel.)

Chopin's girl was George Sand, the noted Parisian novelist,

cigar-smoker and controversial trouser-wearer. Ms Sand believed in free-love, revolutionary socialism and the immediate and preferably violent destruction of the Catholic Church, so it is perhaps not much of a surprise that the God-fearing local peasants regarded her with something like suspicion. Majorca is a place where religious iconography is absolutely ubiquitous, where the Virgin Mary appears on the labels of wine bottles and matchboxes, where every single town you visit has tiled images of the local saint adorning the walls of the houses, where to this day you see people old and young make the sign of the cross when they pass a church. George would have found this difficult to do because she would likely have been trying to chuck a petrol-bomb into it at the time. No, the locals didn't take to George one bit and there wasn't too much love lost on George's side either. Nor was she the kind of gal to pull her punches.

Her deservedly little-known memoir *A Winter In Majorca* is almost amusing in its splenetic hatred for all things Balearic. A Majorcan, she rants, 'is entirely without scruples, more a savage than a man … nothing but a monkey, a creature clothed in human form, vegetating in an aimless existence. He would eat his fellow-man without remorse, were that the custom of his country. He cheats, extorts, lies, insults and plunders without scruple. A foreigner is not a fellow-man for him. He would never rob his neighbour of so much as an olive: for in God's great design of things, those human beings from across the sea exist only to bring small profits to the Majorcan … They are the most stupid people in the world.'

A tad bizarrely, she reserves a special loathing for Majorcan food, perhaps the most inoffensive cuisine on the face of the planet. 'Twenty dishes appear on the table, looking like any Christian food: but take heed, for they are hellish concoctions brewed by the Devil himself … .Their [olive] oil is so vile that every house, man and carriage on the island and even the very air of the fields becomes impregnated with its stench. Since it is an integral part of their cooking, the fumes rise up two or three times a day from their homes and the walls are steeped in it. If, deep in the country, you lose your way, you need only sniff the air, and if a rancid stink wafts past your nostrils on the wings of a breeze, you may be sure to find a house hidden behind some rocks or a clump of cacti. And if in the wildest and loneliest areas this stench pursues you, look up and you will see some hundred paces away — a Majorcan on his donkey.'

Wonderful, wonderful stuff. But Valdemossa has had perhaps the best revenge on Gorgeous George and her consumptive, ivory-tickling boyfriend. Today every souvenir stall, burger shop and tapas bar in the town has on offer an attractive selection of George 'n' Chopin memorabilia: busts, T-shirts, boxer shorts, key rings, shaving mugs and — my own personal favourite — little plastic pianos embossed with Chopin's miserable face that play '*Y Viva España*' when you open their lids.

All in all, northern Majorca has a lot to recommend it. Far enough from the fleshpots and disco-bars of the south to guarantee peace for the soul and a good night's sleep, it is still only forty minutes from Palma airport. And once you get there, there's all the wildness and isolation you can handle, long walks, deserted coves, mountain tracks, verdant valleys. The only problem is those damn house prices, really. It's just not fair, when you think about it.

The Land Of The Free —
Or At Least The Very Cheap

Friday 13 September

Look, I'm tired, OK? I am hot and exhausted and hungry and stressed. I only got off the plane from Dublin to New York two hours ago. I have jetlag the way Noddy Holder had spangles. I am in a bad mood and it's getting worse.

'Why did you write *Sweet Liberty*?' the television reporter is asking me, for only the fifteen-hundredth time. 'I mean, this book about all the towns named Dublin in the United States? What exactly is it that you feel you are *saying* about the Irish in America?'

'One, two, three, four,' I reply.

She nods in a solemnly encouraging fashion.

'Five, six, seven, eight,' I continue.

'Really?' She flashes a smile that must have cost thousands to achieve. 'How *very* fascinating. Will you share more of that story with us?'

'Oh yes indeed,' I affirm. 'One, two, three, four. HA HA HA. And four, three, two, one, as a matter of fact. But then again, when you really think about it, ten, nine, eight, seven, six, five, four, as James Joyce would have put it.'

'Marvellous,' she grins. 'And you tell it so beautifully. You Irish folks have *such* a wonderful way with words.'

I should explain that we are doing cutaway shots. 'Cutaway shots' is televisual jargon for annoying the very LIFE out of people being interviewed. How this works is as follows: having answered all of the interviewer's enquiries, they then take the camera off you and point it at the interviewer and do portions of the interview all over again, now filming the person asking the questions. Only this time round, as the sound engineer has explained to me, it would be much easier for editing purposes if I didn't actually answer the questions in an intelligible manner, and if I just said 'one two three four' in response. Do I think I can do that? I confirm that having spent five whole years studying English in UCD I think I can just about manage it, yes. In fact I say 'one two three four' better than anyone else in the literature business. I am known all over the world for that. Not even Seamus Heaney says 'one, two, three, four' the way I do.

'Looking forward to your book tour in America?' the interviewer asks.

'Well, Donna,' I smile, 'I'm really glad you asked me that question. Because one, two, three, four, five, six, seven ...'

I feel as low as tits on a giraffe. My tongue is a yellowish-grey sock. My head is pounding like the Manic Street Preachers are rehearsing therein. My feet have swollen in my brand new book-tour shoes.

'One two three four, one two three four.'

Sometimes being a writer seems very glamorous indeed.

Saturday 14 September

Up early and get a taxi dowtown to my interview at Radio Free Eireann.

I know you will be surprised to hear that Radio Free Eireann takes a broadly Republican line when it comes to the Irish national question, but it is all done with refreshing irreverence and a good deal of self-mockery. The presenters are two extremely friendly and funny fellows who fall around laughing when any of the phone-in contributors says anything at all. One of them takes me to task for criticizing a New York Irish priest who said in a sermon that Portlaoise Prison should be immediately destroyed by God. I point out that I am all in favour of God destroying Portlaoise Prison, once he destroys the rest of Portlaoise as well.

Later in the day I turn up to do a reading at a bookshop in Woodlawn, which is in the Bronx. Tens of thousands of Irish people live in Woodlawn. Unfortunately only five of them come to my reading.

The silence in the shop is astounding, as we all stand around and look at our shoes and fervently hope that nobody breaks wind, because the resulting echo would be utterly deafening. The manager explains that today many of the local populace are engaged in 'A Day On The Bog'. This is an important annual cultural event, involving the shipping into Woodlawn of several tons of Irish turf, the spreading of same on a local race-course, and its subsequent and celebratory digging up. Why anyone in even half of their right mind would want to go all the way to New York to dig turf is beyond me, but there it is. 'Give me your tired, your poor, your needy,' said Lady Liberty, 'and I will let them dig turf in the Bronx.'

Woodlawn is also famous for having a large cemetery, which contains what is left of Irving Berlin, Oscar Hammerstein, Herman Melville and the great Duke Ellington. Peripatetic Irish authors, please note — if you ever do a reading in Woodlawn, do it in the boneyard. You just might get a livelier crowd.

Sunday 15 September
Day off. Go for a stroll in the attractive and thriving neighborhood of Times Square. Very friendly locals. Extremely outgoing. So friendly and outgoing that many of them walk right up to you in the street and shout 'GIMME SOME FUCKIN MONEY RIGHT NOW' in your face.

As well as the touching hospitality of its *habitués*, Times Square is noted for the breathtaking variety of its exciting cultural institutions, such as Petie's Porno Palace, The Lap Dance Lounge, Murray's Thai Massage and Big Benny's Bazoom Room ('Fifty Pretty Girls and One Ugly One').

I notice that one of the nearby artistic cinemas is currently showing a sensitive and delicately crafted work set in the deep South, about the affecting relationship between an elderly white lady and her poor black chauffeur.

It is called 'Driving Miss Daisy Crazy'.

What a nice town New York is.

Monday 16 September

Get up early and fly to Washington where my book-signing session at lunchtime goes OK. I meet two folks from Roberts Rinehart, the American publishers of *Sweet Liberty*. These are Jack Van Zandt and Shelley Daigh. Shelley will be accompanying me on the rest of the tour. It is her job to drum up publicity for the book and to make sure that the rest of the tour goes smoothly, but most of all it is her job to make me get receipts for any expenses I may incur. She seems absolutely adamant about this. There will be no expenses pay-out for anything that doesn't have a receipt. She says this quite a number of times and does not look like a person to be trifled with at all. Her nickname back in the office is 'The Bulldog', she tells me proudly. Subsequent to this revelation Jack fondly informs me that she is 'the Eva Braun of Roberts Rinehart'.

The Bulldog keeps using the phrase 'the wrath of Shelley' to describe what happens when she gets upset. (For example, when an expenses claim is submitted WITHOUT A RECEIPT.) Pretty soon I decide pretty firmly that the wrath of Shelley isn't something I ever want to see. I actually like having kneecaps, after all, and don't want to have to carry them home from America in a plastic bag.

Washington is abuzz with talk of the forthcoming election, also with memories of the recently deceased criminal fraudster and Nixon henchman, Spiro Agnew. Tonight there is a launch party for *Sweet Liberty* at the Irish Embassy. Big enthusiastic crowd. Bits of cheese on cocktail sticks. Someone tells me that America has really changed a lot since the bad old days of Vice-President Agnew. Yes, I joke, in these days of Clintonism a lying State Governor with severe legal problems can make it as far as the actual *Presidency*.

This goes down very well indeed, as you can imagine.

Tuesday 17 September

Fly back to New York. The American newspapers all carry the epoch-making story that Senator Bob Dole fell over on his backside the other night while campaigning for the Republicans in Chico, California, the only town in the United States to be named after one of the Marx Brothers (apart from Zeppo, Texas). Some journalists have put this forward as evidence that Mr Dole is too old to be still active in politics. They may have a point. Shortly after his tumble he reportedly made a reference to his deep admiration for 'the Brooklyn Dodgers', who actually departed Brooklyn in 1957. Next week he's going to Paris to discuss NATO with Napoleon Bonaparte. Still, Dole seems like a nice old codger. And at least when he met the Japanese ambassador recently, he didn't vomit on him like former President Bush once did. (I am not making this up.)

Back at the hotel in New York a reporter from a tremendously major newspaper such as the *The Staten Island Picayune* or *The Boise Idaho Leprechaun* fails to turn up to interview me. Shelley's eyes take on the expression of Linda Blair in the more memorable moments of *The Exorcist*. He, it seems, 'shall feel the wrath of Shelley'.

I decide to leave the room before her head starts revolving.

Wednesday 18 September

This morning I wake up to the somewhat startling news that the mayor of Dublin, California has issued a statement about *Sweet Liberty*, condemning it as 'a work of fiction'. Hmm. It is an odd country indeed where the worst thing you can say about a book is that its contents are fictional. Someone faxes me the front page of Dublin California's local newspaper, which boasts the screaming banner-headline IRISH AUTHOR DUMPS ON DUBLIN CALIFORNIA beside a photograph of myself looking sulky.

The article goes on to describe how my book 'goes through Dublin, California block by block, like a literary wrecking ball'. My publishers seem very excited about this, on the basis that there is no such thing as bad publicity. I often wonder whether this cliché is true, but Shelley feels it is, and I'm not going to argue. She points out that Hugh Grant's career in the United States actually *improved* after he was caught soliciting a hooker. She then goes on to ponder aloud whether I would be prepared to get myself into a Hugh Grant-Divine Brown-type situation in order to publicise *Sweet Liberty* a little further. I tell her yes but I don't think prostitutes give receipts.

Extremely well-attended reading at the Glucksman Ireland House in NYU. I am introduced to the audience by one of my heroes, the Irish-American journalist Pete Hamill. During his remarks he says I am 'disgustingly young' but I point out that in fact I am merely disgusting.

Afterwards I go for a drink with the wonderful staff and a mate from Dublin, Peter McDermott. We are all in a highly literary state by the end of the evening. Indeed, literature is discussed so very thoroughly that I keep waking up with an awful pain in my head.

Thursday 19 September
Fly to Boston, where I meet my father Sean and brother Eoin. With massive kindness way beyond the call of duty, they have flown over from Ireland to keep me company for a few days on the tour. Poor chaps, this will be very expensive indeed for them.

American hotels seem moderately priced when you look at their rate cards. But when the bill eventually arrives the unwary traveller can get quite a shock. By the time they add on the standard Sales Tax, State Tax, Local Tax, City Tax, 'Room Occupancy Tax' — like, what ELSE are you going to do with a hotel room if not *occupy* it? *Take it for a walk around the block?* — Service Charge, Concierge Commission, Maid Tax, Air-Breathing Tax and Looking-At-The-Waiter-In-A-Funny-Way Tax, the bill for a hundred-and-fifty-buck room can quite easily be $50,003.01

Sean, Eoin and I have an agreeable time looking around Boston. It is a graceful civilized town, if a wee bit snobbish. In other American cities they have drive-by shootings. In Boston they have drive-by shunnings instead.

That night in the bookshop I ask the manager if he thinks many people will show up for my reading. A strangely stressed smile invades his face. 'I'm not gonna lie to you here, Joe,' he says. 'Tonight is gonna be an intimate occasion.'

As I stand at the podium and gaze down at the crowd of nine, two members of which I share actual DNA with, I am struck once again by the great American capacity for euphemism.

Friday 20 September

Today is my birthday.

Well whoop-de-bloody-doo.

They say you're only as old as the age you feel. In which case, I probably died six years ago.

Eoin, Sean and I go to lunch at *Maison Robert* ('It means Robert's House in French, guys,' the Concierge helpfully explains). In the jacks of that fine establishment, I meet an waspish English bloke who proudly informs me that his mother was 'a titled lady'. I tell him mine was too. Leinster Middleweight Champion.

Saturday 21 September

Get up and bid my beloved relatives safe return to Ireland. They decline my bribes to stuff me into one of their suitcases, smuggle me on board and convey me homewards. So me and the Bulldog fly to Chicago where the signing session at The Joy Of Ireland Gift Store is a disaster of almost Biblical proportions. We rack up sales of a massive seven books, four of those to a clearly insane old lady who seems to be under the impression that I am Roddy Doyle.

Mr Richard Kosmacher, who runs the store, is clearly upset that so few people have turned up. I try to console him as best I can, though really I feel it should be the other way around. Yet I do have a genuine sense of pity for Richard, for he too shall soon be undergoing 'the wrath of Shelley'. As he watches her eyes begin to narrow, I hope to God he has made a will.

In the peaceful two-hour gaps between waiting for punters to show up and buy my book I scan the morning newspaper. There is an interview with the great diva of soul Dionne 'Walk On By' Warwick, who is apparently involved with a television channel called 'The Psychic Friends Line'. I confess that I find this somewhat amusing, because only last week in New York I read *another* article about Dionne Warwick, pointing out that she had recently been injured by someone throwing a brick at her.

With all those psychic friends she has, you'd think she'd have known to duck, wouldn't you?

Sunday 22 September

Day off. I call Richard Kosmacher to see if he wants to meet for lunch, but today is Yom Kippur, the Jewish 'Day of Atonement', and Richard, being of that faith, is consequently busy with Things of the Spirit. I bid him fond farewell and promise to keep in touch. I can't help feeling that God will forgive him a lot sooner than Shelley will. And that Shelley may require more painful atoning.

Monday 23 September.
Me and the Cuddlesome Canine get the train to Milwaukee, which isn't a very exciting town. The streets, in fact, are almost deserted, except for the occasional small group of citizens huddled together in a doorway to watch paint dry.

Very tired as we drive to the hotel. The most positive thing I can say about the room is that it contains a fly-swatter, which comes in handy.

When you buy a book the author receives about one tenth of the cover price. The cover price of *Sweet Liberty* is fourteen dollars.

Tonight at my reading in downtown Milwaukee, I boost my annual income by one dollar forty.

Tuesday 24 September
Fly from Milwaukee to Denver, Colorado.

Here we meet the Bulldog's husband who drives us to Boulder, the commodious city which contains among other things the international headquarters of Roberts Rinehart. I am a tad disconcerted to notice that the first thing Shelley does when we get to the office is whip out a badge of a snarling bulldog and proudly clamp it to her lapel. She really is an unusual person.

I am led around and introduced to all the fine, intelligent and strikingly good-looking people who toil away in Roberts Rinehart for the greater good of literature. I am quivering with anticipation at the thought of being reimbursed for my neatly filed and remarkably comprehensive sheaf of *per diem* receipts. But sadly the company accountant is not in today. She is out stealing the pennies off dead men's eyes.

A pleasant and strikingly beautiful young woman with the

unusual name of Isis has just started working at the office. I ask if by any chance she is named after the Bob Dylan song of that title and am overjoyed to discover that she is. Her second name is Layla — after the Eric Clapton classic. I tell her she got off remarkably lightly. She could have been christened 'I Shot The Sheriff'.

Back to Denver with minutes to spare, then the Bulldog and I take the shuttle to Seattle, where the hotel room is so small you couldn't raise veal in it.

Again I am worried about tonight's reading, but to my considerable surprise it goes quite well, except for the presence of one dribbling loon in the audience. When it comes to time for questions he thrusts his hand roofwards, glares at me, and asks if people in Ireland have ever heard of Seattle?

I kick for touch by simpering madly and swallowing a few big slugs of water. I ask myself if this is a trick question. Does he mean the Native American chieftain after whom this beautiful city is named?

No, he means Seattle.

I say yes, we are a very civilized country, we have flush toilets and we've heard of Seattle.

'You guys get *Frasier* over there in Ireland?'

I say that not only do we get *Frasier* in Ireland, I've actually had a couple of one-night-stands with Ros.

He then asks me who I think should play Brendan Behan in the forthcoming film of that writer's life. I say Sylvester Stallone. Everyone laughs, except this guy.

He's glaring at me like he wants to strangle me with his bare hands, rip out my liver and feed it to his psychiatrist. I am quite glad I have the Bulldog here to protect me.

Back at the hotel I can't get to sleep. It sounds like the room next door is occupied by two Sumo wrestlers with Tourret's Syndrome working their way slowly through the *Readers' Digest Guide To Sado-Masochism and Bondage.*

Finally drift into the arms of Morpheus (my teddy bear) and get a really good night's rest which lasts for, oh, an hour and a half.

Wednesday 25 September

Get up early and watch the TV news. Things are getting freaky in this country. Everywhere you look people are trying to ban things. The people of Oregon are currently voting on something called Ballot Measure Nine — amusingly misprinted 'Ballet Measure Nine' in today's *New York Times* — which will give status of law to the hoary old prejudice that homosexuality is 'abnormal, wrong, unnatural and perverse'.

Personally I've had enough of all these people telling us who it's OK to sleep with. You're gay? Good for you. You're straight? Congratulations. You want to bonk a llama? Hey, if it's cool with the llama, it's cool with me. You're getting it on with your living-room bookcase? Well, bring her down to the pub on Friday night and let's *all* get a look at her! Bro, Sis — if *you're* happy, *I'm* happy.

But here in America that is not how things work. The most multicultural democracy on the face of the earth and pretty soon you're going to need a permit to read *Doonesbury*.

Shelley and me fly to San Francisco. I go shopping for presents. Shelley goes shopping for receipts. Amazingly long queues in all the stores. People are shoplifting to save time, not money.

Mixed memories of San Francisco. Last time I was here I stood on a nail — it's a long and crushingly tedious story — and ended up hobbling to Casualty in a local hospital. There were maybe twenty people in the emergency room, and nineteen of those were holding urine samples. It was like a scene from Octoberfest.

Ah, sweet recollection. I won't say the queue was long but the guy in front of me had a musket wound. The first question the doctor asked me after a four-hour wait was 'How will you be paying for your treatment tonight, sir?' Wincing and groaning and trying not to bleed all over the floor I replied, 'With my life, sweetheart, if you don't pick up the fucking pace.' Tony Bennett may have left his heart in San Francisco, but I left my entire life savings.

This time around things are better. I manage not to skewer any part of my person and tonight's reading goes very well indeed.

Thursday 26 September

At San Francisco airport I bid goodbye to the Bulldog, who gives me a kiss on the cheek and one last bark of affection. She feels the tour has gone well, all things considered. I am in two minds about that myself, but I'm certainly not going to argue the toss. Some people might feel that an eight-thousand mile journey to sell forty-two books might not be a total success, but I am not one of them, and neither is Shelley.

'Main thing is, we got the receipts,' she points out.

And I really have to agree with her there. Particularly because she's biting my leg.

Roll Me Ova, In Mantova

Not that one would wish to be nervous of other cultures. But probably the most important thing to know about Mantua is that the locals do eat some quite mind-boggling things. Frog-leg pasta. Rabbit ragout. Marinated raw eel. Not much spaghetti.

On our second night in this gloriously beautiful place we went to a restaurant where nobody spoke any English at all. I should point out that the only Italian I speak myself is '*Ha scritto un romanzo, andiamo*' — 'I have written a novel, let's go' — which an Italian publisher once informed me were the only words a young single man would need in his country to guarantee a memorable visit. Anyway, there we were, myself and the Missus, in this unpretentious local eatery, ordering dishes just because we liked the sound of them when spoken *mezzo forte* by the friendly waiters. This, we felt, was a brave thing to do, in a city where one of the local specialties is Donkey Stew.

Yes, *spezzatino de Mantova*, while it sounds very wonderful, is made from the flesh of a genuine female donkey. And while it isn't actually served with the two ears protruding TV-aerial-style from the sauce, it is nevertheless, one suspects, something of an acquired taste. I have to admit I didn't try to acquire it. Investigative journalism is all very well, but presumably even John Pilger would draw the line somewhere.

Apart from mule casserole, Mantua is something of a foodie's paradise. Asking for a deep-pan pizza here, or a plate of spag bol just like Momma used to make, is a way of not acquiring too many friends. Those exceptions aside, the menus are amazing. You name it, you can find it to eat here in Mantua, cooked to perfection and at a third of the price you'd pay for it in Dublin, in one of those trendy new restaurants that feels like a boutique. Though, be advised, it's a very good thing to like pumpkin if you're coming here, because *tortelli di zucca* (ravioli stuffed with pulped pumpkin and almond) is so ubiquitous that it's sold on the street corners, the way dodgy watches and fake designer jeans are in England. So awesomely popular is this humble globose fruit that the city recently held a three-day festival of celebration at its most important cultural centre entitled '*La citta delle zuche*', featuring art shows, documentaries and installations about pumpkins. (I swear to God I am not making this up.) One gets the feeling that if Cinderella had come from Mantua, her coach would have turned into something else at midnight. Possibly a Lamborghini.

Here in Pumpkin City, eating is organised a bit like a boxing match. Full of fight, you spring from your corner and gamely attack the *antipasto*, which in other parts of Italy is small enough to be served in a saucer, but in Mantua is often so big that it comes in a veritable upturned dustbin lid. Next round is the *primo piatti*, your starter, basically, a mound of melt-in-the-mouth risotto the size of a soccer ball or a hunk of prosciutto from a pig so athletically proportioned that you really wouldn't want to meet it down a dark alleyway. Weak with satiation you retire to your corner, silently wishing you could throw in the towel. But you can't, the tender pummelling of the taste buds is about to continue. The bell sounds and in comes the *secondo*, enough for a Borgia, or at least a minor Pavarotti on a bit of a diet. You dodge, you weave, but you're up against the ropes. Then come the vegetables, then dessert, then cheese, then coffee and a liqueur, very possibly a *grappa*, a particularly muscular local brand of hooch stewed up from the grape skins left over from winemaking. Reluctance to follow this historically ordained pattern is met by waggings of fingers from waiters, or, even worse, understanding and tolerant smiles that say 'Ah, these poor northern Europeans, with their meagre appetites both sexual and culinary.' Ordering a light salad was met with ribald laughter.

It is a wonder to me how so many Italians are thin, graceful and phenomenally attractive. After one long weekend spent in Mantua I would have been afraid to strip off and sunbathe on a beach, lest I be struck on the head with a bottle of champagne and officially launched by Romano Prodi.

After all this gorging, you will need a good walk. And Mantua is a blissful pleasure to ramble around by day or night, its narrow cobbled streets abounding with dusty antique shops, little cafés and, of course, delicatessens, practically singing with agreeable aromas. The thing about the great Italian cities most beloved by tourists is that there's just so much of them. On and on they go, with their *piazzas* and *duomos*, their *Vias* and *Museos*, their hot streets named after recently discredited Communist leaders in the pay of the Mafia or significant dates from long-forgotten wars. Wandering around Venice, for example, can feel oddly like being force-fed on luscious chocolates. Utterly magnificent as they undoubtedly are, your Florences and Romes can wear you out — an important ruin here, a Renaissance masterpiece there, spit on the street and you hit a Leonardo. But Mantua is a town built small and neat, a modest little place, nestling around four squares and tucked into a space between two lakes, named, with a minimalist approach to adjectival language quite startlingly un-Italian, Lago Superiore and Lago Inferiore. Even here you are never far from culinary concerns. The pleasant grassy banks abound with fishermen, seeking the bass, pike, perch and sander with which the waters happily teem. Here you may stroll on a Sunday afternoon, eat ice cream, watch Italian families being somehow both traditional and cool at the same time and generally feel like an extra in a Fellini movie. Yes, all the traditional Italian activities may be enjoyed in the lakeside parks. Drinking wine. Discussing Dante. Riding your Vespa.

Forming a new coalition government.

Back in town, the most important building is the Palazzo Ducale, which was built by the local ruling dynasty, the Gonzagas, in the days when modest understatement wasn't really the thing. Begun in the 13th century and never truly completed, with 500 rooms, a floor space of 40,000 square metres and a total population of almost a thousand, it was, at one time, the largest palace in Europe, a gaff so utterly over the top that you could quite easily imagine the Duchess of York living there now. Only a small portion of this town within a city is open to the public — its restoration, like its original construction, is a never-ending story. Indeed, to see it all would take several days. But rooms that fall into the must-see category include the Sala delle Sinopie, where important sketches by Pisanello have recently been discovered beneath the frescoes, and the tapestry apartment, boasting magnificent work by Raphael. Elsewhere the palace features an entire scaled-down model of the Saint John Lateran cathedral in Rome, something no tasteful home should be without. This miniature oddity is sometimes described by the locals as 'the midgets' room', because way back in the days of yore one of the more crazy elderly female Gonzagas used to collect male dwarves as a hobby. (The guidebooks all say that they used to entertain her, though specifically how is mercifully not detailed.)

A pleasant twenty-minute stroll out of town, past the home of the greatest locally born artist Andrea Mantegna, is the rather more humble and manageable Palazzo Te. Designed by Giulio Romano for Duke Federico II Gonzaga and his main floozie, with a moat surrounding it to keep the Duchess away, this is a place you can see in an hour. Duke Federico seems to have been sixteenth-century Mantua's equivalent to Austin Powers and this, verily, was his shag-pad, baby.

The first thing you see when you enter is a panel of

paintings celebrating the life of King David. Biblical scholars among you will recall that King David murdered his lover Bathesheba's husband, so he could have his wicked way without having to suffer the inconvenience of spousal objections. This particular mural was commissioned very shortly after the Duke's girlfriend's husband was mysteriously tossed into Lago Inferiore in several untidy pieces. You can't help wondering if other Mantuan husbands were being told something subtle here.

The most fun room in the palace depicts the mythical battle between the Titans and the Gods, which was won by the Gods in a controversial penalty shoot-out. This vast mural is a kind of Renaissance Marvel cartoon-strip, spreading from the walls all over the ceiling, the whole scary effect considerably augmented by the fact that the Duke had an expert on acoustics design the room with a tremendous echo (before, no doubt, bonking his wife and murdering him). If you dropped a button on the floor in here, the resulting boom would be heard five chambers away. It is said that Federico and his moll were particularly fond of doing it in the Titans' room. It must have made quite a commotion.

But when they weren't getting jiggy, the early Italians were saying their prayers. And if there's one thing Italian Catholicism loves, it's a relic. This a country where bits of saints are stored in crypts like chops in a freezer. Mantua can rightly claim a certain smug superiority in this regard because when it comes to relics it trumps everyone else. Not for this place the fingernail clippings of Saint Theresa or the left cheek of John the Baptist. No, no, here they have THE BLOOD OF CHRIST! Which in Catholic relic terms is very much the big enchilada.

The blood was reportedly brought from the Holy Land by the soldier who pierced Jesus's side on the cross, which was nice of him, I suppose, though it can't have made the Donor feel much better. But sadly I have to report that you can't actually see Our Lord's solidified blood itself, at least, not without making an appointment with the Sacristan. It is kept deep in the bowels of the rather stern Basilica di Sant Andrea, where, miraculously, a bit like the Italian lire, it goes into meltdown three times a year.

All in all, then, Mantua is marvellous, a place that's just about ideal for a long peaceful weekend or a short romantic jaunt. Just, please, do remember one vital thing. In Ireland, it is sometimes said that a person is so hungry he would eat somebody's ass. But only in Mantua is that literally true.

The Irish Male Does It
Inishowen Unique Way

It is said of Saint Columba, the patron saint of poets, that as he was sent into exile from Ireland, on a bitter day in 563 AD, he stopped his boat one last time by the shores of his beloved northern Donegal. He climbed the cliff at Inishowen Head, near a stark, wild place that's now called Portkill. There he wept with longing as he blessed the landscape, knowing he would never see it again.

A plaque marks the spot of his final teary benediction, with a simple inscription in medieval Gaelic.

Do-ell Erinn, indell cor,
cechaing noib nemed mbled.

Which, roughly translated, means 'We do bed and breakfast.'

Okay. okay, I'm joking about that. Actually it means:

He turned away from Ireland, entered a pact,
He crossed the sea in ships, the sanctuary of the whales.

When you stand here now, fourteen centuries later, you realise the view probably hasn't changed too much since. Yes, there are cottages, two or three holiday homes. The lights that twinkle across the bay at night are those of the British Army base at Magilligan Camp in Co Derry. But you really do see what upset the poor saint. It must have broken his heart to leave Inishowen.

Donegal is an astoundingly lovely region, but Inishowen, the peninsula that forms its northeastern tip, is the most beautiful area anywhere in Ireland. Visitors have been coming here for centuries, drawn by a landscape so hauntingly desolate that once seen they never forget it. With its lakes, mountains, bogs and ancient ruins, it's one of the last places left in Ireland that looks like a location for *The Quiet Man*.

Our hotel turned out to be one of the most expensive in Inishowen. But the charming staff could not have been more helpful. The night we arrived we were too late for dinner so they offered us food upstairs. We looked at each other and actually beamed. How lovely it was to be here in Donegal.

But upstairs was where the problems started. The miniature bed in the minuscule room had been arranged so as to completely obscure one's path to the minute window, which, when you scraped off the grime, offered remarkable views over the gracious sweep of the car-park. This is a hotel in the Irish countryside, with a view of mountain, water and fen. It is the loveliest setting for a hotel I have ever seen anywhere. It boasts the kind of view that would make even Ian Paisley stop in his tracks and start humming a tune by Clannad. If only the rooms didn't face out on the car-park.

The wife, who is English, seemed to find all this sweet, and somehow profoundly, authentically Irish. I, on the other hand, thought it mystifying. Was it possible, I wondered, that the entire building had been put up the wrong way around? I was standing on the bed, craning my neck out the window for anything resembling a view, when dinner arrived. The main course — either a very small chicken or a very large bat — was overdone. I took a bite. On the balance of probabilities it was probably chicken. It had all the flavour and consistency of a cornflakes box.

Still, we weren't fussy. You don't come to Inishowen for *cordon bleu* dining or luxury accommodation (though little extras like light-bulbs would have been nice). Having eaten and imbibed and enjoyed a chat, we decided to have an early night. But the bed was too small for us both to get into it and not have an argument.

The wife suggested that she go out to the landing and fetch the cushions off the sofa so I could sleep on those. There was a bit of discussion at this point, but our marriage counsellor says we will get over it eventually. The final compromise was that she got the rather grimey duvet and the mattress, which we dragged onto the floor by the door to the bathroom, and I got the wooden base of the bed with the sofa cushions, and my overcoat. Out in the car-park a drunkard was singing:

I wander her hills and her valleys,
And still through my sorrow I see,
A land that has never known freedom,
Where only our rivers run free.

As you can imagine, this cheered me up a great deal.

Next day, bright and early, I skipped out of bed — or, at least, off the base of the bed — whistling a traditional Irish lullaby I had personally composed while lying awake all night getting cramps in my limbs.

Toora Loora Loora,
Toora Loora Lie,
Toora Loora Loora,
Yes, we're going to die.

A barefoot woman was at the door, wondering if we had a leak in our bathroom, because water was pouring through her ceiling. I stepped over the wife and entered said room. We did have a leak. In fact, we had a river. But at least it was running free.

No view, no sleep, a leaking toilet. A dry chicken and a wet bathroom floor. (In fairness, it must be noted that a mild complaint to the manager led to the bill being waived, and not in our faces.)

Things improved when we checked out. Inishowen has countryside you have to see at least once. You think it's as heartbreakingly beautiful as it's going to get and then it gets more beautiful again. Frankly, if you can drive through the Mamore Pass without stopping at least twice to just sit there and go 'WOWWW', there is probably something wrong with you. Outcrops of ferocious-looking rock seem to sweep down from the mountains like frozen waterfalls. Bog flowers and sea birds, carpets of wild fuschia and rhododendrons, turf stacks like sleeping dragons, silhouetted on the brows of the hills. Dolmens, stone crosses, megalithic tombs and fairy forts. Ruined castles everywhere, brooding in the fields. Odd, really, the number of castles. Was there ever a country more fortified than Ireland, only to get itself invaded so often?

Even the place names resound with beauty, the unpretentious poetry of local speech. Carrowmenagh, Carrowbeg, Craignahulla, Gortnageeha. Ballyliffen, Bally-clamsy, Bulbinmore, Altnadarrow. Reading aloud from a road map is fun here. It makes you feel like you're Seamus Heaney.

Heaney himself is a frequent visitor to Inishowen. Brian Friel has made it his home. You can see the attraction for literary types; narrative and geography are intertwined all around you. Every feature of the landscape seems to have its own legend. The cross-shaped mark in that boulder was carved by a saint's finger, the two shallow indentations over there in the graveyard the miraculous prints of a praying hermit's knees. If you're a sucker for a story, as I am myself, then Inishowen is the place to be. You see a hole in the pavement dug by a council worker, and someone will tell you it was Saint Patrick's wine cellar.

But it's not all wilderness and misty-eyed mythologising. The peninsula is speckled with pretty little towns like Cardonagh and Malin, Moville and Culdaff. The fishing port of Greencastle offers B&B and seafood, and an opportunity to visit the eccentrically constructed St Finian's church, which like certain Donegal hotels, appears to be facing the wrong way around, with the 'east' end actually pointing west. St Finian's was built by an endearing local whacko, Bishop Frederick Harvey, 4th Earl of Bristol. He ordered the workmen to position the entrance porch in such a way that he could view it by telescope from his home across the lough in Co Derry. If the numbers were low on a Sunday morning, or he didn't like the look of the congregation, he'd take a rain check and get back in his bed.

Way up the top of the peninsula near the Malin Head meteorology station is the storm-lashed bit of rock known as 'Banba's Crown', named after the Irish goddess, Banba. (On a similar basis Waterford is 'Queen Maeve's Coccyx', while Limerick, of course, is 'Cuchullain's Nob'.) This is the most northerly point on the island of Ireland. During World War Two, to advise passing aircraft of the fact that they were now over a neutral country, local people spelled out the word EIRE in enormous letters on the ground here, using the white quartz stones that litter the field below the cliff-top. A quaint tradition grew out of this; modern-day visitors use the stones to write out their names or messages of love. The day I was there, I saw a NOEL, an EMER and a DUBLIN LADS. It was kind of sweet. Though having spent two days in Inishowen by now, I also expected to see BED & BREAKFAST AVAILABLE HERE.

Yes, Inishowen has B&B galore. Hotel accommodation is thin on the ground, so every other bungalow you pass has a sign in its window and a shower rigged up in the spare room. But this is probably your best bet for a bed. People in Donegal are amazingly friendly, they take great pride in their beautiful homeland and they'll treat you as though you were one of their own. Almost literally. At one fully booked guest house we tried, the owner offered to shift his own grandmother out of her room so we could have it ourselves. We were deeply touched by the offer, but naturally, we declined. We said we'd be happy for Granny to stay.

Once she slept on the floor and we got the bed.

Fondling Foreigners In Frankfurt

(for Lar Cassidy, in fond memory)

The flight from London to Frankfurt is full of publishers. You can tell they are publishers because they are weighed down like pack-mules, with briefcases and hold-alls and supermarket bags full of thick typescripts. Modern technology, which has put a man on the moon, cannot produce a novel typescript that does not look and feel and weigh like a telephone directory. Often, of course, they read like a telephone directory also, but that will not stop these airborne publishers from selling them to other publishers, who will in turn sell them to *more* publishers, who will print them up and sell them to wholesalers, who will sell them to bookshops, who will finally sell them to unwitting members of the public, who will hurl them into the bin after reading one page. And a key part of this wonderful process is that annual form of madness known as the Frankfurt Book Fair.

I arrive, get off the plane and gaze upon the attractive foyer of Frankfurt airport, which is roughly the colour of a cancerous lung. I am looking for the person who is supposed to meet me. He, she or it has failed to turned up.

Hmm.

I look around and consider my position. Most of the German I know is of the comic-book variety. But I imagine that phrases such as *Donner und Blitzen*, *Achtung Achtung* and *HANDE HOCHE, BRITISCHER SCHWEINHUND!!* may not be all that useful in booking a hotel room.

I start to walk around the terminal, attempting to look like a published Irish novelist. This is more difficult than it might initially sound. Spiritual angst crossed with traces of faint residual hope is the mix you have to try your best to project. But quite often it comes off as violent constipation.

After a while I bump into another lost and bewildered Irish writer, Belfast's own Mr Glenn Patterson. I don't know what it is Glenn is trying to look like, but if it's a pitiful Dickensian orphan he certainly is succeeding. He tells me his own driver has also failed to show. So Glenn and myself get a taxi to our hotel, which he happens to know is in a town called Raunheim.

Raunheim is a small town to say the least. It is, quite frankly, a bit of a kip (*eine kleine krappendümpf* in German.) Many places in this area were bombed by the Allies during World War Two. Raunheim escaped the bombing because the Allies looked down from their Spitfires and assumed they must have bombed the shit out of it already.

We pull up outside The Best Western Wings Motel. The building has all the beauty and charm of something stuck to your shoe. 'Thank God,' Glenn comments, 'it isn't The Second Best.'

I should explain that Glenn and myself are here as part of the 'Ireland And Its Diaspora' festival which is being held at the Frankfurt Book Fair this year. Every Irish person who has ever written a poem, published a novel, or sat half-drunk in a pub and merely *wished* they had written a poem or a novel, has been airlifted to Frankfurt at the expense of the German and Irish governments to discuss what they feel about Ireland and its diaspora. They are all staying at the Best Western Wings Motel, an hour's drive from the centre of the city.

This is an impressively cunning exercise in crowd-control by the main organizers, the Irish Arts Council. Knowing a thing or two about young Irish writers, they realise full-well that putting forty-seven of them in a hotel in downtown Frankfurt on an expense account would be a recipe for an irretrievable breakdown in diplomatic relations between Germany and Ireland. But *this* hotel is so far out of downtown

Frankfurt that I seriously wonder whether it is not actually in Belgium.

I know the person in the room next to my own must also be a young Irish writer because I can hear him pacing the floor in iambic pentameter. Meanwhile my television is switched on, and the screen is flashing out the message WELCOME TO RAUNHEIM HERR O'CONNOR. I lie on the bed and look at this for a while, thinking intensely literary thoughts, such as 'I wonder if there is a minibar?'

After a while the flashing message starts to annoy me. I get up and try to switch it off but I can't. There is a small sticker on the table warning people NOT TO BE SWITCH OFF THE TELEVISION FOR NO REASON AT ALL PLEASE. I contemplate simply chucking it out the window, plug and all, in true rock 'n' roll style, but decide this would not be good for the image of Ireland, not to mention its diaspora. So I pick up the remote control and make another attempt to make the offending screen go dark.

I now notice that it is possible to receive in-room pornographic movies, all of which have arrestingly alliterative titles. So I am now terrified to change channels in case I accidentally order up 'Lipstick Lesbians Get Lusty In Leipzig,' 'Horny Heidi Humps Helga in Heidelburg' or even 'Fondling Frisky Foreigners in Frankfurt'. I mean, yes, to be absolutely candid, I don't have anything against fondling foreigners in Frankfurt, *per se*, you understand, in fact if the opportunity were to present itself I might even ... never mind. It's just that I don't want to watch a film about it, particularly one that might show up on my bill.

The person in the room above me, however, clearly doesn't feel the same way. To judge from the wild gasps, lascivious whoops and low guttural groans coming through my ceiling, either he is energetically availing of the in-room entertainment or he is a more enthusiastic literature fan than you often find.

'Oh my God,' a voice cries. 'It's so *big*. Oh, Jesus! I've never seen one so huge before. *Oh, God, yesss! It's FUCKING ENORMOUS.'*

Of course, he might not be watching pornography at all. He could be talking about John Banville's latest advance.

I leave the room and amble down to the lobby, where Glenn is having a cup of coffee. He has just read in today's newspaper that Gerry Adams is among the Irish writers who will attend the Book Fair this year. I ask Glenn if Mr Adams will also be staying at the Best Western Wings. 'No no,' Glenn jokes. 'The Provisional Wings.'

Myself and Glenn take a taxi into Frankfurt. I discover that I left my money in my bedroom, so being an all-round decent segocia, Glenn munificently stumps up the fare. But the Best Western Wings Motel is so far from the city of Frankfurt that the sum comes to almost fifty pounds. Glenn then realizes that he has lost his complimentary entrance ticket to the Book Fair and will have to buy another to gain admission. He has only been in Germany for two-and-a-half hours and already he is seventy smackers down on the deal. It is lining up to be one hell of a weekend for him.

People tell you that the Frankfurt Book Fair is big. Indeed they struggle to find adjectives that can possibly convey just how staggeringly, awesomely, implausibly large it is. You could take all those superlatives and multiply them by infinity and you still wouldn't even be half-way close. It is vast. It is massive. It is momentously humungous. There are many whole towns in rural Ireland where people get born, grow up, meet partners, fall in love, have children, retire and die, that are a good deal smaller than the Frankfurt Book Fair. It is actually quite macabre, from a young author's point of view, to wander the halls and gaze upon the hundreds and thousands of books that get published in any one year. I confess I had expected, as a young Irish author, to be greeted by mobs of screaming literature fans, all falling to their knees before me, sprinkling my path with fresh rose petals, thanking me for the continuing regular production of critically acclaimed, yet commercially successful, literature. But no. An author at the Frankfurt Book Fair is basically an inconvenience. Which is funny. Because none of these people would be here if it wasn't for us, as I explain to Glenn, as he stares into his rapidly emptying wallet with a look of considerable emotion on his face.

'*Gott in Himmel*,' he says. But in a very literary way.

Several hours later and several kilograms lighter, Glenn and I manage to find the Irish Pavilion. I reflect how it is so heart-warming to take part in these events which challenge outmoded and unhelpful stereotypes of Ireland, as I stare at the posters of thatched cottages, round towers and red-haired colleens dancing jigs beside tractors. The posters have been supplied by the Germans, apparently. They must have thought the Irish Pavilion, staffed and organized and designed by Irish people, and full of Irish writers, and made of Irish materials, and paid for by Irish taxpayers just wasn't quite Irish enough. And hey — who can blame them?

A thirty-foot-high blow-up doll of Lemuel Gulliver is standing proudly erect outside the pavilion, like a gigantic bouncer in period costume. Mr Gulliver, as you will know, is the central character in the classic novel *Gulliver's Travels* by Jonathan Swift ('Verily I could not putte it downe' — *Ye Iryshe Tymes Booke Supplemente, December 1726*). I can't help wondering, however, whether Swift would have liked his famous creation being used in this way. After all, his own views about Ireland were somewhat mixed. He left money in his will for the building of the first mental hospital in Dublin, adding, in a pithy codicil, that had he been richer he would have bequeathed enough dough for a twenty-foot wall to be constructed around the entire country.

After a time I bump into Gunter and Klaudia, whom I met at a literature festival in Berlin three years ago. We all go along to a Thai restaurant for dinner. The stunningly attractive waitress is clearly not a literature fan and thus fails to recognise either myself or Glenn. 'Be careful, it's hot,' she keeps saying, whenever she places a dish on the table. After a while Glenn seems to feel that the only adequate response is 'Me too, baby'.

After dinner we all go to the *literaturhaus* (German for 'pub') where the brilliant Frank McCourt is giving a reading from *Angela's Ashes*, the German title of which is '*Limerick, Nein Danke*'. (It isn't really.) 'A happy childhood isn't worth a fuck,' he says, in answer to a question from the audience. I laugh so loud that it gets a bit embarrassing. I intend to tell my children this at least once a day.

The night is just beginning to hot up nicely when the man with the Raunheim bus turns up and sternly explains that we have to get onto it. Grumbling and moaning, we all do.

Back at the Best Western Wings Motel we are overjoyed to discover that there is a night-club in the basement. The poor barman looks very worried. I would estimate that on average the night-club in the Best Western Wings Motel gets about four people on a Friday night; three Austrian businessman and one hopeful local hooker. Tonight it is crammed to the doors with Irish writers, drinking, dancing and discussing poetry. Indeed, we are all in a highly poetic state by the end of the evening.

Up early the following morning. My head feels like something died in it. My tongue looks like it needs to be scrubbed clean with a toothbrush. Glenn and I get the bus into the *literaturhaus* where we are doing a reading together. The reading goes well and afterwards there are questions. One girl wants to know why so many wonderful writers come from Ireland. I feel it is probably the weather. It is always so cold and rainy in Ireland that there is very little to do all day except stay at home and produce literature.

When the event has finished, I have some meetings. I have meetings with my Swedish publishers, my Italian publishers, with the foreign rights department of my British publishers, with my Japanese publishers, with my French publishers and, accidentally, with Maeve Binchy's Norwegian translator. The day begins to feel like a strange and terrible nightmare. Before too long I have no idea who I am talking to any more, nor what language I should be apologising for not being able to speak. I bump into Glenn again. By now all his money is gone and he is considering selling his body so he can afford a cup of tea. I am considering selling mine too. But where Glenn is considering selling his by the hour, I am considering selling mine by the kilo.

We go for a walk and discuss the hell out of literature. Outside the Irish Pavilion, we notice a group of three Germans staging some kind of demonstration. The word 'OUT' is printed on their T-shirts. I wonder if they are from a Gay Rights group. But no, on closer examination we see that the word 'BRITS' also appears on the T-shirts, conveniently positioned just before the word 'OUT'.

Yes, it appears that these three Germans are the Frankfurt chapter of the Free Ireland Campaign. Glenn goes over to explain that while he actually lives and works in Belfast he is absolutely sure that Fritz, Heidi and Heindrich, who have once been to West Cork on a bicycling holiday and who actually own several Planxty CDs, not to mention some Aran jumpers, have a much more profound and sophisticated understanding of the many complexities of the Northern Ireland situation than he does himself. But they do not seem to recognise irony when it presents itself. Every time they use the phrase 'ze six counteez' I am showered with saliva.

People have begun to gather at the pavilion for the next

event. Suddenly a strange and disquieting thing happens. A long, loud hissing sound can be heard. Naturally I assume it is the Free Ireland Campaign being rude. But no, it is actually the giant inflatable Gulliver. Some appalling disaster, possibly involving cigarette burns, has befallen him. He sags, begins deflating and tilts over face-forward, like a drunk leaning his forehead against a urinal wall. I can't help but feel that this is an omen. The endlessly genial Lar Cassidy, who has organized this event, starts looking around for a bicycle pump. I try to avoid making eye contact with him. I love Ireland as much as the next man, but I do know where to draw the line. If Lar cannot find the bicycle pump it certainly won't be myself who ends up giving Gulliver a patriotic blow-job.

Inside the pavilion a large crowd has turned up to sit there in awed silence while Glenn, myself, Anne Enright and Evelyn Conlon discuss Ireland and its diaspora, live and unplugged. We do this for some time. Glenn says the word 'diaspora' sounds like some disease you might get from a toilet seat. But that is facetious. It actually sounds like the name of one of those small emerging statelets produced by the break-up of the former Yugoslavia.

When the diaspora has been vigorously discussed to the shattering fulfilment of the German public, the event ends and I visit the stand of my British publishers. There I meet three people from my American publishers. They are busily trying to buy the rights to my next novel. I am somewhat bemused by this, since I have not as yet got around to the tedious business of actually thinking it up and writing it down. But this does not matter at the Frankfurt Book Fair. This is a place where people actually have huge auctions, involving telephone-number sums of money, for two or three pages of a new novel. For one page, sometimes. For a single paragraph. A blurb. A title. A word! Sometimes they will have an auction for *the idea for a novel*. I swear to God I am not making this up.

Frankfurt is an event where highly-paid professionals buy and sell what does not exist. I myself made a quick fifty thousand Deutschmarks by telling a Japanese publisher about an idea I don't intend to actually *get* until 2013. I also sold the translation rights to an afterthought, movie rights to an attitude, and serialization rights for several irrational prejudices and a vague hunch.

That night I go out with my German editor, Hans-Jurgen Balmes, and two of his *freunde*. We drink beer, shoot pool, tell rude jokes, discuss whether the linguistic strategies of the contemporary novel can play any truly radical role in the new millennium, y'know, guy stuff. Hans-Jurgen explains that all the prostitutes leave Frankfurt during the Book Fair, because publishers are too mean to pay for sex.

After dinner we go to the bar of the Frankfurterhoff Hotel. I am now in a state where saying the word 'Frankfurterhoff' is proving quite a challenge. This is the hotel where very rich publishers and mega-successful authors stay when the fair is on. The hotel is booked up many years in advance. It is said that someone in publishing has to actually die before you can get a room at the Frankfurterhoff during the Book Fair. Indeed, just to get a seat at the bar requires a senior editor to have a mild heart attack.

My English agent, Carole Blake, is here, chatting with my French agent, Maggie Doyle. They buy me many drinks and indulge my insane, exhausted ranting about the sheer size of the Book Fair. Although they have been working at an inhuman rate — Carole's diary looks like a train timetable — they look like they've just had ten hours sleep. I, unfortunately, look like downtown Limerick on legs. I am so tired that I could cheerfully lie down in the Gents' toilets and go to sleep.

Except I can't even get into the Gent's toilets. Not until Frank McCourt dies.

Amore In Amalfi

The driver we have arranged to meet us at Naples airport is an hour-and-a-half late 'because there is much traffic today'.

I glare at him. By way of response he gives one of those large, nonchalant Italian shrugs. The kind that says: 'I am a relaxed Mediterranean type but if I have to kill you for business reasons, I will.'

Me, I would have thought there would be much traffic *most* days in a city such as Naples. That if you were a person who made his bloody *living* from driving you would bear this little fact *in mind*, you know, that you might even *leave your house a bit early*, or perhaps even … My first wife and current travelling companion tells me not to go inflicting my own cultural standards on people whose nonchalant philosophy of life is not the same as my own so I apologize to the work-slacking Latino lounge-lizard and he thoughtfully allows us to carry our own luggage to the car. (I wouldn't mind, only the wife is six months' pregnant so she finds it hard to manage my golf-bag.)

In we clamber and off we go, and an hour later, after a knuckle-clenching drive up the cliff-top roads and dirt-tracks to Ravello, we arrive at our hotel, the Palazzo Sasso. (Named after a local medieval nobleman, Prince Palazzo Sasso, who invented period costume.)

I don't actually know too much about the geezer, but with pillars and fountains and courtyards and terrazas, his former digs are certainly something to see. The whole place has been recently and thoroughly 'upgraded'. Think Graceland crossed with Government Buildings and you will be close to the interior-design concept.

Obviously the upgrading has not quite reached its completion. Our room — featuring allegedly 'free' champagne and fruit — offers a stunning view of the Gulf of Salerno, not to mention the building site (*sito de contructione* in Italian) which is conveniently located beneath the balcony (*balconia*). But Antonio, the baby-faced and very pleasant desk-clerk, assures us that this is nothing to worry about. The work is almost completed; the workers are very quiet. 'You will not even know they are there,' he smiles. I don't know why we believe him but poor fools we do.

We unpack our clothes and the large library of childcare books which Once Twice Three Times A Lady feels we should read on our weekend away. We do indeed read, for at least four seconds, and then at my insistence we go out for a stroll around the neighbourhood.

Ravello is the kind of unspeakably pretty little Italian town that looks like it came in a flatpack box from a stage-set warehouse. It has small dark cafés, ice cream parlours ('the best ice-cream in the world'— Jacqueline Kennedy), a couple of spooky churches, a small piazza where toddlers play football with nice old duffers. Couples stroll. Fiats buzz. Old ladies in black sit gossiping on the benches. It is so Italian it's just not true. You expect to see the youthful Robert De Niro skulking about in the shadows, planning to pitchfork various people who once offended Mama.

One admirable thing about people of the Italian persuasion is that they do seem to love a pregnant lady. My first wife and myself remark on this fact as we stroll the neat and dusky streets. Women passing give her empathetic smiles. Men rush to open doors and offer chairs. 'When will you be three?' one waiter graciously asks. This is all quite nice when you come from Ireland, a country where pregnancy is still occasionally regarded as a vaguely embarrassing minor ailment. (The day before the holiday a photographer at a wedding — not our own I stress — had suggested that Herself might like to move out of the front row and conceal herself at the back since 'Yeh know like ... I mean ... y'know ... the aul bump like.' I asked if he'd had a mother himself, before venturing the opinion that it was a pity she hadn't crossed her legs in mid-delivery and choked him.)

As we saunter along, arm-in-arm, we talk about the many responsibilities of parenthood. It is hard to describe the cocktail of feelings exactly but it is a subtle mix of joy, angst and impending poverty.

That night we eat in the hotel restaurant (*restaurante de hotelia*). This is the kind of place where you get sorbets between the courses but you don't enjoy the food because you are worrying about the bill, not to mention the bewildering selection of tableware — which features lobster-crackers, crab-disembowellers and something that looks like its principle use might well be the debollocking of horses. When I see the menu I understand the veritable arsenal of cutlery. You don't come to the Palazzo Sasso for coddle and chips, nor even that jewel of Dublin cuisine, the batherboorga. If ever it crawled, scuttled, slithered and wriggled along the sea-bed, or adhered itself to a rock/hull/drowning sailor's leg, you can eat it in Ravello, usually half-raw.

But the wine is really exceptionally nice. The Face I Can't Forget, of course, has been eating for two in recent weeks. And I, for my part, have been drinking for two. (It is nice to be supportive at a time like this.)

By the time we retire I am in a thoroughly Italianate state, as happy a dog *con due mickiz*. I totter onto the balcony and look out at the moon, the stars, the tiny fishing boats in the waters below. 'Isn't it beautiful, Dear,' I call to My Sexual Plaything.

'Zzzzzzzzzzzz,' she replies.

Hmmm. I suppose I had better get used to this. I have been told by associates who have already reproduced that connubial bliss tends to happen a good deal less frequently when there is a new baby residing in the house. I drift off to sleep and have a strange dream. There she is in the bed, my Main Squeeze, and I have only whipped off my night-shirt when the whimpering, then the screaming starts. 'You better pipe down,' I tell her. 'Or you'll wake that baby.'

At 8 a.m. we are awoken by a phenomenal noise (*uno racketo stupendo*). The stereotype of Italian workmen is that they are lazy and inefficient, but oh no, not here in Ravello, oh *no*, that would be *asking too much!* By 8.03 it sounds as though the Colosseum itself is being strenuously erected outside in the garden. I stagger to the shutters and haul them open.

Below I see a veritable army of labourers doing extraordinarily noisy things with large bits of industrial machinery. Diggers and trucks and cement mixers are pounding, while a jackhammer is busily mincing my brain. For no reason at all obvious to me, a very fat man is repeatedly hitting a tree with an iron bar. The hem of his shorts has slipped half-way down his ample buttocks, resulting in a remarkable example of that unforgettable phenomenon known on London building sites as 'The Dagenham Smile'.

The Other Half Of My Soul is already on the phone, calling around all the other hotels in the area to see if they will take us in. We pack up our clothes and our child-rearing books and go down to the lobby to say goodbye to Antonio.

He couldn't possibly be more charming or understanding about the fact that we are leaving early. He tells myself and Mi Chica Bonita 'When you have your baby, you must all come back'.

We taxi down the hill to the local town, Amalfi, which in medieval times was the regional capital of a major city-state and is now the regional capital of tour-buses, souvenir shops and *al fresco* heckling of girls. The bones of Saint Andrew are lodged in the cathedral and a great big statue adorns the square, of local boy Mr Flavio Gioa, who invented the compass, thereby guaranteeing that whole generations of aspiring orienteers would have something to argue about at weekends.

We stagger into the Hotel Santa Caterina and throw ourselves at the desk-clerk's feet, begging for hospitality at any price. Foolish move, as it turns out. He turns his beady eyes upon us in the manner of a Roman Emperor in a Hollywood epic who is about to lazily intone: 'You there, Centurion — the fat one amuses me. Have him stripped, washed and brought to my tent.'

'Do you have a reservation?' he wants to know. I am tempted to reply: 'Several, actually, but we're prepared to put them aside if you give us a room.' He scrutinizes his book, softly shaking his head. I feel like a sinner at the gates of paradise. (*Los gatos de paradiso*.) They do have one room left, he finally says.

Great!

Well, strictly speaking, it is more of a suite than a room.

Oh?

It costs one million lire per night. Which translates into approximately £402.

Now I don't know about you, but I have had entire *holidays* that did not cost approximately £402, many of them not too bad either when you got used to the scabies. We consider our position, the wife and myself. We do have a little money put by in case our beloved child-to-be ever needs something like an expensive cot. She looks at me. I look at her.

'Sod him,' I say. 'He can sleep in the bath.'

Yes, I think, fumbling for the Visa card, one important thing about international travel is that you make adequate financial preparation for the rainy day. This may well *be* one of those rainy days. In fact, as the wife points out, it is!

Outside the rain has begun bucketing down. Lightning is

cracking the sky in two. A bitter wind is whipping up the waves. A giant black cloud shaped just like a pound-sign is drifting in from over Capri.

Wooooo! it seems to say. I am coming to get *yoooo*.

The suite to which the desk-clerk leads us is the size of a small house and has been decorated with no thought for expense, not to mention taste. It does, however, have its drawbacks. Situated at the very end of the building it is only twenty yards from the main road to Naples, which is not necessarily where you want to be on a relaxing, restful holiday. 'It is a very quiet room,' the clerk announces confidently, over the drone of cars.

'Pardon?' we say.

'IT IS A VERY QUIET ROOM, HONESTLY. IT IS VERY PEACEFUL.'

But it isn't quiet. In fact it is noisy. It sounds as though several juggernauts are actually driving *through* the bathroom. I ask the clerk how he thinks we will get any sleep. The trick, he explains, is to close all the shutters and put the air-conditioning on at full-blast. I can't believe he is telling us this. He truly has a neck like *los bollocks de la jockey* (Frankie Detorri). For £402 a night I would expect the manager to personally make his aged mother go and lie down in the road to stop the traffic, but She Who Must Be Obeyed feels we have no choice and as always she is annoyingly correct.

For the second time in two days we unpack all our clothes and our pregnancy books.

We lie on the bed together and watch a little Italian television. A very little Italian television that doesn't work very well.

We switch to what is advertised as 'the Culture Channel'. Before us on the flickering star-spangled screen, two scantily-clad women on roller-skates shimmy and glide, dancing around to a song called 'Captain of Her Heart'.

'That must have been difficult to learn,' the wife says. No doubt it was. But was it worth it, you wonder.

There follow an episode of 'Only Fools And Horses' dubbed into Italian, which is without even one single doubt the weirdest, most disturbing thing I have ever seen in my life, comparable, I would imagine, to a really bad acid flashback lasting twenty-eight minutes. And yet it does have its educational moments. (For the benefit of linguistically curious readers, *strozzo* seems to be the Italian for 'plonker'.)

By now culturally satisfied, not to say exhausted, we flick to an American cable channel. Over a soundtrack of Richard Clayderman music, two silver-haired old people are strolling arm-in-arm along a sunset beach. 'Are you aged between sixty-five and eighty and thinking about life insurance?'

'*Huh*?' I ask myself. Isn't eighty cutting it a tad fine?

I am reminded of the story of the American couple who at ninety and ninety-one were the oldest people ever to seek a divorce. Asked by the reporters on the steps of the courthouse why they had waited so long, they are said to have replied, 'We were waiting for the children to die.'

After two hours or so the rain stops. The sun peeps out from behind the black clouds. 'Come out,' it seems to say. 'You poor gullible suckers.'

We gather up the pregnancy books and the few little knick-knacks which women seem to need for sunbathing — towel, sarong, flip-flops, hairbrush, straw hat, sun-screen, moisturizer, P.D. James novel, camera, tripod, Swiss Army knife, postcards, pens, nail-polish, laptop, mobile phone, fold-up desk — and lumber down to 'The Beach Club'.

The Beach Club does not feature a beach, as such; nor to be honest is it actually 'a club'. It is a flat expanse of tar-macadam beside the sea, administered by two handsome local youths in tight shorts. The wife seems to think there is something attractive about them but, as I point out, they probably don't have a sense of humour or a fine mind like what I do.

'Mmmmmmm,' she agrees.

I open my copy of *Babies And What To Do With Them*. But I don't have very much time to read because now it is time for lunch.

In the adjacent dining area I notice that the menu offers such thought-provoking savouries as 'Baby Octopus Drowned in Tomato Sauce'. Perhaps impending fatherhood is making me a wuss but I decide I'm not really in the mood for cruelly murdered squidling and order instead a tuna and tomato sandwich. Said item along with two glasses of fruit juice and one small chicken salad which, without any doubt, once had a piece of chicken waved over it, brings the bill for lunch to £36. At this stage our son's Harvard education is beginning to look dubious. (We will have to pretend he is thick as a plank but quite rich so we can get him into Oxford.)

Now depressed and downhearted I repair back up to the room. Outside there is 100-degree heat and blazing sunshine. But I am in bed, in a haze of despondency, under the covers to protect myself from the rattle of the air-conditioner, trying hard to read *Loving Discipline* which is not a sex manual for Tory MPs but a handbook for aspiring parents who don't want to beat their children. The noise of the traffic gets louder and louder. The walls are so thin I can hear our next-door neighbour's inner doubts. Tension rises. Tempers are frayed. The Wind Beneath My Wings and I have an argument. I don't speak to her for a couple of hours. (Well I don't want to interrupt her, after all.)

That night we get a taxi back up to Ravello where we intend to have dinner in a local restaurant (*restaurante de locale*). This five-kilometer journey sets us back £20. But that's not the bit that really gets us. Two hours later, faces stuffed and wallets depleted, the taxi driver breaks the startling news that to go *back* to Amalfi costs £28! I will not say that Ravello's taxi-drivers are robbers, as such. Just that they should be wearing tights over their faces.

Still at least we are back in our lovely suite. And at least things seem to be looking up. And at least we have abandoned our plans for judicial separation. And it is, of course, at that precise moment that the disco begins in the restaurant above our bedroom.

Now I am as fond of disco music as the next person. But I do have to admit that by one in the morning I am starting to get just *a little* irritated. Again and again my ears are assailed with cheerful exhortations to boogie awn down, shake my thang and put mah funk into various people's faces. Given the choice of putting anything into anyone's face right now, I think I would choose a loaded Magnum.

Louder it gets, the bass throbbing. 'It's fun to stay at the YMCA', I am repeatedly assured through the ceiling. By now I am wishing that *is* where we're staying. At least we might be able to get a bit of kip and it wouldn't be costing us £402 a night.

But is when the karaoke kicks off that I really do get angry. I feel my throat-muscles begin to tighten as the raucous chorus commences above me — 'When the moon in the sky is a big pizza pie, that's *amore*.' But that ISN'T *amore*. That's fucking DRUGS!

I pull on my dressing gown and go complaining to the reception desk, or, as it is known in Italian, *el desco de receptione*.

I try to explain to *el portero de la notte* that I can't sleep. He smiles and says there is nothing he can do for the moment.

'But there must be something?'

'No no. Nothing.'

Sad, isn't it? Italians once built the Roman Forum, subjugated the mightiest armies in Europe, ruled a vast and awesome empire encompassing almost all of the known world. Now they can't even stop a singalong of pissheads.

Next day we rise in a bad mood, but cheer ourselves up by setting out to arrange that greatest of all holiday pleasures, hiring a car which you know you are not going to use, but that's not the point — it's there if you need it. The car is delivered, a nifty little Fiat. We drive smugly up and down past the Amalfi taxi rank for a while, making hand gestures of a vaguely Italian nature out the window.

Since we would like to be in a position to feed the child at least sometimes, we decide not to have lunch in the hotel today, but to bring our custom to one of the *trattorias* in the town. We pull into the local car park.

'*Buongiorno*,' I say. 'How much?'

'Italian?' asks the attendant.

'No.'

'From where?'

'Ireland.'

He thinks for a while. 'Five thousand lire.'

I hand over a bundle of notes.

'Would you like to buy me a cup of coffee, my friend?' he smiles.

I wonder if the parking attendant is propositioning me sexually. But no, it soon becomes quite clear that the invitation is a euphemism, a colourful romantic Italian way of saying 'Give me a gratuity or I will vandalize your car'.

Off we go for lunch, following which the wife discovers that a large bottle of mineral water which costs four pounds back at the hotel is available in the town for just under one pound. I suggest that we buy a few extra bottles and see if we could claw back some of the weekend's unforeseen expenses by selling them on to the other guests. Then it's into the car and off for the day-trip!

See Naples and die, they say. Having now driven in that

city, I understand what they mean. One is always nervous of lazily repeating stereotypes and perhaps we were there on a bad day, but I would rather have my eyeballs prised out by the teaspoon of Beelzebub than ever drive a car in Naples again.

Trucks actually speed *at* us, as though in attack. Motorbikers seemingly intent on hari-kiri crisscross in great roars of diesel. Little old ladies on scooters zoom into our path, cackling and scowling like demented Valkyrie. Motorway exits loom up and disappear. In the distance Vesuvius keeps flashing by. Before long I am feeling pretty Vesuvian myself.

We pass a sign that says BIENVENTO A NAPOLI on a mural depicting an armour-clad legionaire. The banner in his hand reads SPQR, an acronym of the ancient motto of Naples ('Some Parts Quite Revolting.')

Somehow we end up in a grimy backstreet. Two staggeringly large ne'er-do-wells looked up from their antipasto and began lurching across the alleyway in our general direction, dragging their knuckles in the dust as they walk.

'Lost, *si*?' one monster grins.

'Yes. I was wondering if you could give us directions. Back to Amalfi.'

He thrusts out his hand. For one awful moment I wonder if he wants me to hold it.

'Money,' he says.

'Don't you DARE ask me for money, you unshaven, dog-breathed cutpurse,' I reply immediately. In my mind.

'How much?' is what I actually say.

'Twenty.'

'Twenty lire? Gosh that seems very reasonable, doesn't it, Dear? If you hold on a moment, I …'

'TWENTY THOUSAND!' he barks.

I reach into my emaciated wallet and give him thirty. He pockets the notes and glares at me for a while.

'The traffic in Naples, she is bad today, *si*?' he says.

'Oh yes,' I simper. 'Yes, very bad. But it's really a terribly nice place, after all. We're really finding it thoroughly enjoyable, myself and my six-month pregnant wife who would be all alone in the world if anything were to happen to me, murder for example.'

He looks at me and sniggers. '*Strozzo*,' he says.

Then he turns around and walks away.

The Special Occasional Irish Male

Christmas would bring out the bollocks in anyone.

Patrick Kavanagh

Many Unhappy Returns

It was my thirty-seventh birthday last year and my siblings had a little problem deciding what to get me as a gift. They discussed various interesting possibilities, but couldn't come up with anything concrete. Well, they could, but I didn't actually *want* anything concrete, so it was back to the builder's suppliers with that half-ton of crazy paving — and from there back to square number one pretty pronto. 'What do you buy for the man who has everything?' a sister enquired. 'A course of penicillin?' a brother helpfully suggested.

Of course, birthdays are not the most important thing in the world. (The Republic of Ireland qualifying for the next World Cup finals is the most important thing in the world.) But still, there is nothing quite like a birthday to concentrate the mind. Thirty-seven whole years. 13,505 days. Or 324,120 hours. Or 19,447,200 *minutes!* (And if you're reaching for a calculator to work out whether all that is correct, you are really terribly sad indeed.)

My birthday falls, or rather plummets, on the 20th of September, on which memorable date, as you no doubt know, various parts of Bold Robert Emmet, the late darling of Erin, were efficiently separated from each other in Thomas Street, Dublin by representatives of the English public service. Thus was I almost christened Emmet by my patriotic parents. But a difficulty arose at the baptismal font when it became clear that the priest, a fine Dubbalin man, had acquired the local linguistic habit of dropping the final 'T' in the word. My parents decided that Emma O'Connor would not be much of a name for their eldest son. So they changed their minds at the last minute and called me Joseph, after the noted mass murderer and former seminarian Joseph Stalin. But it could have been worse. September 20th is also the birthday of the fine Italian thespian, Miss Loren, so I might well have been christened Sofia O'Connor, which probably wouldn't have helped me much at school. (Although actually I attended a Catholic all-male boarding school, so hey, you never know.)

Being born on the 20th of September makes me a Virgo. This is not a good sign to be. Virgos are the uptight malcontents of the Zodiac. Fussy, pernickety, morally superior, perfectionist, nervous, shy and fundamentally annoying, you can always spot the Virgo male at a party. He will be the one in the corner examining the potted plant and biting his fingernails down to the knuckles, while secretly watching everything you're doing and making detailed notes to photocopy and send around to all your friends.

So I decided last year that I was fed up being a Virgo. Damnit, I thought, I just want to be something else. In weary desperation I turned for enlightenment to an ancient book on the Chinese Horoscope, which chops up the months in quite different ways, each one having its own emblematic animal.

In Chinese terms, I had always thought I was a rat, as had so many of my former girlfriends. But no. Those of us who had the enormous privilege of bouncing into this world on September 20 1963 are in fact — get this — *rabbits!*

Bloody typical. I go from being fussy virgin to fluffy vegetarian quadruped in one ungainly little hop.

The book further informed me that suitable professions for a rabbit would include philosopher, diplomat, politician or, of course, cartoon character. And funnily enough, I have tried all these callings so far, but without any true or lasting satisfaction.

It also revealed that my ideal spouse would be either a dragon or a dog. And I feel certain there is a joke in there somewhere. But if you think I'm going to make it, you've another thing coming. (I would quite like to live to be thirty-eight.)

Jingle Bills: The Post-Millennium
Irish Family Christmas

Whenever I tell foreigners, and particularly English people, that I am the eldest of eight children they smile understandingly and sometimes quite enviously. 'Ah,' they say, with a wistful sigh, 'the typical Irish Catholic family.'

I think they have a mental image of the eight of us sitting around a turf fire with our gentle, grey-haired Mammy and gruff but oddly poetic Da, all of us strumming banjos, crooning 'Boolavogue' to each other and writing long poems in Irish about fishermen. The Von Trapp family meets Ógra Fianna Fáil.

In fact there were four children in my parents' marriage, which ended when I was thirteen years old. My father is happily remarried to a wonderful woman who had three daughters in her own first marriage. She and my beloved father have a son of their own and I very much think of him as a brother. That makes eight kids. At least I think it does. Sometimes I have to stop and add them all up. Yup. Eight. At the last count.

We don't all keep in constant touch. We often forget each other's birthdays. Only rarely have we all been in one room simultaneously — and that's probably the reason we manage to get along.

Yes, we have our ups-and-downs. Some of us argue, others fall out for a while. But there is one thing which always gives me true hope for the future:

WE HAVE MANAGED TO SPEND ALL OF CHRIST-MAS DAY TOGETHER WITHOUT ANY SINGLE ONE OF US BEING ACTUALLY STABBED.

And it's coming again. You know it. Don't fight it. There is really no point in your pitiful denial. It doesn't *matter* when you are reading this book. It might be August. It might even be January. But it's coming again.

It's *always* coming.

Yes, Christmas actually comes but once a year. Thanks be to God and Her Holy Mother. The season of jolly jangling music in the streets, and styrofoam snow piled up in shop windows. Crackers that don't crack and fairy lights that don't light and Christmas trees all shaggy with smug aplomb. Office parties and television repeats and perpetual hang-overs and Grandad in the corner sucking the vodka out of his jumper as he wistfully recalls to the dazed company, all smacked out of their heads on the angel-dust in the spiced beef, how he got a ball of tinfoil for a Christmas present every single year until he was forty-seven and he was happy as a hogget in SHITE with that, not like these young pups today with their Nintendo machines and micturating Barbie dolls and mountain bikes and Playstations, not that it matters anyway because it's his last Christmas on this earth, and won't he be happy as Larry to go.

Then there is the purgatory of Christmas shopping. Come — gaze into the crystal ball. There you are, head pounding, in the subterranean torture chamber that is your local branch of 'Toys Я Bloody Expensive Considering They Break So Soon'. Your companion is a hysterical nine-year-old relative who is screeching that her entire life will be ruined and she will grow up unhappy and never be able to form stable and meaningful relationships AND IT WILL BE ALL YOUR FAULT unless she is immediately supplied with a large inflatable hirsute animal that makes a farting noise when you pull the string attached to its navel. At this stage, you have actually surrendered. You are weeping openly. You have your cash in your trembling sweaty hands. You would willingly throw your money and the deeds of your very soul into a bucket wielded by Satan, if only you could find a Sales

Assistant who would release you from this tinselled gulag. But you can't. Because there isn't one. They're all having the day off. And you know *why*?

TO DO THEIR CHRISTMAS SHOPPING, THAT'S WHY!

Buying for children is bad enough. Buying for children can give you a breakdown, reduce you to a wreck, destroy your mind for ever. But buying for women?

Be afraid.

Men, of course, are useless at this. The Irish Male's idea of a romantic Christmas present is a collapsible monkey-wrench or new carburettor. Even the New Man can get it wrong on this point. A woman I know told me quite recently that she had broken it off with her former boyfriend because of what he bought her last Christmas.

A tennis racket.

Now in truth it seemed to me that a tennis racket was actually quite an original present, a well-thought-out non-sexist gift, a token of egalitarian love in the new century, a subtle tribute to her athleticism and strength. But no, she corrected me, it was a BLOODY TENNIS RACKET!! She then levitated towards the ceiling, spitting thumbtacks and bullfrogs.

As well as ending many promising relationships, the holiday season also affords the opportunity for playing all the old favourite traditional Christmas games, such as Musical Chairs, Lick The Bowl, Find The Christmas Pop Song That Doesn't Make You Punt Your Muffins, Avoid The Carollers, Find The Taxi, Snog The Weird Ex, Make The Returning Emigrant Feel Vaguely Uptight In The Pub On Christmas Eve, Fight Off The Mugger and — because it's really for *the children* of course — Leave-the Slice-of-Cake-Out-For-Santee-Or-He'll-Give-All-Your-Presents-To-Somebody-Else.

And speaking of Santee, how did HE ever catch on?

Wouldn't any healthy society have him locked up immediately? I mean, just hang on one second and let me get this straight. An ancient, overweight Norwegian alcoholic in a red suit and kinky boots, with no visible means of support despite his massive wealth, is going to slither down my chimney in the middle of the night and creep into my bedroom to fill my stocking?

I have a gun. And I'm waiting, Fatboy.

Ah yes. Jolly old Christmas. All those lovely cheerful songs.

On the twelfth day of Christmas my true love sent to me:
Twelve ulcers throbbing,
Eleven puddings burning,
Ten letches letching,
Nine drunkards puking,
Eight grabbers goosing,
Seven Richards Cliffing,
Six toddlers screaming,
Five crOOning BINGS —
Four bawling aunts,
Three French strikes,
Two Ninja Turtles.
And a repeat of The Partridge Famileee.[1]

'Still,' they will tell you, the Christmas-loving monsters, 'It's a family time, isn't it? All the family together. What on earth could possibly be better than THE FAMILY ALL UNITED AT CHRISTMAS?'

How about having cocktail sticks stuck into your eyeballs?

This Christmas, when you see an image of the Bethlehem

---

[1] From Charles Dickens, *'Twas the Night Before Christmas and Daddy Was Smashed*. (Oliver Twisted Books).

manger, have a good long hard look at it. It's an icon of the supposedly perfect family. OK, OK, so it doesn't stand up to even basic scrutiny. *She's* an unmarried mother from a religious minority, *he's* a semi-skilled migrant labourer with poor employment prospects. And Jesus Christ Almighty, that cute little kid in the swaddling clothes is gonna grow up to wander around the desert in a frock, cause enormous civil disturbance, vandalize a temple and come into serious conflict with the law before being arrested, tortured and nailed to a tree. I mean they're not exactly The Waltons, are they? But no, no — this is a *family* time. Nothing to do with screwing money out of you, honest. We just want you to enjoy YOUR TRADITIONAL FAMILY.

Years ago when there actually *were* traditional families — if, in fact, there ever were — perhaps all this ludicrous mumbo-jumbo was fine. But nowadays things simply ain't so simple.

You waken on Christmas morning feeling like Death-in-a-Duvet. You try to remember who you snogged last night at the office party, after you all got ossified and photocopied your bottoms. There were so many cows, dogs and asses in the room, you thought you had stumbled into the moving crib. You definitely remember getting off with *somebody* earlier in the evening. You're sure of that. Who could it have been?

Oh no.

Oh Jesus, no.

As the theme music from *Psycho* begins stabbing through your mind, the terrible memory slowly dawns. Your former girlfriend caught you in the pub jacks busily snogging YOURSELF in the mirror.

Your stomach is churning. Your bedroom is spinning. Next time it spins your way you're going to avail of the centrifugal force and jump. Oh *Christ!* Your brain is melting. What did you ever do to deserve such pain? You lurch down the stairs, and there it is. Gathered by the tree. Waiting for you.

The traditional Irish post-millennium family unit.

Yes, gone are the days of the Irish family being the Ma, the Da, the kids and the dog, all of them Catholic, conservative, heterosexual, faithful if married, and virginal if not. There are seventy thousand separated people in Ireland these days, buddy! That means a whole heck of a lot more Christmas complication.

In addition to relations both full-time and temporary, the room is crammed with boyfriends, girlfriends, exs, foundlings, waifs and strays, children and pets. So nice to have those children around at Christmas isn't it? So lovely the way they skip and chant and sing the jolly Yuletide song they wrote especially just for YOU:

Hear the Christmas bells all jingle
Pity that you're fuckin single.

If the composition of the Irish family has changed, the power structures within said constitutionally protected entity have mutated also. This all started a few years back when the Irish family began to *communicate*. What a disaster. Make no mistake about it; open, honest, uninhibited sharing of feeling has no place whatsoever within the family unit, as fans of *The Godfather* can well attest. As soon as Irish parents started 'to rap', 'chew the fat' or 'shoot the breeze' with their children, the whole institution of the family subjected itself to unwithstandable pressure. And Christmas in Ireland is not a good time for pressure.

Used to be, one word from Dad and everyone nodded their fervent agreement while secretly resolving to do exactly as they liked. But the day after the divorce referendum was passed, Dad packed his bags and promptly legged it. Off to a

Buddhist monastery down in West Cork to get in touch with his inner child. Sometimes he sends the occasional letter, signed Bhagwan Shree Majooma Gosht — though your Mum always knew him as Mickey-Joe Mooney. Now it's one word from Stepdad and he's given a long lecture on the patriarchy by Auntie Vera, who's come to stay until New Year's Eve, and who's never liked your stepfather anyway, and who has a beard that Castro himself would be proud of since she accidentally took an overdose of Nandrilone bodybuilding steroids instead of her HRT.

Your mother doesn't like your eldest sister's boyfriend. But he had to be invited to dinner this year because last year he wasn't, and it all ended with a tearful punch-up in the cake. This year Mum went along with it, but she's unhappy. Hey, call her old-fashioned, and yes, just because he's done four years for burglary, that doesn't *necessarily* mean he's not a nice person. But does he *have to* pour his soup out into a saucer before swigging it? And does he *have to* keep referring to the dog as 'that bitch'. And if he absolutely *must* wear his mirrored sunglasses inside the house, couldn't he at least brush the dandruff off the lenses first?

No, Mum is uneasy about your big sister's boyfriend. But she ain't too crazy about your younger sister's girlfriend either. Carly, she's called, and she turned vegetarian the same year she discovered her clitoris, as she's happily explaining to Grandad, who's choking on his dentures with the excitement of it all. Live and let live, that's what Mum tries to practise. But did Carly really *have* to turn up to Midnight Mass last night in her QUEER NATION sweatshirt? Back in Mum's day, choice of orientation means using a compass instead of a map to find your way to Sodality meetings. A dyke was something vague in geography class: something Dutch boys put their fingers into. Now, it seems, Dutch girls *also* put their … No. STOP! She doesn't want to go there.

Three-year-old nephew Tarquin is bludgeoning his sister because Santa forgot to bring the batteries for his cute little Machine-Gun/Learning-Aid. Four-year-old niece Madonna is fashioning postmodernist sculptures from bits of dog turd she found under the Christmas tree — her mother warns you not to intervene and accuses you of trying to stunt her creativity. As for the Christmas tree, it isn't the best. Your stepfather totally forgot to buy one this year. He was too busy concentrating on scoring some coke. So it was up to the attic at one this morning to search out the ancient bri-nylon model that looks like a mouldy toilet-brush stuck to a tripod.

Granny's here too. Temporarily released from the Old Folks' Home, allegedly on an experimental care-in-the-community scheme, but actually because she keeps trying to burn the place down. Look at her, paper sombrero clamped over the heated rollers. Absolutely no idea of where in the name of Jesus she is. But what the Hell. At least she's happy. And if you were on the drugs *she's* on, you'd be too.

Grandad wants to tell you what's wrong with the Michael Collins movie that's on the telly AGAIN tonight. He knew Michael Collins *pairsonally*, you see, him and Mick were *like dat*, he knew him well and he was *a daily communicant* and the very idea that he'd be leppin in and out of the scratcher wit dat tart Julia Roberts is a heinous blasphemy. Stepdad tells him to put a sock in it. Mum tells *him* to do the same. Grandad insists that he knows what he's talking about. He was 'out' in 1916. Little sister and Carly stop playing footsie under the table and perk up at this point. Is Grandad saying he too is part of the QUEER NATION? No no, of course he's not, he's saying he was 'out' in the General Post Office in 1916. 'AND DAT FILLUM IS A DAMN DISGRACE.'

Food, too, is now a source of utterly explosive Yuletide ructions. In the good auld days of turkey and ham, menu planning was admirably simple. All anyone had to argue about back then was whether or not to have Brussels sprouts. (Actually nobody has ever argued about that: everyone on the planet *loathes* Brussels sprouts. That's why it's compulsory to have them at Christmas.)

Nowadays Granny's food has to be minced, and little Tarquin's has to be pulped, and little Goneril's has to be mashed and wok-fried because she's hyper-active and allergic as well as dyslexic, and your brother's vegan girlfriend has to have desiccated lettuce or broiled tofu-burgers guaranteed to be produced in a country where they've never even shown a cow on television. She's studying politics in UCD and she's very Left-wing and after oh, a vat of red wine, she wants to know how anyone has the loik audacity to eat this amount of fewd when people in the thord world are loik storving. (She almost caused a fistfight earlier when she told your two-year-old cousin Lucretia that Santa's little elves work in loik Fascist conditions and are TEWTALLY non-unionised.)

Auntie Vera is GAGGING for the want of a drink. She's only staying with you because she was fecked out of the chronic alcoholism unit in John Of God's, so it's Carly's home-made vegan lemonade for her, until she can sneak up to the jacks where she's hidden a dishcloth saturated with gin in the cistern. Your mother heard full-throated sucking sounds coming from the bathroom earlier, but given the various hair-raising possibilities implied by the range of overnight guests she didn't really feel like investigating too closely. She had other things on her mind anyway. She's not allowing herself to have any Christmas pudding this year because she's on a diet. She says she's on a diet 'for herself,' as a 'life-affirming, self-nurturing, holistic experience'. She's actually on a diet because last night, when he reeled in from the next-door neighbour's sherry and pornography evening, your stepfather grabbed her, dragged her under the mistletoe and told her she could wear her stomach as a kilt.

Sisters start fighting. Babies start crying. Brother starts sulking. Mother starts screaming. Auntie Vera starts drinking. Stepdad starts singing:

> *Away in a manger, no-ho crib for a bed*
> *The little Lord Jesus lay down his sweet head*
> *The stars in the bright sky, light up you and me.*
> *The little Lord Jesus*
> *On P.A.Y.E.*

Bah, as somebody once put it, and humbug.

And as for New Year's Eve? *Don't get me started.*

Should old acquaintance be forgot and never brought to mind? Take it from me, the short answer is YES!

Patrick Pearse And The Easter Bunny

You know, I recollect my dear old Granny talking to me once when I was a lad. Well, two or three times actually to be strictly accurate. But this particular time was just before Easter one year. I think I would have been five or six.

'Joseph,' she said — her memory was admirable — 'Joseph, if you are very good, and if you do not be giving lip out of you to the poor nuns beyond in the school, and if you eat up all your greens, do you know what will happen to my nicens little man?'

I glanced up from my biography of Proust and replied in the negative.

I recall Granny smiling then, and giving me a big huggly-wuggly-snuggly and confiding that if the above conditions were fully satisfied, and if I tried to be that rarest of things, 'a good boy,' a giant rabbit would hop into my bedroom on Easter Saturday night and give me a large egg made out of chocolate.

She grinned. She nodded wisely. And I can clearly remember thinking, as I stared at her loving face, how absolutely great it will be when I am a grown-up, because then I too will be able to take powerful hallucinogenic drugs, just like Granny.

The Easter Bunny?

The WHAT?!

Something in our culture has gone terribly wrong when we celebrate the miraculous arrival of Spring by inventing a character which even John Lennon in the post-Pepper years would have found a tad on the spacey side. Santa Claus? The Easter Bunny? Honest to God, the role models we give children. And we wonder why they grow up robbing cars.

Apart from long nights lying awake feeling terrified of giant lagomorphine invaders, my other childhood memory of

Easter is the Easter Parade. Younger readers will not remember this, because a number of years ago a government of what I suppose one might call the revisionist persuasion (though 'uptight Blueshirt scuzzballs' is the technical term) decided that the best way to deal with the Easter Rising and its attendant, if uncomfortable, symbolism for our country was to completely ignore it and instead make RTÉ put on 'The Best of the Two Ronnies' so we could all celebrate Easter *properly*.

The thinking was that if we had a parade to mark the Easter Rising, all the inhabitants of our poor windswept rock would immediately rush off to join the Provisional IRA, just as in modern France, as we all know, people don period costume and behead aristocrats every Bastille Day. But anyway. There used to be an Easter Parade, and my parents used to bring us to it.

Oh, how we looked forward to the Easter Parade! Forget Mayday in Moscow or East Berlin, here was a display of military might. You could see the entire Irish army pass by — all seventeen of them *and* their bikes. Also marching would be those valiant praetorians, the FCA or 'Free Clothes Association'. If you were really lucky they would have on display many pieces of high-tech equipment, such as penknives, compasses and complicated knots.

Now, seven-year-old boys do not have much of an understanding of Ireland's important tradition of neutrality, nor of the essential and courageous work of our international peace-keepers. When you are seven and possessed of a Y-chromosome, you do not want to see your country's army wielding hurleysticks. You want to see them carrying THERMONUCLEAR MISSILES. So the Easter Parade, like most things in childhood, was more exciting to anticipate than to actually experience.

Except for one aspect.

Every year it would be the same: out of the middle of the

ranks of soldiers he would come capering, some poor unfortunate recently recruited private, dressed up in that most secret of all deadly weapons — the Irish Army's Easter Bunny suit. To see him gamely lepping about O'Connell Street, flapping his arms and chewing his giant plastic carrot, would make the parade seem worth a whole year's waiting.

Yet for all his absurdity the Easter Bunny is quite a revealing beastie, if we think about him for even a moment. The plain fact is that before Christianity appropriated the pagan festival of spring for its own highly specialized ends, Easter was actually a celebration of the one activity at which rabbits truly excel. And I do not mean going 'Nyeargh, what's up, Doc?'

Yes, Easter was the rite of renewal and birth, and, in that beautiful spiritual context, was very much about shagging. If we could enter a time machine and go back a few millennia to see what our ancestors were doing on Good Friday, they would not have been saying the Sorrowful Mystery, I'll tell you that much. Easter is the one festival that truly belongs to us all, not to any single church or sect or Party. It is a milestone that says life is worth the living, its secret meaning still sometimes capable of being read, even through the layers of pietistical sludge with which we've beslobbered it.

I mean, come on — *chocolate EGGS?*

What do you want? A telegram or something?

The Secret World Of The Irish Mammy

A few years ago St Patrick's Day and Mother's Day happened to fall on the same Sunday. Well a thing like that can make you think. Particularly if you can't be bothered to get out of bed.

What do we really feel about mothers here in Mother Ireland, the world capital of po-faced devotion to mammydom? Oh yes, we sing about the mammy when we're rat-faced drunk and we bung her a bunch of daffodils every Mother's Day morning, which we stole from the forecourt of a garage down the road. And musha, why wouldn't we? She's our mammy, after all.

Many traditional Irish ballads celebrate the special role of mothers, including the following beautiful and poignant example from the 1920s in South Kerry. It is sung to the tune of 'Spancil Hill', with a tremendously deep feeling of beer:

Oh Mammy, you're a livin' saint,
An angel in a dress.
You always have a lovely smile
When you're sweepin' up the mess.
When I'm loadin' up me weapon, boys,
For to aim it at a Brit,
I think about me mammy's smile.
And I shoot the little shit.[1]

Such stirring examples of native song expressed our patriotic feelings about the Mammyland. And our mammies had a unique place in our affections. For example, as Gemma Hussey's book *Ireland: Anatomy Of A Changing State* points

---

[1] Quoted in *Five Hundred Songs of Mother Ireland* by Dr Oedipus O'Beard (Maam Cross Publications).

out, if you look up the word 'mother' in the index to the 1937 Constitution, the document on which every single Irish law is predicated, you will notice the words, '*Woman — see family and sex*'.

Nice, huh?

Must have been really convenient for Irish mammies to be shown with such clarity just what they were for.

Oh begob, we were historically, hysterically, mad about the mammy. On Mother's Day we cooked the lunch. Well OK, *she* actually cooked it the day before but at least we managed to heat it up without setting fire to the kitchen. Because we *loved* our mammy. We LOVED HER TO DEATH. And just to really prove our love, a Dail motion of 1925 stopped her getting divorced; a law of 1927 excluded her from jury service. Well, we didn't want our mammies sitting in the courts or anything. Sure it's *men* who decide what crimes are, not ladies! And when it came to setting up the Censorship Board, our mammies were once again excluded. We wouldn't want our mammies reading dirty literature, vile sweaty guff about lezzers and malcontents. It might take their minds off washing our pants.

Strangely enough, a great number of books which the male censors thought were acceptable promoted an image of our mammies as victims or virgins. But that didn't worry us. 'Sit back there, Mammy, it's Mother's Day,' we cried. 'Here's a box of chocolates and a few balls of wool. Would you ever knit us another jumper?' Our mammies were helpfully banned from the civil service in 1925, to allow them more time to clean up our bedrooms. Ten years later they were told they couldn't have any of those nasty English contraceptives. We liked them being our mammies so much, we decided they should be mammies over and over again!

Yes, we sent her a card every year. It expressed our gratitude and profound appreciation in heart-warmingly sentimental little verses such as the following:

Mammy, how I thank you;
You really are my friend;
All the love you give me —
Love without end.

And when you get to Paradise,
Our Lord Himself will say:
"Welcome, dearest Mammy —
NOW WHERE'S ME SHAGGIN' TAY?!"[2]

OK, so we didn't *always* feel as well-disposed as that. Occasionally we thought our mammies were getting strange modern ideas. We didn't like some of the clothes they wore. When a mammy is a mammy she should *dress* like a mammy. So we got the Bishops to write a few Pastoral Letters about 'immodest fashions in female dress'. And the priests would put on their nice lacey frocks and flowing silken gowns and read to our mammies from the altar, telling them not to be dressing like tarts.

By 1937 the Bishops were busy with other things. Yes, they were happily writing the new Constitution with the occasional bit of interference from the actual government. There were three TDs at the time who were mammies. But these were naughty, *unhelpful* mammies. They wouldn't just shut up and make the sandwiches, the way a proper mammy should. No, they kept on making speeches, yapping out of them — you know the way the ladies do. They went so far as to claim that mammies had rights! Well we had to talk a bit of sense into them. So we got the newspapers to do that for us.

---

[2] William Butler Yeats, '*The Song of the Wandering Mammy*'.

Here is an absolutely genuine quote from an *Irish Independent* editorial of the time:

> 'Many men (including, it is whispered, the President) think that a woman cuts a more fitting and more useful figure when darning the rents in her husband's socks by the fireside than she could hope to cut in a Parliamentary assembly ... '

Now. That softened their cough for them, didn't it?! We didn't send *those* mammies a Mother's Day card. Naughty mammies. *Bad* mammies.

For thirty years after that, there was barely a peep out of the happy Irish mammy. She was busy at home, where she needed to be. She had fourteen children, after all! And every Mother's Day we brought her breakfast in bed, where she was happily giving birth to the next babby while simultaneously ironing us a shirt in which to emigrate. All this feminist nonsense about our mammies being oppressed. All that liberal hokum about miscarriage and still-birth rates being the highest in Europe. Our mammies *loved* their wonderful lives. And didn't they have their own mammy in heaven — The *Blessed* Mammy — to put in a word for them when things got a bit tiring?

No, the Irish mammy had a wonderful time. On Mother's Day, Daddy would give her a little break. Or sometimes even a compound fracture. But that was a terribly rare occurrence. In fact no Irish mammy *ever* had to live in a violent marriage, so there was no need at all to give them legal aid, or change the laws to allow them to have abusive husbands removed. So that was handy! They were *never* deserted or abandoned with their children, so the taxpayer never had to give them welfare. Think of all the money we saved! As for the few *very* bad mammies who did run out on their husbands just for punching them every night for ten years — well you will always get the rotten apple. (As Eve found out!) But even *then* we didn't turn our backs on them. Oh no. In order to protect that misguided mammy the Criminal Conversation laws were introduced, entitling her ape-like geek of a husband to prosecute anyone who gave her a cup of tea and a sandwich. I ask you, what could be fairer than that? *Every* day was Mother's Day here in Ireland!

Admittedly our mammies were considered their husbands' property. But that was what our mammies *wanted*. And what man in his right senses wouldn't look after such a valuable possession? This is what the young women of today completely fail to understand — our mammies didn't *mind* that until 1965 they could be disinherited by their husbands. Not at all. They thought it was great! And they didn't *mind* that they weren't entitled to the dole, or that their only legal status was as dependents of males, or that Children's Allowance payments were made to fathers and not mothers. And as for getting equal pay for equal work?

They were mammies, for God's sake! *Their* work was being walked on!

Late last year, I was listening to Marian Finucane's radio programme, when a young woman called to say she wanted to take up boxing but was having difficulty finding a trainer. Would any of the listeners have any advice? A much older soft-spoken reticent woman rang to say she found the idea utterly horrifying. It was undignified, common; so unladylike.

'I mean, Marian,' she implored, 'can you imagine the Blessed Virgin Mary in a boxing ring?'

I have to confess I found the picture intriguing. *'In the Red Corner, ladies and gentlemen, wearing the black trunks, the undefeated heavyweight champion of the world — Iron Mike TYSON! (Booooo). And in the Blue Corner and wearing the sky-blue veil, tonight's contender — something of a newcomer but she's full of grace, an immaculate little mover with some good combinations. Make no assumptions, she's virgin on a title! Your appreciation please — FOR THE MOTHER OF GOD!'*

Now that would be a fight worth getting Sky Sports for.

Ms Finucane had to point out that young Irish women did *lots* of things these days which it might be hard to imagine the Blessed Virgin Mary doing. As indeed they do. Things like vote. Or watch *Ally McBeal* on a Wednesday night. Or employ other modes of transport than assback. It was a funny moment. But it was poignant too.

The historian Dr Margaret McCurtain has remarked: 'Around Irishwomen, as in a cage, were set the structures of family life.'

You won't be seeing that on a Mother's Day card.

Nor the words of the great Irish socialist, Hannah Sheehy-Skeffington: 'Ireland will never be free until Irish women are free.'

But sure there you go. That's women for you now. Never bleeding happy, are they?

Taking His Pleasure:
The Irish Male And His Hobbies

*So long as a man rides his Hobby-Horse peaceably
and quietly along the King's highway, and neither
compels you or me to get up behind him — pray, Sir,
what have either you or I to do with it?*

Laurence Sterne, *Tristram Shandy*

Flicks, Chicks And Getting In A Fix

The very first film I ever saw in a cinema was *War And Peace* starring Henry Fonda and Audrey Hepburn. The cinema stood on the main street in Dun Laoghaire. It isn't there any more, and I can't remember its name, despite much brain-racking and carpet-pacing (The Adelphi, maybe?). Anyway, it was fantastically exciting to be going to the pictures at all, and I was knocked out by the storming sound and fabulous fury of the movie with its epic battle scenes and colourful costumes and generally swashbuckling style. But what was even more gripping than the film itself was the fact that it was so long it had to be shown in two parts. Part One ran for one week and you couldn't see Part Two until *the week after that*!! For a nipper reared on the ten-minute culture of children's TV this was an astonishing and quite revolutionary concept. Over this I could not get.

Apart from the fact that the film concerned Russians and people bayoneting each other and glamorous women flouncing around in crinoline, I couldn't really follow the story of Part One much, but I loved it anyway. I spent the whole of the ensuing week salivating with anticipation at the thought of returning to the cinema for Part Two, in which, as I recall it now, Audrey Hepburn looked even more beautiful than she had in Part One. Well, perhaps I had grown a few more hormones in those seven days. Anyway, 'Natasha' was the name of the character she played. I promised myself that if I ever met a Natasha when I grew up I would marry her. And I did, once. But that's another story.

Shortly after this experience my parents and I went to see *Butch Cassidy and The Sundance Kid* in the same cinema. It which wasn't as good as *War And Peace* because it was only in one part and it didn't feature Audrey Hepburn, or, indeed, any characters at all called Natasha or dressed in furry hats or bayoneting each other. But it was still pretty good.

The other cinema in Dun Laoghaire was the Pavilion, a vast, pastel-coloured, ornately corniced building which was as quintessentially Fifties as a little red Chevy. (Sadly the Pavilion is now also defunct, transmogrified into a yuppy apartment block.) You could see a film on a Saturday afternoon in the Pavilion for ten pence, and my brother and sisters and I often did. I suspect that many a marriage in the greater south Dublin area was saved, or at least prolonged, by the existence of the Pavilion Cinema.

In school there was a film every Friday night at seven o'clock in the hall. A gentle, compassionate priest called Father Al Flood was in charge of this event. At the start of each year he would select two or three boys for film duty, and one year myself and my pal James Boland were the lucky winners. The job involved Father Flood driving us into town after school on a Friday in order to collect that night's film from the distributor's office, which, as far as I remember, was just off Westland Row, and then driving us back to the school, where we would get the reels out of their big metal circular boxes and set up the projector and generally think we were really something.

The Friday night films were typically such fine intelligent works as *The Guns Of Navarone, The Great Escape,* and *Tora! Tora! Tora!,* which is a deeply educational and multiculturally sensitive work about the bombing of Pearl Harbour by evil Japanese loonies. From time to time Father Flood would tire of this kind of thing and for a few Friday nights there would be films with religious themes, such as *The Ten Commandments* and *Brother Sun, Sister Moon*. These were not nearly so entertaining, although it was rumoured that several people had ACTUALLY DIED during the making of *The Ten Commandments*. It was a lot of fun watching out for those bits.

Father Jarlath Dowling was another wonderful man. He taught music in my school for many years. I seem to recall that he actually *lived* in the music room; his small bed, which always looked as if it had been recently savaged by a wild animal, sat looking forlorn in the middle of the floor, surrounded by trumpets and tubas and drums.

Father Dowling was fanatically interested in old movies. He had a pull-down screen and a rattling projector in the music room. Often he would show us a Laurel and Hardy short or a Marx Brothers feature when we should have been listening to Beethoven or Brahms. He was a plump, passionate, fiery man with a head as bald as a billiard ball. Whenever he either lost his temper or laughed for any length of time he would sweat heavily, and his face would go red and heat up, with the result that the sweat on his scalp would turn into steam. When this happened — and it happened not infrequently — it looked like Father Dowling's head was oozing smoke. It was quite an effect. It really was. He could have sold tickets and made a lot of dough.

I remember one time during a music class Father Dowling decided that we really should see *A Night At The Opera*, which had the blissful virtue of combining his two greatest enthusiasms. The screen was pulled down, the chairs were pulled up, the curtains were drawn and off we went. Father Dowling was sitting just down the row from me. And about five minutes into the film, he started to laugh.

It was what comic-books call 'a titter' at first, and then it grew to a strangled chortle. Shortly after this he began to guffaw and then to snort. He tried to control himself. He sat sculpturally still, his legs tightly crossed, his face scarlet, the occasional apologetic cluck of mirth bursting forth from his massive frame. But it was no good. Before long he was rocking back and forth on his chair, slapping his thighs and actually honking with helpless unrestrained laughter. And then the poor man just lost it completely.

He couldn't stop. What I can only describe as a blast of laughter exploded out of him. It sounded like one of his beloved trumpets being played by a lunatic with gargantuan lungs. He howled. He bawled. He groaned. He cackled. The Marx Brothers cantered across the screen and Father Dowling opened his mouth and ROARED and bellowed with laughter. He jumped to his feet and lurched up and down the music room clutching his enormous stomach, barking with sheer abandoned joy, big tears of gaiety rolling down his chubby cheeks. Thirty seconds later the entire class of nine-year-old boys was in utter hysterics. The Principal must have heard the noise because he burst in shortly afterwards to find out what was going on. He glared astonished at Father Dowling, who was now uncontrollably sobbing with hysterical glee and leaning on a radiator with a hanky stuffed into his mouth — and then he glared at *us*, and then he glared up at the screen, where the Marx brothers were now doing a dance. And then the Principal started laughing. Which made Father Dowling laugh even more. And then the smoke started coming from Father Dowling's head. Which made us nearly *widdle* with laughter. And so on. It was astonishing. The Catholic Church introduced me to Marxism. It's the happiest memory I have of school.

Another movie recollection, less pleasurable although more poignant, is the first real date I ever had. It involved the Forum Cinema in Glasthule, a large bag of popcorn, a lot of hope and Denim deodorant and a very nice girl from Monkstown Farm. Her name was Patricia Keegan and she had gorgeous hair. I had met her the previous Saturday night at 'Prez', the Presentation College Disco, Glasthule. She, like me, was sixteen-and-a-bit. (She a bit beautiful. I a bit nervous.)

The movie we went to see was *Midnight Express*, which turned out to be about an unfortunate American youth called Billy Hayes who gets imprisoned for twenty years in Turkey for smuggling drugs. To say the work portrays negative images of that country would be something of an understatement. The people who run the Turkish Tourist Board must have shat themselves when this was released.

Let me tell you, if you are trying to make a good impression, this is NOT a good movie to see on a first date. Poor Billy Hayes. Torture, gang rape, nudity, squalor, filth, cockroaches, endless cursing and public masturbation — *Midnight Express* featured all these thought-provoking themes and more. Every five minutes, it seemed to me, Patricia emitted another near-puking noise, or plaintive wail of abject disgust, and scowled in my direction like I was some sort of pervert for bringing her to see this hideous gore-fest. I, for my part, kept my eyes locked on the screen. Because by now pure shock had drained the power from my neck-muscles.

The film climaxed with a scene of a prisoner biting a fellow inmate's tongue out and spitting it across the room in glorious Technicolour slow-motion. If I live to be a hundred-and-fifty, I will never forget the sound which issued forth simultaneously from the darkness beside me. It was the sound of Patricia Keegan going 'oh *Jeeeeeeeeeeeeeeezis*.' As I watched that tongue flying through the air I somehow sensed that the chances of my own tongue making any contact whatsoever with Patricia Keegan's later on in the evening were receding fast. And I wasn't wrong.

She broke my heart when she finally dumped me. Every time I see *Midnight Express* I still think of her. And the funny thing is, after all these years, I still reckon Billy Hayes got off lighter than me.

Saying *Yesss* To Europe

At this time of the year — at *any* time of the year — we are all thinking about our holidays. I have just returned from my own well-deserved vacation, a better man if a poorer one. I went to Italy for a week, a country for which I have a deep love. I find that I always feel strangely at home there, though I haven't a clue why that might be. After all, with its long history of Catholicism, organised crime and political corruption, Italy isn't at all like Ireland.

Italy is perhaps the most stereotyped European nation of all. There is, for example, the myth that all Italians are good-looking. Well, yes — many of them are. But I may tell you candidly, I have seen creatures dandering about the *piazzas* of Florence for whom you'd need a licence if you wanted to keep them in the house.

There is also the notion that Italians without exception are inherently stylish. Well, if gangs of drunken carbuncular teeny-boppers publicly interfering with each other and screaming '*Ciao bella*' at your girlfriend is your idea of style — and perhaps it is — you would love Italy as much as I do.

But nevertheless I have many happy memories of that fine country. Last Easter Sunday morning in Rome was a marvellously spiritual experience, I have to admit. It was lovely being in Saint Peter's Square, all of us together, singing hymns, reciting rosaries and queuing up to kiss the Papal ring. (The lip ointment is really working well now, *Deo Gratia*.)

In my own view there is only one thing seriously wrong with Italy and that is the currency, which can drive you insane. The current exchange rate for the lire is about 2700 to the punt. This makes life very difficult indeed. A newspaper costs several hundred lire, the price of a beer is nearly five grand. In Italy a person would need to be a billionaire to be an alcoholic. Not that *that* seems to stop some of them.

But the mental calculation needed to purchase anything at all is phenomenal. Many's the night, as I propped up the wall of some dodgy trattoria, singing ribald choruses of '*Bandiera Rossa*' or '*Nessun Dorma*' with the locals, I found myself — and not for the first time — disagreeing with the British government on an important aspect of fiscal policy. Reader, I found myself saying: why can we not all just accept the Euro?

Now, as regular disciples will know, I am not exactly blessed when it comes to the study of matters financial. When the other boys were doing double-economics at ten past nine on a Monday morning, your present scribe opted for art instead. Art class was an agreeable way to start the week. There was one boy who was actually talented at art, plus three or four indolent little skivers; the remainder of the body comprised twenty-five saddos whose eyes were just a *little bit* too close together and who delighted in fashioning turd-shaped objects from plasticine and attempting to ignite each other's gaseous emissions with cigarette lighters. Intuitive readers will already have discerned the category into which I fitted myself.

But anyway. Where we were? Oh yes — economics. It isn't one of my many areas of expertise. You could tell me that John Maynard Keynes was a blind blues guitarist from the Mississippi Delta who once jammed with Muddy Waters and Clarence 'Gatemouth' Brown on a scorching live version of '*Ah Can't Get No Grindin' Baby (What's the Matter With the Mill?)*' and I would believe you. To me, Supply Demand And Curve was a Progressive Rock combo from the mid-Seventies. All I know about the ERM is that 'Losing My Religion' is a catchy little number to warm up a party attended exclusively by social workers. But one thing I do know. After many visits to the European mainland, I am all in favour of the Euro coming in.

In the old days the Euro was known as the ECU, which

signified 'European Currency Unit'. But it stood for other less-pleasant things too. I always had ambivalent feelings about the ECU, ever since a friend who works in the film business confided to me that the acronym 'ECU' in pornographic movie circles (and this is apparently gospel) stands for 'ejaculation close-up'.

Thus, even if we *had* introduced the ECU, considerable caution would have been required in using it. You would need to be pretty careful, for example, sliding up to the bar and calling out to the attendant, 'Please let me have an ECU, I need to make a phone call'. Particularly if you didn't know the barperson very well, and hadn't been out to the pictures with him or her — well, *him* I guess — at least twice. I've come across a lot of angry barmen in my time. But I wouldn't want one of them coming across *me*.

But introducing the more hygienically named Euro all across Europe would cut out an awful lot of bother, would it not? In the whole sorry business of foreign travel, there is nothing quite as trying as the worry about the currency. It doesn't matter how cosmopolitan you are, you are doomed by the fates to get it wrong.

Picture the scene. It is the end of a pleasant evening in the *bodega, bierkeller* or *brasserie*. You are feeling very post-Maastricht indeed, if you get my drift. You get out the wallet, extract a suitable banknote emblazoned with many zeros and a portrait of some moustachioed old Fascist. You shell out the tip, only to find when you have returned to the hotel that the amount you have so blithely donated would pay off the national debt of Zimbabwe and still keep the landlady in stockings for about thirteen years.

Either that, or you will have erred on the side of ferocious meanness; and the next time you visit the premises, the staff will regard you the way they would a basin of warm effluent. In addition, not having spoken any English whatsoever the night before, they will have suddenly and mysteriously acquired such phrases from the great and ancient tongue of Shakespeare as 'tight-fisted old shit' and 'parsimonious gimp'.

The Euro would solve all these distressing problems and more. It would give us the power to be tight-fisted old shits in up to twelve languages. And if that isn't European integration, I just don't know what is.

Tongue-Fu For Beginners

If music be the food of love, get stuffed.
Sir Francis Bacon-Butty, *Hamlet Sandwich*

It is sometimes said by gastronomes that a really good dinner has quite a lot in common with sex. And you know something? They're not all barking loons.

Think of the stages of a great and memorable meal, those dizzying rituals of build-up and preparation that are so much a part of the total experience. The spine-tingling titillation of the first course — the *amuse bouche*, for God's sakes! — exciting foreplay if ever there was, as that happy little body part, the tongue, wakes up and comes to twitchy and significant life. Then a pause. The odd little nibble. The heady drama of provocative anticipation, the longing, the wishing, the wanting, the waiting for that blissful and magical arrival of the … er … *entrée*. Ah, the tastes, the sensations, the aromas, the textures, the mutually shattering smorgasbord of pleasures. More? Second helpings? Oh well, why not? Then the luscious climax of a fine dessert. The cigarette afterwards. The arguing about the bill.

And think of the other things both experiences have in common: puritans and skinny-arsed Health-Fascists frown upon each, while happily rounded people like a lot of both. Each is best enjoyed with someone else; preferably, if at all possible, with someone you love (but sometimes in large drunken groups at parties). The French and Italians famously excel in both fields, whereas the English, bless their hearts, have never been much good at either. As for ourselves, in the past we Irish weren't very interested. It used to be the case in Ireland that the terms 'food' and 'sex' rarely met, except for having a kebab on the bus on the way home afterwards. But nowadays, of course, we can't get enough. We seem to have discovered our appetites lately, and Janey Mack are we hungry or what?

Food and sex. Eros and Epicure. Surely these shared roots of desire go way back into early infancy. The sages and psychologists tell us that one of the first identifiable sensations experienced by newborn babes is that of taste. We're aware of our mouths before we're aware of anything else. We associate food with nurturing, love, acceptance, security, wantedness, the primal desire for physical closeness that wakes us up screaming and crying in the night.

But in time, of course, our childish feelings of infatuation with food fade and are replaced by something more mature. Gone is the craving for the simple spirit-shocking flavours of infancy, fled the solitary and solipsistic snacking of adolescence, replaced by the intimate desire for *dîner à deux*. If you know what I mean. And I think you do.

Literature has always been aware of this mysteriously delicious connection. Think of Proust's madeleine, Yeats's 'honey of generation,' Nabokov's rendering of Lolita's 'peachlike' bottom, Donne's arch appetizer to his mistress, 'suck'd on countrey pleasures'.

But far from being the province of the highbrow and academic, the association of taste with physical desirabilty melts into the language of everyday life with such effortless ubiquity that we scarcely even notice it. The argot of Fifties American movies taught a whole generation of swinging lovers to call each other Honey, Sugar, Cup Cakes, Muffin, Candy, Sweetie and Cherry Pie, Sweet Potato or just plain Sweetness. To this day, Londoners woo each other as 'Treacle' or 'Sweets,' describing one another as 'tasty' or even 'edible'. A Texan will happily serenade his girlfriend as 'Lambchop' or 'Pumpkin'. The ultimate accolade of earthily colourful Dublin slang is of course the expressed desire to eat *pommes frites* out of the desired one's *lingerie*.

We sometimes describe a suggestive remark or person as 'saucy', 'spicy' or 'fruity' — the French say '*piquant*' for the same thing. A certain type of muscularly desirable youngfella is meaty, beefy or, simply, 'beefcake'. Conversely we speak of those we don't like as sour, bitter, salty, cheesy, those who leave 'a bad taste in the mouth'.

From religion to pop, every aspect of our culture thrives on the connection between sex and food. Think, for example, of the Eurythmics' bold image — 'The language of love drips from my lover's tongue/cooler than ice cream and warmer than the sun'. And then ponder the words of the Song Of Solomon: 'Sustain me with raisins, refresh me with apples, for I, my beloved, am sick with love.' Then go downstairs and put the kettle on. Because I'll be round in half-an-hour for a rasher and a roll.

There's One Yawn Every Minute

Gentle reader, you have probably guessed that as a fully-trained, youngish, award-winning novelist — albeit that the award was for ten-pin bowling — I frequently receive letters from the unwashed *hoi polloi*, many of whom want to write Irish fiction as a hobby. Other correspondents are far more serious in their aims. They too would like to be young, award-winning novelists (YAWNS for short) and would like me, perhaps the greatest YAWN in the country, to give them 'some advice'. My main advice would be the following: never sleep with anyone who has an annoying laugh.

But it turns out this is not the kind of advice they want. No, what they want to know about is literature and how to do it. So here are my top ten tips for literary success:

1) Dealing With the Desire to Write

Ask yourself if you really do want to write. It is true that most Irish Males have a book in them, but in most cases that's exactly where it should stay. Few people are suited to the life of the YAWN, involving as it does a good deal of solitude, angst and gratuitous wearing of black poloneck sweaters. If you do find yourself experiencing a deep and burning inner desire to express yourself creatively, try eating something and often the feeling will go away.

2) When To Start

If you really do want to write, start young. It often occurs to me that when Keats was my age he had been dead for eleven years. This clearly gave him an unfair advantage with the critics.

3) Writing Comedy

Always remember the profound words of Groucho Marx: 'An

amateur thinks it's funny to dress a man up as an old lady, put him in a wheelchair and push him down a hill towards a stone wall. For a pro, it's got to be a *real* old lady.'

4) Writing Serious Literature
A work of serious literature is a book with a lot of weather in it. In serious literature wind does not blow. It *howls, shrieks, weeps* or *screams*. To the serious YAWN, rain does not merely fall. It *spatters, patters, spits* or *surges*. Snow invariably lies on the grass *like a coverlet, blanket* or *continental quilt.*

5) Sex
It is often difficult for aspiring YAWNS to handle scenes of sexual activity. This is mainly because they know that Granny is going to read the book when it is published and they do not want to hasten her departure from the corporeal realm, at least, not for the moment. But be brave. Grab hold of your courage in both hands. Remember that it is compulsory to use all of the following words in your sex scene, in whatever order suits your purposes, and indeed your morals: *pulsating; trousers; steaming; Wellington boots* (if applicable); *quivering; tongue; again and again; deeper, tumescent; proudly pert; inwardly; downwardly; swirling ectoplasm of anguished desire; baby oil; heaving; heart-stopping series of Vesuvian eruptions; cigarette; taxi home; chips and batterburger* (salt and vinegar optional).

7) Sending Your Finished Typescript to the Publisher
Most aspiring YAWNS take the time and trouble to enclose a large, stamped-addressed envelope with their first novels. I know from bitter experience that this is a terrible mistake. It is far too much temptation for the publisher to resist.

8) Public Readings

The best audience for your work will be intelligent, well-educated and only slightly drunk. But these days some audiences at literary events can be quite aggressive, going so far as to staple their rotten vegetables to lengths of elastic so they can hit you twice. There is an old English Music-Hall song which goes 'They made me a present/ of Mornington Crescent/ They threw it one brick at a time.' For some reason, those lines frequently come into my head when I am doing a reading.

9) Handling Hecklers

When you begin your career as a YAWN, you will be doing many readings in places like Thurles, which I know quite well because I spent forty years there one night recently. The indigenous peoples of these primitive settlements are not well known for their love of literature. So it is always a wise strategy to prepare a few witty put-down lines for abusive hecklers. One response which has been good to me over the years is 'Listen, pal, I'd like to help you out. Which way did you come in?' If all else fails just open your mouth and scream 'THE DEVIL MADE ME DO IT!' Then simply continue reading as though nothing odd has happened.

10) Book Signings

It is important that you at least *try* to listen to what the kind person who is buying your book has to say. Failure to do so may cause embarrassment, offence or even assault. I am indebted to the fine novelist Mr Colum McCann for the story of the young Irish author who was sitting proudly behind the table at his first signing in London. There he is, a vision of loveliness, pen in hand, as the queue shuffles up to purchase books and get them signed. A young woman approaches. He beams, flourishes the biro and asks for her name.

'Emma Chisett,' she smiles.

He signs the flyleaf with a graceful swirl — 'To Emma Chisett, with warmest best wishes.'

The woman peers at this heartfelt inscription, distaste now graven on her lovely face.

'Whatcher write that for?' she asks.

'Well … Is your name not Emma Chisett?'

'Naow,' she snickers, in finest Cockney. 'I was askin' you 'ow much is it? *Emma Chisett?*'

A Load Of Old Balls: On Being A Student

I noticed in the paper — yes, the other day — that there have been problems in recent years with the annual Trinity College Ball. Basically, nobody wants to go to it.

Back in the days of my own undergraduation, Trinity Ball tickets were as the rarest of gems. People begged for them, forged them, robbed them from their friends. Duels were often fought in the public thoroughfare for them. In 1984, questions were asked in the Dail when a Second Year science student infamously *swapped his own liver* for a Trinity Ball ticket. But such passionate devotion is a thing of the past.

There are a number of theories about why the demand no longer reaches that legendary level. One is that students have become too serious these days. Students, we are told, have somehow discovered the point of attending university is actually to read the odd book, not merely to sit about wearing vast flares, quaffing scrumpy, listening to garage music, snorting cocaine, giving lip to their betters, picking their noses, sizing up potential sexual partners and discussing, y'know, oppression, in the bar.

Except these days they aren't discussing oppression. According to a recent report in *The Irish Times*, the new generation is 'More Me than Marx'. In the Sixties, students demanded a thirty-two-county socialist republic, an end to the arms race and liberation for Vietnam. Now they are more likely to demand a new coffee machine for the Common Room. (With *decaffeinated* espresso — Yeah! Right *ON!*)

Academics and former students of Trinity have been pining for the glory-days when the Red Flag fluttered over the elegant campanile, Che Guevara's likeness overlooked the quads, and the time-worn halls once strolled by Edmund Burke echoed with muscular choruses of 'We Shall Not Be Moved', 'Give Peace A Chance' and 'All Kinds Of

Everything Remind Me of Mao'. In those now dead and distant times, students weren't undergraduates — but undergrudguates.

Ah, the Sixties generation at its most fervently radical! They've all grown out of that phase now, of course. Some have acquired Armani suits, love-handles, balding pates and Fine Gael memberships. But boy oh boy, could they occupy an office in their day, and still be home in time for Mater to heat up the din-dins.

My own theory is that students were secretly every bit as conservative back then as they are now. It's just that in the Sixties they had better songs — certainly better than the tunes of my own generation. In the Sixties they had Hendrix, Dylan and the Stones. Readers who were scholars at the same time as I, what did we have in the Eighties, eh? Man, *you* try smashing society and establishing a new revolutionary order to 'Karma-Karma-Karma-Karma-Karma-Chameleon' by Culture Club, 'Really Saying Something (A-Bop-Bop-Shoobie-Do-Wa-Hah)' by Bananarama and 'Too Shy-eee-eye' by Kajagoogoo. (Or was it 'Kajagoogoo' by 'Too Shy-eee-eye'?) See what I mean? Tricky, isn't it?

And my theory about the Trinity Ball is pretty simple too. To wit (too-woo) that asking punters to shell out sixty-five smackers for the temporary right to slither about the puke-spattered cobblestones of Trinners in a sweaty pickle of extreme sexual frustration, a hired piece of sartorial suicide and a sordid state of almost tragic inebriation is really a tad optimistic.

OK, look, I'll tell you the truth. I'm biased.

I went to the Trinity Ball three times, and each time I went was worse than the last. But the last time was even worse than that.

That year I invited a woman I completely adored. I had sensed a degree of friction between us in the past, and was hoping there would be a good bit more before the night was through. Alas, Reader, it was not to be. For some reason she deserted me about an hour after the ball began — I mean, I only fell into a drunken sleep for a *few minutes*, for Christ's sake — after which I spent the entire night searching for her, before eventually finding her at 'the dawnrise disco', slow-dancing (to 'Too Shy-eee-eye' by Kajagoogoo) in the manly arms of my best friend's brother. Kissing is not quite the word for what was going on. Had she been sucking his face any harder, his lips would have peeled off.

Ah, bitter memory. This is what the Trinity Ball means to me. Betrayal, remorse, exhaustion, disappointment, drunkenness, poverty and rank injustice. (Student fun, I think it is called.)

A Rub Of The Relic: On Churchgoing

It is the eighth of December, 1966, a holy day of obligation for Roman Catholics, the Feast of the Immaculate Condescension. The toddler's mother is in hospital today, having just given birth to a beautiful baby girl. So the toddler's father and grandmother are looking after him. And they decide, poor things, to take him to Mass.

The church is packed. Our three heroes are jammed into the porch. Picture, if you will, an exhausted, stressed-out thirty-two-year-old man, and a deeply pious, gentle old lady, each of them struggling to quell a yelping, barking toddler with a fine pair of lungs, a bad attitude and the digits 666 emblazoned on his soul.

At the appointed time, Dada goes up to Communion, leaving cute wittle diddums kicking in Grannywanny's arms. When he returns, some moments later, Nana conveys her nicens little bunnykins into Papa's care, then goes up herself to partake of the Divine Feast. Granny returns, head suitably bowed. Confidently the child awaits his own turn. But it doesn't come. The priest ascends the steps to the altar. He puts the chalice back in the tabernacle. Well, this is outrageous. This is an affront. The beastly nipper draws himself up to his full height and begins to screech like a demented banshee:

'He's lockin' it all away, Daddy! … *AND I DIDN'T GET ANY!*'

You might think that such an experience represents the beginning of a difficult relationship with the Church. And you might be right. A long time was to pass before I would be allowed into one again. (I was the only child in Glenageary who made his First Communion under armed surveillance by a SWAT-team of Franciscans.) And yet the odd thing is, I grew up to love churches. And to this day I love them still.

If I'm stuck in the centre of Dublin with half an hour to

kill, I'll often drift into a church. (And not to rob the poorbox.)
Clarendon Street, Adam and Eve's, St Anne's in Dawson
Street are some of my faves. I like their quietness, their sense
of calm.

When Auden went to Spain during the Civil War it
bothered him greatly that the churches of Madrid were being
bricked up by the Anarchists. A lifelong pagan, it wasn't that
he wanted to go into them himself: it was just that it made him
happy to know he *could* if he changed his mind. I suppose
that's more or less how I feel too. I'd hate them to be turned
into basketball courts. You see them around the Irish
countryside now, small Protestant churches abandoned, falling
down — being converted into offices and Internet cafés. I
can't help but think it's a sad sight.

Last year on a book promotion tour in Boston, I found
myself in conversation with a wealthy Irish-American. She
had put in a bid on a tumbledown Protestant chapel in rural
Cavan, she told me, and wanted to turn it into a holiday home.
But she'd changed her mind when the Church authorities had
refused to include the adjoining graveyard in the sale. 'I had to
take a stand,' she confided. 'I mean, for the money they were
asking, you'd really want the graveyard too.' It was probably
the most obscene thing anyone has ever said to me. (It is
sometimes unfairly rumoured of people from Cavan that they
would sell you their grannies. I was glad to learn it isn't true,
at least not literally.)

I'm always conscious of the love that went into building
churches, the craftsmanship and care of their design and
construction. When the great Catalan architect Antonio Gaudi
first showed his drawings for the tops of the steeples of his
doomed *Sagrada Familia* cathedral in Barcelona, the local
Bishop was disapproving. Such detail was unnecessary and
would cost too much, said the Bish, and after all, the patrons

would never be able to see it. 'I have only one Patron,' Gaudi replied. 'And He will see it every day.'

But my fondness for churches has nothing to do with being religious. You'll probably have gathered by now that I'm not. Jesus and me got off to a bad start. Perhaps it was just that I didn't like some of his more extreme followers. Holy Christ, why is it that people you wish had never been born are always the ones who get born *again*?

When I was a kid I thought Jesus spoke with a rural Irish accent. I thought he was possibly from some place like Roscommon. I thought of him as a slightly frightening Irish Catholic, not a Middle-Eastern Jew with a cracking selection of one-liners. As for his appearance, I was influenced by the traditional imagery. I thought he looked like Jon Bon Jovi, when in reality he probably looked more like Yasser Arafat.

Still and all, you can't forget Jesus completely. He's inspired paintings and sculptures, cathedrals and poems, country songs and oratorios, movies and rock operas. Has anyone else ever lived whose very name is both prayer and curse? Well, Charlie Haughey obviously. But you know what I mean.

Growing up in Ireland, he was part of our childhood. (Jesus, I mean, not Charlie Haughey.) A crucifix hung on every classroom wall. The grotesquely sadistic apparatus on which he died was the most powerfully sacred symbol in the culture, an image so shockingly pornographic you wouldn't see it in a snuff movie. I mean, come on, I don't mean to be disrespectful — but a half-naked dead bloke nailed to a plank?! I've seen some stuff, but *that's* scary.

The main source for learning about his life was the Bible. The priests in my school would read bits out. Yet I remember feeling frequent unease when they did so, and wondering could you *really* trust this stuff as the literal word of God? This is a book which casually informs us: 'from that day forward [the day Eve sinned in the garden] the snake was condemned by the Lord to crawl on its belly in the dust'. But hang on a second. If it was condemned to crawl 'from that day forward', what the Hell was it doing before that? Up until that point, what was the snake's preferred form of transport? Taxi? The Dart? Did it walk on the tip of its tail? *What??*

The Bible doesn't tell us when Jesus was born, nor anything at all about his childhood. It's likely, though by no means certain, that he was brought up in Nazareth. According to Mark's gospel, he had four brothers, 'Keith, Stephen, Mikey and Shane'. OK, so those might not have been their *actual* names. We just don't know. We aren't told. But in a way that's the point. When it comes to Jesus, we *don't know anything* much. The gospels were written a century after the time in which they place him. They're not eye-witness accounts by people who were there. Putting it bluntly, they're works of fiction. You make up your mind which bits to believe.

Not that you have to be a believer to find Jesus inspiring. In Managua, Nicaragua, in August 1985, for example, I conducted an interview with Tomas Borge, Minister of the Interior, leader of the hard-line Marxist wing of the Sandinista Front.

Commandante Borge was the only Government Minister I have ever met who kept a Kalashnikov in his office desk. (At least, the only one prepared to admit to so doing.) Another thing that surprised me about him was that an entire wall of his office was covered with crucifixes — an unusual interior-decor feature for a rampant Commie. Many of the crosses were vivid and garish, made of coloured glass or bright stones. Christs in native Indian costumes beamed down over the filing cabinets, grinning like babies, rays of lights streaming from their open hands. There were Christs crucified in the robes of emperors. There were female Christs, black Christs, yellow

Christs with oriental eyes. Some were battered and broken, with limbs and heads missing, ancient twisted bodies agonizing in oak and black ash. There was an abstract white steel cross in a black steel circle; there was a Christ in jeans and a punk-rock T-shirt, with syringes jabbed into his bleeding wrists and feet.

I asked the Commandante which one he believed in most.

'Oh, I'm an atheist,' he shrugged, 'so I believe in them all.'

And I guess that's the kind of believer I am too. If there's anything out there, I'll be pleasantly surprised. But I don't think there is and it doesn't bother me. In a way, I kind of hope there isn't. The prospect of everlasting life is vaguely disconcerting when you could end up sharing a cloud with your bank-manager. Yet for the contentedly atheistic such as myself, churches are still temples of human desire, monuments to the heroic attempt to understand what can't be understood in any language. Perhaps more than any other public building, a church is finally about utter mystery. And I like it that every single town in Ireland has a building whose purpose is utterly mysterious.

Limerick, of course, has several. God bless it.

Pitched Battles:
The Irish Male On Football

As flies to wanton boys, are we to the Gods;
They kill us for their sport.

William Shakespeare, *King Lear*

I asked [the Christian brother who warned me against
non-Gaelic games] what he had against soccer? What
was wrong with soccer, a game like any other? The man
who ran our soccer team was studying to be a priest, so
what could be wrong with playing for the team?The
Christian Brother stared me straight in the face
and said 'Judas was an apostle'.

Peter Sheridan, from *Invisible Dublin,* Ed. Dermot Bolger

Slimboy Fat And The Beautiful Game

As those of you who are not ignorant savages will already know, the late Mr Orwell was no daw. In his celebrated 1945 essay 'The Sporting Spirit', he has the following wisdom to impart: 'Serious sport has nothing to do with fair play. It is bound up with hatred, jealousy, boastfulness, disregard of all rules and sadistic pleasure in witnessing violence: in other words it is war minus the shooting. And what's more, many people who play sports professionally are nothing but brainless, drug-taking mutoids who couldn't find their own hairy arses in a darkroom.' Well, OK, I made up the last sentence. (He actually wrote 'brainless, Neanderthal geeks'.) But I think you get the drift all the same.

So it will come as no surprise to you, darling readers, to hear that I have precious little interest in the majority of sports. The allegedly great festivals of the sporting calendar are as welcome to me as a dose of the galloping piyakers. No, I regard many sports as activities practised by individuals with whom I share nothing but a relatively small number of Constitutional rights; and in the case of rugby players I'd have to reconsider even those.

In this distaste I am far from alone. The great majority of the planet's population has absolutely no interest whatsoever in sport. But take a decko at your telly schedules and see what's in store for you any weekend of the year. Tennis, golf, Formula One, snooker, bowling, boxing, bungee-jumping. Mark my words, it'll be tiddlywinks soon.

Most sport simply leaves me cold. Yes, yes, I do go to the gym. Lately I have taken up jogging on the treadmill, which is one sure way of getting to hear heavy breathing a few times a week. But at least I don't take pleasure in it, no way.

Yet even in the gym a person has to be careful. 'Experts' say that physical exercise is healthy; yet it is a well-known statistical fact that more people utterly banjax themselves in gymnasia than in bars, night-clubs and street-fights put together. The other night I was leaving my own Fitness Emporium when I saw this covey stretched out on his back in the car-park, moaning in pain as he clutched his calf. (The back of his lower leg, I mean, not a baby cow.) Piteous the cries which were issuing forth from him; dreadful the groans and scatological oaths. I was terribly concerned by what was going on, mainly because I couldn't get my car out past him. He gawped up at me with an expression of heartbreaking vulnerability, hot tears of agony dribbling down the kisser. 'Excuse me,' he said. 'I'm a little stiff from badminton.' I told him I didn't give a fish's tit where he came from, he better stop cluttering the place up like that.

Football is the only sport I can watch with true pleasure. The game itself is a thing of blissful majesty, only slightly diminished by the ubiquitous pundits and commentators. What about the insane, inane way they talk, the violence they do to the English language? A football match, for a start, is never described as a football match. It is a *fixture*, a *clash*, a *tactical confrontation*, a *long anticipated battle*, a *high-level struggle*, an *epic*, a *gala*, a *meeting of giants*, a *drama played out in this crucible of champions*. Call it anything you want except what is is. Never use one word where seven will do.

And a player never scores a goal, oh no. *He buries it in the back of the net, punishes a lacklustre and casual defence, lobs it home, leaves the keeper standing, sinks it in with a decisive power-header, slams it through on the half-volley, shows exactly why AC Milan have paid out fifteen million pounds for him, Alan, sneaks in from the edge of the box like a shorts-wearing stealth bomber and answers his critics in the only language they understand. He makes no mistake from that kind of distance, runs rings around the unimpressive and disorganized back four, seriously ups the ante, adds to his tally, or* — if the player is German — *finishes with cruel, almost clinical precision.*

If the player hails from South America *he displays silken skills, or moves as though the football is glued to his boots.* If he is a member of an African nation, *he shows delightful spirit, proves his side isn't here just to make up the numbers, entertains the good-humoured and colourful crowd with his cheeky brand of puckish irreverence or adds greatly to proceedings by his mischievous presence HA HA HA.*

Now that Rupert Murdoch personally owns English soccer, look what else the TV bosses have in store for us. Cricket! This is a game created by English religious fundamentalists to vividly convey the concept of a living hell to the non-Christian peoples of the formerly British empire, who at least have the gumption to beat them stupid at it.

And golf? As the great Jack Benny once so wisely said: 'Give me my golf clubs, fresh air and a beautiful partner and you can keep the golf clubs and the fresh air.'

Tennis? What's that about? A game invented by King Henry VIII, whose other useful contributions to suffering humanity included the Church of England, 'Greensleeves' and Marriage Guidance Counselling.

Need we say more? I don't think we do.

Is Football Actually Better Than Sex?

It is sometimes said, and said quite insistently, that football is actually better than sex. At first glance, this seems a strange and highly debatable statement. The two activities are so utterly different. One involves sensuality, passion, emotion, commitment, selflessness, the speechless admiration of sheer heart-stopping beauty, rushes of breathtaking, ecstatic excitement, followed by shattering, toe-curling, orgasmic pleasure.

And the other is sex.

Certain women who are not football fans — I am reliably informed that there are one or two such creatures left in the world — sometimes fail to understand the subtleties of this connection. They simply do not relate emotionally to the blissful anticipation of the game, the sacred ritual of preparation, the joyful build-up to the main event, the veritable foreplay that is the brisk booing and tribal barracking of the opposing team and its supporters, the plateau phase of the contest itself, as it thrusts first this way, then that, the feverish mounting excitement building up to … YES, HE SHOOTS!! … AND HE SCORES!!…with the attendant bubbling-over of pride and raw emotion, not to mention Furstenberg. And then the worry. Let's hope we didn't peak too early.

At this point, let me say to women readers: It isn't that he *prefers* his football team to you (although I would hesitate before forming the question in such a way that he might actually have to choose). It is just that his football team is better at playing football. He's not saying he doesn't *like* you or anything. But would you stand a chance in the World Cup finals? Be honest. Not even if you adopted the four-four-two formation. Come on, you couldn't even beat one of the minor teams, such as Iran, South Africa, China or Scotland. (Well, OK then. *Maybe* Scotland.)

It is true, of course, that not all football fans are men. In recent times, more and more women have come to the realisation that their mothers were completely wrong about football, that really it is a wonderful thing. Yet far from being happy about this modern development, many men actually find it threatening. Quite understandably. In the old days, you knew what women thought about football. It was crap. It was boring. It was deeply unpleasant. It was as quintessentially male as you could get without the aid of illegal hormones. But these days things are different. As more and more women switch on to the game of two halves, you now face the serious possibility that your girlfriend will know more about the sweeper system than you do. Imagine! *Women* discussing blistering runs down the touchline, pinpoint crosses into the box, deft little passes in the centre of the park! To many men, this is all quite horrifying.

Everyone knows that in the past football provided the perfect focus for that most sacred of courtship rituals: male droning. This practise is a crucial element in any lasting heterosexual relationship. Male droning occurs when the male blathers on and on *ad nauseam* about nothing important and the female switches onto emotional auto-pilot, nodding understandingly and throwing in the occasional frown of feigned interest while secretly thinking about getting the cat spayed. It is particularly pronounced in very young men and very old men, but a completely drone-free male is so rare as to be considered officially extinct. Good subjects for male droning include:

- teenage progeny, poor examination results and employment prospects of
- lads in the office, considerable drinking capacity of
- all politicians, fundamental uselessness of
- God, existence or non-existence of
- modern popular musicians, inability to write a tune of

(not like in our day)

- Inland-Revenue officials, unspeakable cruelty of
- 'this', what he may/may not have done to deserve
- your mother, eerily unpleasant aroma of
- the dog, elimination of, if it tries to screw the sofa just one more time.

But of all subjects for male droning, football is probably the best.

That's how Mother Nature intended it. From time immemorial that's how it has been. I expect that if we could decipher those ancient scrolls the archaeologists recently discovered in Southern France, they would say:

CAVEMAN ONE: 'Now, dear, you see if the player is *in front* of the ball when it is played, then he is *offside*. Whereas if he …'

CAVEWOMAN TWO (to herself): 'I wonder when he will get up off his arse and go discover fire.'

But to return to my central point — the tired old truism is, of course, that men prefer football to sex because they're not good at expressing their emotions. They don't show their sensitive side or talk about their feelings. They don't share. They don't cry. (Unless they're supporters of Queen's Park Rangers, in which case they cry till they get to *like* it.) But this hackneyed accusation is based on a profound female misunderstanding of the true nature of male communication. Sport is often the *way* men communicate. If you doubt my contention, consider the following:

All over the country this coming season, the same scene will be re-enacted innumerable times. A couple will visit another couple to spend a sociable evening. The women will talk about relatively unimportant matters, such as the destruction of the rainforests, the depletion of the ozone layer and the almost amusingly remote chance of life continuing on the planet past Tuesday week. And then, at a certain point in the proceedings, one of the men will surreptitiously glance at his watch. Then at the other man. Then towards the door. Their eyebrows will twitch. Their hearts will speed up. Small, almost imperceptible nods will be exchanged. They cannot help it. We are dealing with the call of the wild. Like tiny, confused forest-creatures obeying the command to hibernate, both men will slowly but inexorably drift into the other room to watch an international football match played by two countries they have never been to in their lives and could not find on a map for a million pounds. But to say they won't be communicating would be wildly inaccurate. 'Grand bit of pace on that striker,' they will mutter. Or, even, 'Give me another beer.'

The sad truth is — for some men at least — that in the match between sex and football, football will always scrape home on goal difference. For Heaven's sake, look at the simple facts. A game of football lasts for a whole ninety minutes! And afterwards, you can invite your friends around, order a pizza, and watch the whole thing again on video, pausing the tape to analyze the most exciting bits. What could be better?

I mean, yes, I suppose you could do that with sex also. (I know *I* do.) But you run the risk that it might affect your relationship just a tad, for example when the wife arrives home early from her mother's with the Parish Priest in tow. Phew. Nice to see you, Father. Put down the collection box and pull up a chair, why don't you, there's a really GREAT bit of dribbling coming up.

Sex, the Italians say, is the poor man's opera. But unlike most things the Italians say, this is baloney. *Football* is the poor man's opera. There on the classic stage of the pitch, in the immortal gaze of the floodlights' beam, is all the emotion, commitment and feverish excitement — not to mention sheer physical violence and bloody awful acting — of a great Puccini masterpiece. (Puccini was a composer, by the way, not a brand of sportswear.) What musical maestro could ever have invented a character as insolently noble as Roy Keane, as brilliantly flawed as David Beckham, as dashingly heroic as Zinadine Zidane, as magnificently fat as Paul Gascoigne?

You want memorable music? We got it, and how. For awe-inspiring passion and poetic majesty, could Verdi's 'Chorus of the Hebrew Slaves' possibly ever compare to the rousing hymn with which supporters of South-East London's Millwall FC so sportingly serenade the fans of their opponents: 'You're Goin' Home in a Fark-in' Ambulance.'

Did the great Wagner himself ever pen a line that could beat the battle-cry of USA 94: 'Ooh. Aah. Paul McGrath, Say Ooh-Aah, Paul McGrath'? And where in the collected recordings of Callas and Domingo can you find a sentiment expressed with the terse Yeatsian precision of 'The Referee's a Wanker. The Referee's a Wanker. Ee-Eye-Adio, the Referee's a Wanker.'

But quite apart from its artistic appeal, there are other reasons why men like the game so much. There is a lot of talk these days about how football's real attraction is that it enables supporters — particularly men, emasculated by the tremendous advances of feminism, such as equal pay and the push-up bra — to feel included in a vast extended fraternity of fandom. Once upon a time men left behind their womenfolk and lumbered off together into the primeval forest to bang drums, chant bloodthirsty slogans and paint their faces the colour of vomit. Now they go to the football stadium instead, where they can also get hot-dogs and tasteful souvenir items.

There is an important spiritual dimension too. Thinkers and contemporary commentators of great intelligence (also Glen Hoddle) have posited that the central dramatic narrative of football has about it something of the power of great fiction, the ability it confers to step outside the self, the conveying of the sacred right to belong to something larger than one person, a communal and unified entity which finally becomes more than the sum of its parts. This is a point of view with which most male football fans would enthusiastically concur, by loudly exclaiming '*duh*?'

People will sometimes tell you that such a desire for communality is unhealthy and xenophobic, or even potentially Fascist; that we must all struggle bravely to build a world without borders or tribes, a world of maturity, respect and tolerance, where our children, not to mention our children's children, will live in mutual understanding and harmony for evermore. And that is, of course, fine. Once we beat the English.

We must always remember that football is the most truly democratic game of all time. Indeed, it is the only genuinely international sport there is. Almost totally unencumbered by considerations of class, geography or social standing, it is played on street corners, in car-parks, on vacant lots, and in massive stadia, in every corner of the globe. It is as universal as Coca Cola and the Roman Catholic Church, but usually not quite as bad for your health. Visit any country in the Third World and you will certainly not find the local children playing croquet, rugger, polo or golf. (Not that golf qualifies as an actual sport so much as a stomach-churning form of masochistic torture, but you take my point.) You don't need a swimming pool, a nine-iron, a graphite racket, a horse, a noseful of cocaine or any of the other paraphernalia so many sports seem to demand these days. A ball, and a couple of shirts to act as goalposts, and you are, as they say in the West of Ireland, suckin' diesel.

For all the corruption of owners, the venality of managers and the Machiavellian scandals that have haunted the beautiful game in recent years, all the greed of agents, the manipulation of players, the tragedies of Hillsborough and Hysel, the hooligan hatreds of the lunatic fringe, football remains one of the last great public embodiments of the spirit of human innocence. The legendary Liverpool manager Bill Shankly was once asked whether he saw football as a matter of life and death. 'Oh, no,' he replied, 'it's much more important than that.' But I like to think he was joking. If he wasn't, I like to think he was wrong. Because what is ultimately important about football is that it is ultimately not important at all. You can dress it up as much as you like, but in the end it is twenty-two rational, sentient human beings (and formerly Vinny Jones) chasing an inflated bladder around a field and kissing the face off each other when they kick it between two bits of wood. The fact that people can get so excited about something so fundamentally stupid is really one of the most marvellous things you could imagine. Sex is quite stupid too, when you look at it closely, as I often do. But you do not win the Jules Rimet trophy for sex. Unless you are very good at it indeed. (I have never won so much as a book-token for it myself.)

I know many women honestly feel that men are besotted with their football teams. But that is quite laughable. I mean OK, perhaps they were *once* besotted with them, just as they were with other seductive aspects of teendom, such as heavy metal, flared trousers and born-again Christianity. All these passing delights proved tempting to males when they were younger and more silly and impressionable. But over time, their youthful feelings about their football teams have developed into something more meaningful than mere infatuation.

Yes.

Love.

A man may love a woman — indeed he does, as often as possible — but he can get *involved* with a football team in a more deeply spiritual way. Oh, he's fond of the wife and he wouldn't deny it. As a hobby she's grand, though he wouldn't want to take her too seriously. (Marriage, after all, is only a game.) But he *loves* his football team for better or worse, for richer or poorer, in sickness and in health, till a sudden death penalty shoot-out doth them part. And even then, the parting is often only temporary. After a proper period of grief and mourning, he may somehow learn to love again. Yes, such a lifelong commitment isn't easy. He does have to work at it. There will be ups-and-downs along the way. But when things get difficult and they fail to win promotion AGAIN, he tries to remember his sacred vows of fidelity. In the end, the thought of growing old together is a great consolation. 'You'll Never Walk Alone,' he reflects. United forever. AND DOWN WITH CITY!

As for his partner, she is a woman of many qualities. But a football team does not leave its tights and bra on the bathroom floor. A football team does not shave its legs using his special razor (although it would be more than welcome to do so should the need ever arise). And perhaps most important of all, a football team does not keep wittering on and on about how great and handsome and wonderful George Clooney is, when everyone knows George Clooney has never played football in his life and is consequently only a man in the strictly biological sense.

So do men really prefer football to sex? Well, no, of course not, although it does sometimes appear that way; certainly, it may seem a sad state of affairs when the answer to the question, 'Darling, what's your favourite position?' turns out to be 'Probably centre-half'. But then, it is vital to remember that most men sincerely believe that their personal support of a football team is in some way vital to its sporting success. Football Vs Sex? It is really quite simple. A man believes he can influence the outcome of football. And only rarely can he influence the outcome of sex.

Yes, it may seem inexplicable to a woman that her man can truly care in the very core of his being about eleven millionaires he does not personally know, when she, despite her best and continuing efforts, can't even get him to stop biting his toenails in bed. But hey, try to understand. Make a little effort. As Billy Bragg once so wisely asked, 'How can you lie back and think of England, when you don't even know who's on the team?'

I know it can be annoying. A man can sometimes appear to his partner as though his main interest in life is getting a bit drunk and reciting the names of all the players who took part in the epoch-making Shamrock Rovers vs. Bohemians first-round nil-all draw of the 1957 League of Ireland. But be gentle and patient with him. If you dig down really deeply, and bring him a ham sandwich, you will find that actually, what he is *really* interested in, on a more profound and philosophical level, is getting a bit drunk and reciting the names of *all* the players who played for Shamrock Rovers *ever*. And then wondering why *he* never did. And then crying for his Mammy. And then falling asleep.

This is, of course, the marvellous thing about men, or at least, about the majority of male sports fans. Often they do not have deep feelings about anything much, and when they do, they don't want to analyse them at great length. This is probably the category you women readers are in.

Listen, he idolizes you. He has put Georgie Best on his fantasy football team, but he has put you on a pedestal. He worships the ground at which Arsenal play, but also the ground upon which you walk. He loves you so much that most of the time he simply can't figure it out. You are the best thing that has ever happened to him, and he deeply adores you. But he *understands* football. He knows how it works. And above all else, a man such as the one I have described above really needs something to understand. Because Christ knows he doesn't understand *you*.

It's a close-run thing, but football, better than sex with someone you love? Ha! Please. No way in the world.

Unless it is played by Leeds United, of course. Then we are into a different league.

THE MATCH

a short story

EDDIE VIRAGO had a serious case of the shakes.

He swept back his straggling, greasy quiff, leaned over his desk and continued meticulously forging the expenses docket for his training course in junior bank management at the Royal College of Banking, Peckham Rye. The sun roared in through the office window, making him feel sweaty and not quite alert. Unscrewing the cap of the Tipp-Ex bottle, he began to apply the white fluid to the dotted line, with the devout delicacy of a mediaeval monk. One of those feckers who did the Book of Kells. That's what he thought. He was in a bad mood.

The telephone rang, making him start and fumble.

'Yeah?' he snapped.

'Eddie,' said the voice. 'It's me. Patricia.'

'Patricia.'

'Your sister Patricia.'

'Oh, right. Jesus! How's tricks?'

'Great, Eddie. And you?'

'Grand, grand. Too bloody hot though.'

'London's always too hot in the summer.'

'How's Paris?' he asked.

'Fine. Are you looking forward to the match?'

'Can't watch it. Have to go to some crummy wedding with Siobhan today.'

'Ah well. Sure it's only a match.'

'That's what *she* said. Bleeding Ireland Vs England in the European Championships and muggins here has to go to a bleeding wedding.'

'Eddie, stop swearing and listen. I've got a bit of news.'

'What's that?' He picked up his coffee. 'You and Penis-Head finally getting engaged?'

'His name is Philippe.'

'Well? What about him?'

'This news, Eddie. It's kind of big.'

'Don't tell me he's finally managed to impregnate you.'

'No … Just … Look I had this accident the other night. I'm in the hospital over here.'

'Hospital? …What kind of accident?'

'Well … don't go spare now. But I got run over on Saturday night.'

'You what?'

'Run over.'

'Jesus, that's … Are you OK? Did you get his number?'

'It wasn't a car.'

'It wasn't?'

'No.'

'So what was it?'

'Well, that's the thing, Eddie. It was a train.'

'… *What*?'

Her voice started to crack with tearfulness. 'Well … I was a bit plastered, you see. I'd been out with Philippe and we'd had a row on the way home …'

'And the bastard pushed you under a *train*?'

'No, of course not … We were … we were just a bit pissed, see. We'd had a row. I don't know what happened but I fell over onto the train tracks … Just as this train was coming into the Gare du Nord …'

'Patricia. Please. Tell me you're pulling me wire.'

'Eddie,' she sobbed. 'I'm after losing a leg.'

He spluttered a mouthful of coffee over his desk. 'You WHAT?'

'I lost a leg, Eddie. They had to amputate it.'

The line crackled and bleeped a few times. He heard the sound of her pushing coins into the callbox. Sweat was beginning to soak through his shirt.

'Jesus,' he said. He couldn't seem to think of anything else to say. 'Jesus. Oh my Jesus. Oh Jesus H Christ.'

'I'm so scared, Eddie,' she wept. 'Can you ring Dad and tell him for me?'

He heard himself whinny with high-pitched laughter. 'No way,' he said.

'Please, Eddie. He'll kill me if I do it. You know what he thinks of Phillippe.'

'Patricia, look …'

'He'll make me come home. I couldn't face it, Eddie. Go on, will you, please?'

'Patricia …'

'I have to go, Eddie. The nurse is here with my morphine.'

'Wait a second … Patricia … *Wait*!'

The line went dead and began to burble. He put down the receiver, shaking, sweating. He went to the window, trying hard to concentrate. One of his sister's legs was gone. His sister Patricia had only one leg. It was the twelfth of June, 1988. It was just after eleven o'clock in the morning. He was on the fourteenth floor of an office block in central London. Ireland would play England this afternoon in Stuttgart. The team would probably be Bonner, Morris, Hughton, McCarthy, Moran, Whelan, Galvin, Houghton, Aldridge, Stapleton and Paul McGrath. And his sister had just phoned from Paris to tell him she only had one leg. He said those devastating words aloud.

'Stapleton and McGrath,' he said. Aloud.

My sister has one fucking leg, he thought. I got up this morning and I had cornflakes for breakfast and I read the pre-match reports in the *Guardian* and *The Irish Times* and all that time my sister had only one leg. It suddenly occurred to him that he didn't even know *which leg she had*. Was it the right or the left? She hadn't said. He wondered if he could ring the hospital and ask. But which hospital? And which bloody leg?

And how in the name of Christ would you say that in French? *Quelle jambe, Monsieur le docteur, s'il vous plaît? Le droit ou le gauche?* Was that it? Would that do? The Leaving Cert never prepared you for situations like this.

He looked down into the street. Outside Buck Mulligan's Irish Sports Bar, people were already milling around and drinking. A long banner had been hung from an upper window, depicting a squinting malevolent leprechaun about to kick a British bulldog in the arse. GIVE IT A LASH JACK, the banner said.

He came back to his desk. He lit a cigarette. He picked up the phone and tried his father's number in Dublin. It was engaged. His fingers were trembling badly. He tried again, dialing the numbers very slowly, as though that might possibly make a difference. Still engaged. Who could he be talking to?

He tried to imagine the conversation with his father.

'I think you should probably sit down before I tell you this, Frank.'

'Why, Eddie? Nothing wrong, is there?'

'Just … take the weight off your feet for a second, Dad. Both of them.'

On second thoughts, maybe he wouldn't put it like that.

*

The interior of the Tube train smelt of feet and sweat and hot rubber. He was peering over the shoulder of the slim Japanese woman beside him, trying to read an article about Madonna's latest lip job, when the train suddenly shuddered to a stop in the tunnel. The lights flickered and hummed and then there was silence, except for the irritated rustling of several dozen copies of the *London Evening Standard*.

'My sister has only one leg,' he thought. 'My sister is a monopede.'

The engine rumbled into life and cut out again. 'It's a bloody disgrace!' one old lady said suddenly. 'It's an absolute bloody disgrace, that's what.'

'Oh yes,' agreed another old dear. 'It is.'

'They should do something about it,' said the first lady.

'But they *don't*, though, do they? They don't care anymore.'

'Well that's right. Yes. They just don't care.'

It occurred to him they could have been talking about more or less anything, from the price of bread to the threat of nuclear war. This was how the English seemed to converse. The point was to fill in the silence but not to say anything of any importance. Not that that was a bad thing at all. It was a skill he often wished he had mastered, one that would be useful to any member of an Irish family. It was probably the thing he liked best about the English. The act of conversation rarely led to trouble. When they weren't beating up foreign football fans, they were the politest people in the whole world.

He looked around the carriage at the tired red faces. A young couple by the doors began to kiss. The boy slid his arm around the girl's waist, pulled her gently into his chest. She wrapped her arms around his neck. He moved his thigh between her *two* thighs and she gave a soft laugh before pushing him away. A handsome Asian man in a white suit and red turban began to whistle. With a dull throbbing sound, the train moved off again.

It pulled into Leicester Square Station and the doors opened with a disturbing squeal. He climbed the escalator, feeling exhausted and hot, his head now pounding with tiredness and tension. In the vile-smelling tunnel there was an enormous poster of Postman Pat, onto which someone had scrawled a cartoon penis with a fluorescent marker. Jesus, what was the world coming to?

A sad looking busker with a dog tied to his feet was hamming up the words of an old Irish ballad.

Ah, hung, drawn and quartered,
Well that was me sentence;
Condemned as a rebel, a traitor, a spy.
But no man can call me a knave or a coward,
A hero I've lived and a hero I'll die.

Eddie felt the hot diesely air smack his face as he sprinted up the steps to the street and crossed over to the doors of the Hippodrome. Siobhan wasn't there. She was always late. He looked at his reflection in the black glass door. He thought about his sister and her one revealing leg. For some strange reason, he wanted to laugh now. It was terrible news, but he wanted to laugh, the way newsreaders are said to want to when they have to read out something dreadful. His sister had one leg. His sister was hopping. The feeling of hysteria gave way to dull horror.

The tarmacadam street seemed to suck the sunshine into itself. The doleful thud of speed-metal music came pounding out from the packed interior of a nearby Irish bar. He pressed his face against one of the Hippodrome's windows. The dark smooth glass felt oddly cool. He looked at his reflection again; the knot in his tie was the size of an orange. He undid it quickly and tried again — this time it came out the size of a walnut. The armpits of his jacket smelt musty and ripe; when he closed the buttons it felt a little too tight. He thought he heard Siobhan call out his name, but when he turned to look there was still no sign of her.

The Charing Cross Road seemed to shimmer with heat. Light poured from an almost aggressively blue sky. Smells drifted out from the cafés — stewed vegetables, boiling fat, greasy fried onions. Christ, there was nothing the English wouldn't eat. You had to love them for that.

The busker he had seen in the station came out now, dragging the shabby dog behind him. The poor mutt had a length of green tinsel around its neck. His ragged master started to sing again:

> *Bold Robert Emmet, the darling of Erin;*
> *Bold Robert Emmet, he died with a smile;*
> *Farewell companions both loyal and daring;*
> *I lay down me life for the Emerald Isle.*

A long line of Hare Krishnas shimmied around the corner from Leicester Square, all banging their bongos and gaily chanting. A tall languid girl in an open white shirt, black bra and flower-patterned flares ran across the street with a portable television in her hands. Outside the Tube Station, a newspaper man was calling out to passers-by: 'Standard-Ho. Evening Standard!' The billboard beside his stall proclaimed ENGLAND SET TO CRUSH CHARLTON'S IRISH.

The English newspapers seemed incapable of referring to the Irish team without mentioning the manager too. It was as though the name of the actual country had been changed by deed-poll to 'Jack Charlton's Republic of Ireland'. Maybe it should be, Eddie thought. He could think of worse things to have on your passport.

Suddenly he felt arms twine around his waist from behind. 'Hi,' she said.

He turned and kissed her. She had on a dark-green dress that hugged her figure, black lace gloves, a pillbox hat. She looked so lovely that he wanted to laugh out loud.

'I wore green for Ireland,' she said. 'With the day that's in it.'

He loved her accent, its soft Donegal inflections, the music of its exaggerated vowels.

She glanced at the watch he had given her for Christmas.

'Are you right, so?' she said. 'We're wild late, Eddie. My zip went. I must be putting on weight.'

'Siobhan, listen, there's something on my mind ...'

'Maybe I'm pregnant,' she grimaced. 'Wouldn't that be gas?'

'You're not pregnant,' he said.

'No, I'm not,' she said. 'You drink too much. Your sperm wouldn't be strong enough. If I gave birth to anything it'd be a bottle of tequila.'

'Look, Siobhan,' he tried again, 'I got this phone call ... .'

But she had stepped away from him and into the street, standing on tiptoes and eagerly waving her handbag. A black taxi pulled up, leaking plumes of exhaust. The yellow light on the roof flickered out.

'Euston Road Registry Office,' she said.

The taxi inched up the Charing Cross Road, across Shaftesbury Avenue and onto Tottenham Court Road. A bus had broken down at a main junction; other buses and cars were blaring their horns. Telecom workers had dug up a long section of the street outside the Dominion Theatre. A Fire Brigade stood outside the entrance to the Tube Station.

The taxi's interior was stiflingly hot, heavy with the smell of sweaty leatherette and lemon air-freshener.

'Siobhan ...'

She turned to him, licked her finger and ran it quickly along his eyebrows.

'Mammy rang this morning, Eddie, to say Uncle Peter might be over from home. You'll like him.'

'Great. But listen, there was something I needed to say to you ...'

'And Eddie, listen, try to be a bit sociable today, will you? And stay off the politics with Aisling, OK? She's a bit of a rebel and all that crack, but a bride is entitled to peace on her wedding day.'

'… A rebel?'

'Well, y'know.'

'Jesus,' he sighed. 'Not another one of your Provo chums.'

'Her father was interned back in the Fifties,' she said. 'With all my uncles and my Da. In the Curragh.'

'Your dad was *interned*?'

'For IRA membership, yeah.'

'You never told me that before.'

'Course I did, Eddie. Sure, everyone knows that.'

'You didn't, Siobhan.'

'Oh well. Sure what does it matter anyway. Just don't be starting rows, all right?'

She gave him a sexy smile and grabbed his hand, moving it to her bare knees. He turned away from her and peered out through the window. Siobhan had two legs. His sister had one. In the leg department, his sister was singularly deficient.

'What's up with you today?' Siobhan asked him.

'Nothing.'

'You're not still sulking about that bloody match, are you?'

'Who said anything about the match?'

'I don't know why you'd want to go and sit in some awful pub with a load of sad wankers and watch some stupid bloody match when you could be with me. The most desirable woman in London.'

He said nothing.

'Eddie, come on. Please cheer up. Or tell me what's wrong.'

He decided not to tell her about his sister and his leg. He would hang back, save it for later. That would bloody wipe the grin off her mug. He would bide his time. He would say it later. "Oh, by the way, Siobhan, I know you're having a really fabulous day with your hayseed woollybacked refugee-from-Deliverance relations here, but my sister had to have her leg off last Saturday night and I just thought you might like to know before the fucking barn-dance starts." It might come in handy if she was enjoying herself too much. He didn't like Siobhan enjoying herself too much. It always felt vaguely out of control to him.

She poked his thigh. 'Seriously. Are you all right today, Eddie? You look as though you're fretting about something.'

He shook his head.

'Football deprivation,' she teased. 'Bad for your heart, eh?'

He said nothing.

'If you have one of those,' she said.

'You're hilarious, Siobhan,' he told her. 'Really. You crack me up.'

A flash of irritation brightened her eyes. 'Don't be such a dry shite,' she said. 'If you really don't want to come with me, then don't.'

He turned to her, doing his best to appear hurt. 'I do want to come with you,' he said sulkily. 'That doesn't mean I have to *like it*, does it?'

She rolled her eyes, began to do her lipstick. The taxi-driver roared at a passing cyclist. Eddie looked out the window again. Another billboard caught his eye:

ENGLAND SET TO TRIUMPH OVER CHARLTON'S ARMY.

*

The Registrar was a beautiful Pakistani woman who couldn't seem to stop smiling. One of the kids, a boy of about ten, was dressed in a green-and-white Ireland strip with the word STAPLETON across the back of the shirt.

After the brief ceremony everyone clapped and cheered, all except for the bride's mother, who looked as happy as someone coming out of *Schindler's List*. Siobhan turned to Eddie and whispered in his ear. 'Would you look at the mug on Auntie Betty. She's raging because it wasn't a church job.'

'Because the bloody groom is English, you mean.'

Siobhan shook her head. 'No, it wouldn't be that. Uncle Martin'd be more upset about that.'

He watched as people drifted past. Women in large, churchy hats. Men in crumpled, dark-coloured suits.

'Do you actually know all these people?' he hissed.

'There's a lot of them over from home,' she said. 'I didn't think there'd be so many. I hope Uncle Peter comes.'

The boy in the soccer strip wandered over towards Eddie. Siobhan smiled and ruffled his hair.

'Don't you look right handsome today, John-Jo,' she said.

The kid blushed and buried his face in her thigh.

'You're my bonny boy, aren't you,' she said.

'Christ,' thought Eddie. 'It's Walton's Mountain.'

*

Outside the Camden Town Irish Centre the cars were untidily double-parked. A group of young black men in baggy jeans and baseball caps were glumly kicking a ball around. Loud raggamuffin music boomed from a ghettoblaster on the footpath.

The John F Kennedy Memorial Function Room had been decorated with flowers and tinfoil stars, strings of green, white and orange bunting. White plastic tables and chairs had been arranged around the edge of the wooden dance-floor. Plump women in aprons were moving between the tables, polishing glasses, folding tricoloured napkins into cones.

It was Woollyback City. It really was. When he closed his eyes he could practically hear 'Duelling Banjos'.

He sipped tensely at this third pint of Guinness and looked around at the chattering guests. You could tell which ones were Irish, but he didn't know exactly how. A waiter brought in a tray of drinks and put it on a table. The groom's relations were sitting by themselves in a corner, looking determinedly restrained in their hired suits.

For no good reason he found himself wondering about his own parents' wedding day. Sometimes his mother had mentioned it to him, in the happier times, before she and his father had parted. It had been a very sunny day in April, Eddie knew that much. The drink had run out early, and the priest had fainted. They had gone to Barcelona on their honeymoon and stayed in a little hotel in the Placa del Pi in the Barrio Gotic. She always seemed so proud of that. 'Nobody from Crumlin went anywhere like Barcelona on their honeymoon. But your father and I did. We thought we were it.' The thought of his mother's laughing face caused a weed of panic to sprout in his stomach. Someone would have to tell her about Patricia.

He realised it would probably be him.

In another corner, some of the men were watching a small television. It was showing highlights of previous Irish matches. A black-and-white Steve Heighway weaving through a line of defenders. Young Liam Brady, shy and handsome. The great Don Givens scoring four against Turkey way back in October of '75. Johnny Giles with a big bushy perm and sideburns, looking like a member of Lynryd Skynryd.

Where was it now? The leg that had been cut off? Had a bit of it just been left behind, lying on the train tracks? For some manky Parisian perv to take home as a souvenir? Or had someone thought to pick it up and put it in a bag — a shopping bag, perhaps? — and bring it along to the hospital? Would they be able to get her a wooden one? Did they still do that? Or were artificial limbs made of plastic these days? Hadn't he read something a few months previously about some guy who had gone from designing Muppets to manufacturing shit-hot plastic limbs? Out of some unseen place a dreadful memory limped up. The man he had once seen in Earls Court Station, an elegant looking gent in a suit and tie, who had carefully dusted off the bench with his morning newspaper before sitting down to pull up his trouser hem *and unscrew his wooden leg*. Which had a shoe and a tartan sock on it! He had simply unscrewed it, fiddled around with it for a minute, then attached it back to the stub of his knee. But that wasn't the weird thing, although it *was* weird. It was the people all around him. They never looked. They gaped at the sky, down at the tracks; they read their newspapers and examined their watches. He could have shoved his wooden leg up his arse and still nobody would have said a thing. That was the thing about the English. It was why he would never understand them.

Holy Christ. Meet my sister. The one-legged Muppet with the Master's degree.

He gazed around the room, wishing he was somewhere else. Anywhere else. It wouldn't matter. He didn't know where Siobhan was now, and he felt uneasy, already a bit drunk. Guinness had a way of making you feel weary. It was too heavy a drink for daytime consumption. People began to drift in from the bar. Somebody put on a record. A few of the younger guests started half-heartedly dancing. Then two old women began to waltz with each other, even though the music was a U2 song. They waltzed steadily, in a vaguely martial manner — as though they had learnt the steps from a book.

It occurred to him that his sister might never dance again. The thought struck him as utterly appalling.

Across the dance-floor, a young dudey guy in a sharp red suit was efficiently jitterbugging with a beautiful blonde girl. He held her hand, pushed her away, pulled her in close, whirled around her. Suddenly she jumped and wrapped her thighs around his waist and everyone laughed and clapped as they spun.

'Fucking pretty-boy,' Eddie mumbled.

Just as the record was ending Siobhan tottered into the room looking drunk and lost. She beckoned Eddie over to her, took his hand, then tapped the handsome jiver on the back. The blonde girl smiled and said she had to go to the bathroom. They watched her walk away, wiping her face on the sleeve of her blouse.

'Trying to get your end away already, Wiggy?' Siobhan grinned. 'God, where did you pick that dancing up?'

He shrugged and pushed his hair out of his eyes. 'Along the way like.' A Birmingham accent coloured his vowels.

'You're fabulous at it. You must give me a lesson some time.'

'I'll give you one later,' he laughed, then glanced at Eddie.

'Oh,' Siobhan said. 'Wiggy Thompson. Meet Eddie Virago.'

'All right mate?' said Wiggy, shaking Eddie's hand. A sudden ray of sunshine burst into the room from the upper windows. Siobhan said she was going to the bar.

'You're Irish then?' said Wiggy, in his Jasper Carrot accent. Eddie nodded and sipped at his stout.

Wiggy gazed around the room as though he was looking for somebody interesting. 'Terrible what we did over there, man,' he said.

'What's that?'

'What we did.'

'Who's we?'

'Y'know … Britain like.'

'Oh. Right.'

'Yeah. See, I'm in the Socialist Workers' Party like. We're very anti. You know? I mean everything that went on over in Ireland.'

'Oh. Great. Are you?'

Wiggy threw a glance at the ceiling. 'Fucking Tories. Fucking Labour. Eh?'

'Well …'

'And James Connolly, man. Hell of a guy.'

'Right,' said Eddie.

Wiggy closed his eyes devoutly and shook his head.

'Hell of a guy,' he said. 'Hell of a guy. Terrible what went down over there in Ireland. Imperialist bastards. Yeah. That's all.'

*

Lunch was scrawny chicken, fizzy potato salad and slices of greasy ham that stuck to each other. 'Tesco's in Neasden', the waitress said, when Siobhan asked where the chicken had come from. It tasted like it had walked all the way from there to Camden and thrown itself under a bus in the main street. Everybody at the table talked about the match. Having that much to talk about was a relief to Eddie.

The speeches started. The Best Man said he was looking forward to receiving a picture of the happy couple, 'preferably mounted,' and everyone laughed long and loud. The groom stood up and thanked everyone for their help. When he mentioned the bride's mother she looked down at her plate and began meaningfully forking her left-overs.

As the after-lunch drinks were being served, Eddie noticed an old man on a stick come shuffling painfully into the room. He had eczema scars all over his cheeks and a small black patch over his right eye. A few of the guests jumped up and ran to him as he began to limp across the floor, clearly in great discomfort. He shook hands with several of the men, kissed some of the women. Then he nudged one of them, pointed down at Siobhan and put his trembling finger to his lips. He edged over to the table and tapped her on the back with the point of his stick. She turned.

'Uncle Peter!' she cried, jumping up. 'I wasn't sure you'd be over.'

He hugged her hard, kissed her on the cheek and then slapped at his chest, panting heavily.

His high-pitched voice was frail and wheezy.

'Oh well … Johnny Doherty ran me over to Belfast. I got the British Midland … I was treated in fine style.'

'Eddie,' she said. 'This is my uncle, Peter Toner.'

'I'm delighted now to meet you, Eddie. We've heard all about you over at home, so we have.'

'You have?'

'Oh indeed and we have. The big city flyboy who stole my wee girl's heart.'

The old man laughed good-naturedly at his smiling niece.

'Eddie's a bit of an intellectual, Uncle Peter. He was in the university down in Dublin. He has brains to burn. Or that's what he tells me.'

Peter Toner inclined his head and half-smiled. 'S'that, Pet?'

'He was in the *university*, I said. In Dublin.'

'Oh, aye? Isn't that great now. And what's this you were studying, Eddie?'

'English.'

'Speak up?'

'English literature.'

'Novels, is it?'

Well, yeah,' said Eddie. 'Novels and poetry.'

The old man nodded a few times and sighed. 'Funny how they call it English, all the same. When all the best practitioners are Irish. Would that be the right word, Eddie? Practitioners?'

'Yes. I suppose so.'

'Aye. When the monks in Ireland were saving European civilization, weren't the pagan English running around the forest in their pelts.' He coughed a mouthful of watery phlegm into a crumped handkerchief. 'Ah, well. Still. Not to worry, eh?'

Siobhan took her uncle gently by the arm, led him to a chair and poured him a glass of wine. In the far corner, surrounded by her friends, the bride's mother now appeared to be crying. A nun was on her knees beside her, holding her hand and offering tissues.

'What's up with the Mother of Sorrows over there?' asked Peter Toner.

'She's upset, Uncle Peter, that Aisling didn't get married in the church.'

He shrugged, slopping some of his wine over his mouth and chin. 'That one's never happy unless she's miserable,' he said sourly. He pulled out a handkerchief and dabbed his lips.

Siobhan seemed to enjoy goading the old man. 'Auntie Maureen was saying earlier it was an awful thing to be getting married in white when you're in the family way'.

'Oh well, weren't they engaged? And isn't it only the natural thing anyhow. There's nothing wrong with a bit of affection.'

'*Shame* on you, Peter,' Siobhan said with gentle mockery. 'Isn't it against the Church to be up to mischief before you're spliced?'

He clicked his tongue with exasperation. 'Some of these crawthumping Holy Joes — they never *had* a woman and between you and me that's their trouble'

Siobhan laughed, again pretending to be shocked. 'Peter, you're terrible. But poor Darren was saying he's dreading the birth all the same.'

'Who?'

'Darren, Pet.'

'Who's that?'

'Her *husband*, love. He was saying he was nervous of going into the hospital with her.'

'Is he sick?'

'No, love, no. When she's having the baby.'

Her uncle coughed violently and turned away. 'Oh but that's a big thing now, all the young husbands do go in.'

Fondly she slid her arm through his own. 'I wouldn't be too sure you were there with Auntie Moya when Noleen and the twins were born'.

He shook his head. 'I never had that privilege. Though I don't mind saying them were the happiest days I ever had.'

'People say they're great at that age,' Siobhan said.

'Pardon me?'

'They're great when they're young, Peter. That's what people say.'

'Oh, great fellows,' he agreed, squinting suddenly, phlegm catching in the back of his throat. 'But after a few years they're nothing but lip. One word from the auldfella and they go to the fair altogether.'

He pulled a handkerchief from his pocket and wiped his mouth. 'Aye, they do what they like. But there it is. It's all ahead of you, eh, Freddy?'

'Eddie,' said Eddie.

'Pardon me?'

'*Eddie.*'

'Oh aye. Sorry.'

A short, stocky old man with a moustache and ruddy face came up from behind to the table, carrying two pints of Guinness.

'Is it the blaggard Toner?' he said loudly. 'Would you look at the bloody get-up of it. Is the suit paid for yet, Citizen?'

'That must be Sean Moylan,' Peter Toner chuckled, standing shakily and turning around. 'I'd know that ignorant Cork prattle of him a mile off.'

Moylan plonked the pints on the table and took Peter Toner in his arms. The two embraced warmly, clapping each other on the back. 'How's the man? It's great to see you, *a Pheadar.*'

'Oh well, I'm still trotting along anyhow, Sean. You've met my niece, Siobhan Kearney? And her young man, Neddy.'

'I've not had that pleasure,' said Sean Moylan, shaking hands with them both. 'She didn't get the looks from your side anyway, Peter.'

'What's that? Speak up?'

'She's a lovely looking girl, I'm saying, Peter.'

'Oh, aye. Why wouldn't she be? Tell me now, is Maureen with you?'

Sean Moylan shook his head. 'She's not been well since the by-pass, Peter. I had to make her stay at home.'

'Ach, that's a shame. Tell her I said hello.'

'I will of course. But you're looking fit to beat the band. You must be hoping to click with some young one today, are you?'

'What's that?'

'Are you looking for a woman or what? With the cut of you?'

Peter Toner gave a laugh. 'Little point there'd be in that any more. I'm too old for all that caper. Thanks be to God!'

'Siobhan,' said Sean Moylan. 'I could tell you stories about this man here. From the old days. Some Commanche he was. Isn't that right, Peter?'

The old man turned to him, shuddering. 'Speak up there, Sean?'

'I'm saying I could tell them stories, *a Pheadar*. From the old days. The struggle, you know. The yarns I could spin them, eh?' He shook his head in reminiscence. 'Nights we'd be on the run. All night up to the neck in freezing bogwater.'

'Aye. True enough.'

'Still. *Sinn Fein amhain*, eh, Peter? The friends we love are by our side and the Saxon trembling fore us. Hah?'

'God be with the days,' said Peter Toner, in his trembling

womanly voice.

Sean Moylan nodded sadly. 'But sure, won't there be more good days, Peter, eh? And better days than ever was. The Republicans won't always be down.'

'Pardon me?'

'*Better days coming, Peter.*'

'Oh, aye. Please God.'

They stood in silence for a moment while Peter Toner looked around the room.

'Tell me this,' he said. 'Is Maureen here, Sean?'

Moylan gave a gentle smile. 'She's at home, Comrade. Didn't I tell you that before.'

'Is she?' Peter Toner squinted and shook his head. 'That's odd. I could swear I saw her just now. Over beyond.'

'Ah well,' Moylan said. 'There's none of us getting any younger, Peter. Isn't that right?'

'That's right,' Peter Toner said, and laughed. The laugh of a man who doesn't understand.

'Still, you crafty rogue, I never seen you looking better in my life. If my nabs Charlton had yourself on his team we'd run the English into the ground, isn't that it?'

'Pardon me?'

Moylan glanced at Siobhan and gave a kindly wink. 'I'll tell you what, Peter, you and me'll sit down here and have an old jar and a natter, what?'

'I could have sworn I saw her. Standing in the door.'

Siobhan led Eddie across to the middle of the dance-floor; put her hands on his waist and leaned her forehead on his shoulder. The room had grown uncomfortably hot, as though sucked dry of air. She looked up into his eyes and moved closer to him. He could smell her perfume, feel the softness of her body against him.

'He's a bit gaga today,' she said. 'I'm embarrassed now.'

'Don't be,' Eddie said.

'You look lovely, Eddie.'

'So do you.'

They circled slowly in each other's arms, while the disc jockey played a slow song.

'Last night was lovely, wasn't it?' she said.

'We should have used a condom.'

'I'm mad about you.'

He tried to laugh. 'Don't say that.'

'What's on your mind today, though? Are you thick with me or something?'

He said nothing.

'Look,' she sighed. 'I'm sure they'll have the stupid match on in the bar. All the lads here'll be slipping out. I don't mind if you want to go with them.'

'It isn't the match.'

'What, then?'

He sighed and looked around the room. There really wasn't an easy way to put it.

'Well,' he said. 'Patricia had an accident in Paris at the weekend. She had to have her leg amputated.'

She stepped back from him, a gape of disbelief on her face.

'Fuck off,' she laughed.

'I swear to Christ. She rang me earlier about it.'

'Jesus, Eddie … You're not serious, are you?'

'I am. Honest.'

Her mouth was wide open and her eyes looked frightened.

'My God almighty. Jesus, Eddie, that's … Did you not say you'd go over to her?'

He slid his hands into his pockets, feeling awkward. 'I didn't think. She asked me to ring up my Dad and tell him.'

She stared into his face. 'Jesus, Eddie.'

'Yeah,' he said. 'Jesus is right.'

The disc jockey put on 'Danny Boy'. Over at the table, Peter Toner and his friend Sean Moylan seemed to be watching them.

*

His father's phone was still engaged, so Eddie left the lobby and went into the bar. A quick pint by himself might help him calm down. The room was beginning to fill up already: a semi-circle of people had formed around the television. Eamon Dunphy was on the screen, saying that Ireland had only ever beaten England once before. While he continued to talk, excitedly, passionately, they cut to a shot of the Stuttgart stadium. A uniformed brass band was marching in formation up and down the beautiful lime-green pitch, but the tune couldn't be heard because the Irish fans were already singing. 'You'll never beat the Irish! You'll never beat the Irish!' English supporters were waving Union Jacks. Some of them were waving fists in the air. Their chants were being drowned out by the Irish.

There were close-up shots of some of the Irish banners.

SALLYNOGGIN ON TOUR
PAUL MCGRATH — THE BLACK PEARL
DAVY KEOGH SAYS HELLO

Children in the bar were playing on the carpet, throwing crisps and peanuts at each other. He noticed Wiggy sitting with the blonde woman in the corner. He had a pack of playing cards in his hand and seemed to be showing her some kind of trick. Three teenage girls came in, laughing and chatting. Their accents were the same as Siobhan's; they looked like her too, with the same dark eyes and full mouths.

A heavy-set young man wandered in and sat down beside them. 'God, Niall, is it you?' one girl said, kissing him on the cheek. 'I wouldn't recognise you out of the Wellingtons.' The others laughed. One of them half-turned and seemed to notice Eddie. She smiled, then turned back to the others and whispered something that made them giggle.

As he sipped his drink he found himself thinking about the night he had met Siobhan. It must be two years ago, at a gig in the Powerhaus — he couldn't even remember the name of the band. He had noticed her up at the front, dancing with a few other girls. She'd been wearing a black miniskirt, tartan tights, a ragged black T-shirt with the word 'IRELAND' on it. Soon as he saw her, he got the feeling she was a bit frantic. She seemed to laugh too much, maybe that was it.

It was just after he'd split up with his last girlfriend, and he'd gone out to get wrecked with two old mates from college. He certainly hadn't been looking to meet anybody. But there was something about her, he couldn't look away.

Later, in the queue for the bar, the surge of bodies pushed them together. They got talking, shared half a cigarette. She was from Culdaff, in the Inishowen peninsula. She worked behind the counter in the Shamrock Travel Agency ('Where Irish Eyes Are Smiling') in Archway. He told her how he had come to London to join a band, but it hadn't worked out because the others were less talented than himself. Now he was working in a bank, training to be a manager. It turned out she'd once met a friend of his from Dublin, Dean Bean — the best-looking man she had ever seen.

When the gig was over they stood on the pavement talking for half-an-hour. Then she asked him back to her flat for a drink.

When they'd got back to her place it was late and very cold. Her three flat-mates were lying together on a double mattress in the living room, under a quilt with no cover, watching a video — *An Officer and a Gentleman* — while sharing a joint and a bottle of cheap red wine.

They had gone into her room and she'd closed the windows. She put on a tape of The Waterboys singing about the West of Ireland. She really loved The Waterboys, she said, she'd seen them live a few times since coming to London. She wasn't too sure what they'd been up to lately, but there was talk they'd be playing at the Fleadh in Finsbury Park in the summer; one of the lads in work was going to get her a free ticket from a chap he knew who worked on the *Irish Post*. She talked as though to calm some kind of nervousness, and yet it seemed to Eddie that the more she talked the more nervous she became. They talked about music, then films and comedians. When the naggin of vodka they'd brought home ran out, they drank a half-bottle of musty *saki* which one of the girls had won in a spina bifida raffle and which Siobhan said was a very dangerous drink, the reason Shane McGowan had got thrown out of the Pogues.

As she grew more drunk she said she missed Ireland. She got so lonely sometimes, she wished she could go home. But any time she did, she always wanted to get back to London after a week. It was the smallness of Ireland that got to her now, she said, the way everyone knew everyone else. She always felt happy when the plane touched down at Heathrow. She felt free in London, in a way she never did in Ireland. He told her if he ever got famous and had to fill out one of those twatty questionnaires in the Sunday newspapers where you have to name your favourite place in the world he'd put down 'Departures Lounge, Dublin Airport'. She laughed when he said that. He liked her laugh; the way her eyes seemed to glitter in the murky light of the room.

'You're gas,' she smiled. 'I'd say you could be trouble.'

Then she asked if he wanted to share a joint. He told her no, he was trying to give it up. When he looked at his watch it was almost two. He asked if she had a mini-cab number.

She shook her head and looked around the room, avoiding his eyes. 'If you wanted to stay, that'd be all right,' she said.

She had taken off her skirt, tights and shoes and collapsed on the bed in her T-shirt and underwear. When Eddie stripped down to his Nelson Mandela boxer shorts, she laughed at them. They had crawled under the quilt, kissed and touched for a while and then fallen into a drunken muttering sleep. Next morning they had woken with terrible hangovers and had sex, while the sound of the dumper trucks and pneumatic drills down in the street had filled the room, along with the smells of tea and frying grease. They had been going out for nearly six months now, though sometimes they argued about whether 'going out' was the term. Whatever the semantics, they were almost inseparable. Though each continued to keep up a room in a flat, they hardly spent a night apart. They had even gone over to Paris to visit Patricia and Philippe. They were practically living together, but he still hadn't told any of his friends about her.

Eddie changed his mind about the pint and asked for a double whiskey.

'Irish or Scotch?' the barman asked.

'Surprise me,' Eddie said.

When he came back into the ballroom, she was sitting in a corner with Peter Toner and Sean Moylan. All three of them seemed very drunk now: she was laughing loudly with her hand to her mouth. As he sat down beside her, he had the odd feeling that the conversation had stopped because of his presence.

The plastic chairs had been arranged in a wide, untidy circle around the tables, which had been cleared of dishes, cups and glasses. A few hairy youngfellas had guitars and fiddles, and one was half-heartedly banging on a bodhrán. He looked like Jesus on the shroud of Turin. It was that particular stage of an Irish wedding where people argue about who's going to start the singing.

'Any luck with your Da?' Siobhan asked, peering at him.

Eddie shook his head. 'Still engaged.' He took a long sip of his drink.

'Get up there Martin Hannon and give us a song,' shouted Sean Moylan to the bride's father.

'Ah now, stop,' the man replied. 'I've no voice on me these days.'

'The Men Behind The Wire,' someone called.

'The Boys Of The Old Brigade,' another shouted. But the bride's father shook his head and started into another pint of Guinness.

'Well someone better bloody sing,' a male voice called. 'There's a match on soon that I want to watch!' Everyone laughed.

'Martin Hannon, get up and get it over,' shouted Sean Moylan. People cheered and rattled spoons against their glasses.

'Jesus, all right, all right,' the bride's father sighed. 'I'll give you a few quick verses of something. And on your own heads be it.'

He stood up to a chorus of jeers and whistles. Someone handed him a microphone. He tugged up the sleeve of his jacket and made a great show of looking at his watch.

'Well,' he began, smiling modestly and blushing, 'Ireland do battle with England shortly now. And God knows it's not the first time in history that's happened.'

'Nor the last,' someone yelled, down at the back. He smiled again and nodded.

'Yes, today is a happy day. In a short while there's a certain match going on you might have heard about.' A few of the men cheered. 'And I suppose, when you think about it, with Aisling and Darren — that's another match between Ireland and England.' People laughed appreciatively. 'I've a fair idea who's going to win both of them,' he said, to more laughter.

But then his eyes took on a serious expression. 'I want to take a moment today to think about some absent friends.

Absent comrades too, I'm not ashamed to say it. Brave men I thought would be here at my only daughter's wedding. But who won't be.' His voice suddenly quavered. He took a sip of water. When he looked up again, his face was pale. 'No need to dwell on it. They gave all for their country and were happy to give it.' A silence had fallen over the room, broken only by the cry of a baby. 'Sometimes,' he continued, 'my Aisling here, she'll say to me, "Daddy, forgive and forget." The young people now, they think that's the way forward. Maybe they're right and maybe they're wrong. I'd not claim to be better than them. But all I know is this one thing: I might forgive one day, when there's justice in my country. But I don't think I'll ever be able to forget.'

People shifted in their seats and began to look uncomfortable. As if he sensed the unease, he forced a smile.

'Anyhows, I think you can all imagine what Betty and myself said when Her Ladyship here arrived home one fine morning and announced she was marrying an English lad.' People laughed nervously. 'Well, of course,' he went on, deadpan, 'we were thrilled skinny.' People laughed louder. 'Personally,' he continued, 'I think it's Ireland's revenge for eight hundred years of colonial oppression and I therefore give it my blessing.' There was a great roar of laughter and a round of applause. Even the groom's family were clapping, Eddie noticed.

'Seriously,' he said, 'I have to say that Darren seems a quiet, down-to-earth sort of lad, and for what it's worth I welcome him into the Hannon family. As for his being English, well, I think of the words of my late noble lord, the Duke of Wellington, who was once asked was it true he was born in Ireland. "Indeed I was," was the answer he gave. "But just because you were born in a stable, doesn't mean you're a horse".'

'Ah, shut up and sing will you,' someone shouted over the

laughter.

'A rebel song,' another yelled.

'I was thinking this morning about what I might sing today,' he said, 'with the match being on, and something occurred to me. And I hope our English friends won't be embarrassed, if I tell you that when those lads in green go out on that field in a short time — there's another field I'll be thinking of, closer to home.'

Complete silence came down over the room. 'What's this is the way it goes?' he murmured, staring up at the ceiling. He closed his eyes then, and began to sing very slowly, in a faltering baritone.

What did I have?
Said the proud old woman.
What did I have?
This proud old woman did say.
I had four green fields,
And each of them a jewel
Till strangers came,
And tried to take them from me.

One of the young men started to strum his guitar, trying to gauge the key. Some of the others turned to him, scowling and shaking their heads. He rested the guitar on his knees, lit a cigarette and began to listen.

But my fine strong sons,
They fought to save my jewel,
They fought and they died.
And that was my grief, said she.

'Lovely, lovely,' whispered one of the guests as he reached the end of the first verse. Siobhan stuck her fingers in her mouth and whistled. Over in the corner, the groom's family began to look distinctly uncomfortable.

Long time ago,
Wept the proud old woman;
Long time ago,
This proud old woman did say

He leaned forward and splayed his fingers on the table, leaning his weight on it.

There was war and death;
Plundering and pillage;
My children died,
By mountain, valley and stream.
And their wailing cries,
They shook the very heavens
And my four green fields

He paused and raised his hands, palms upwards. Some of the people joined in the song, singing loudly, their voices soaring, seeming to fill the room.

Ran red with their blood, said she.

The bride's father stopped and gave a nervous laugh. Suddenly he seemed to have forgotten the words. He glanced down at his wife. She whispered something to him, but he didn't appear to hear what she was saying. He began to sing the next verse, then stopped again, blushing deeply, rubbing his lips with the back of his wrist. His wife stood up slowly and took his hand. She looked into his eyes, smiling fondly, as she started to sing. He nodded as they sang together now, her voice very high and nervous, quivering on the grace notes.

Long time ago,
Said the proud old woman;
Long time ago,
This proud old woman did say;
I had four green fields,
But one is still in bondage;
In strangers' hands,
They tried to take it from me.
But my sons had sons,
As brave as were their fathers;
And my fourth green field
Will bloom once again, said she.

He turned and threw his arms around his wife, kissing her hair, burying his face in her neck. She wrapped her arms around him, quietly crying now. The bride jumped up and ran to her parents, hugging them both. Her father's face was blood-red, tears streaming from his eyes as he sat back down. Cheers and wild applause filled the room. He stood up again, trembling with emotion.

'Up the Republic!' he shouted, to a roar of appreciation.

Eddie felt Siobhan's eyes on him. 'It's a great song, isn't it?' she said. 'It's awfully sad.'

He felt the drink pulse through his veins, the small muscles tighten in the back of his throat. 'It's a load of shite,' he said. 'Four green fields, my hole.'

Her face purpled. She tried to smile. 'Don't say that, Eddie. People have strong feelings.'

He scoffed. 'If they've such strong feelings about it, what are half of them doing living over here? If it's so awful why don't they shag off back to the bog they came from.' In the corner of his eye he could see Sean Moylan staring at him.

'It's only a song,' she said. 'What harm is there in it?'

'It's bollocks,' he said. 'And that's all it is. The fucking Nazis could have sung it about Germany.'

She stared at him, her lips trembling. For a moment he was sure she was going to cry. Instead she turned away defiantly and spoke to her uncle.

'Do you hear this West-Brit, Uncle Peter?'

The old man turned to her, his one eye bleary. 'What's he saying, love?'

'He's saying it's all shite, Peter, about the four green fields. That's what they all think down in Dublin. Too busy thinking they're cool to give two damns about anything else.'

Peter Toner said nothing. He gazed around himself looking confused, like a man waking up in a strange room.

'These lovely Dublin so-called liberals,' she snapped. 'All very liberal, in South Africa or Nicaragua. When they'd hand the whole country back to the Brits tomorrow. That's what they really want.'

'What they want is peace,' Eddie said.

Peter Toner tried to smile, a thin ribbon of saliva moistening his chin. He raised his shaking finger and wagged it from side to side. 'Ireland and England should never be in bed together, son. There's no peace down that road, nor never will be.'

Eddie scoffed. 'What are you on about, man? They *are* in bed together.'

'Pardon me?'

'And what good ever came of it, Eddie,' said Sean Moylan suddenly. 'Can you answer me that? In fairness.'

'Ah, would you go back to sleep,' Eddie muttered.

Siobhan stood up, trembling with rage. 'How dare you? How fucking *dare* you speak to him like that.'

Sean Moylan laughed as he reached out and took her by the hand. She sat back down, folded her arms and looked away.

'Maybe we'll leave the politics for another day,' he said.

'Politics?' Eddie scoffed. 'Shooting people in the back of the head? Smashing their kneecaps with concrete blocks?

Eighteen hundred people murdered — most of them Irish? Beautiful politics *you* have, man.'

The smile froze on Sean Moylan's face. 'Hold on there a second, buck,' he said. 'Nobody's saying mistakes weren't made. That happens in any war situation.'

Eddie laughed bitterly. 'Mistakes like Enniskillen? Blowing up pensioners for a United Ireland?'

'That was a mistake. It was caused by the Brits.'

'Whole lot of mistakes, weren't there, pal?'

'It's not for me to say what military operations should be. That's a thing that's for others to say.'

'Listen, man, with respect — you're talking through your arse.'

'That's lovely talk now, from an educated person,' Sean Moylan said. 'The young people today, they haven't a notion of what had to be done, do they, Peter?'

'Pardon?' said Peter Toner.

'No,' Eddie said. 'They do. It's just they've got the brains not to care any more.'

'What's that?'

'They just don't give a flying shite. Ireland against England? To me, man, that's a football match. That's *all* it is.'

Peter Toner looked at Eddie and attempted to smile, his head quivering, his eye half-closed. 'Maybe that's what we fought for,' he said. 'So you'd have the freedom not to have to care. If you didn't want to. To sit in a pub and watch a football match without a care in the world. Ever think of it that way?'

Eddie drained his drink. 'No, man, I didn't.'

'You dirty West-Brit,' Siobhan snapped.

He slammed down his glass, stood up and made for the door, bumping into the groom, who was staggering around in a drunken embrace with the Best Man, crying bitterly and telling him how much he loved him. Half-way across the empty dance-floor she caught up with him and grabbed his arm.

'If you walk out that door you can fuck away off,' she said. 'I don't ever want to see you again.'

'Oh dear,' he said. 'I'm really scared now.'

She turned away from him, suddenly sobbing; bowed her head and wiped her eyes. He reached out and touched her face but she slapped his hand away. 'You had to spoil everything,' she wept. 'You just had to. Didn't you?!'

'Oh thanks. Jesus, thanks a bunch. *What about my sister's leg?* Like, I'm really incredibly sorry here, Honey, but I've got more on what's left of my mind than you and your four green shagging fields. All right?'

Tears were trickling down her cheeks. Her smudged mascara had given her eyes a bruised look. 'If it wasn't that it'd be something else. *You always have to take the good out of everything ...*'

'Siobhan ...'

'Just get out and leave me alone!'

*

His father's phone was still engaged, so he went into the bar to get another drink.

The room was packed to the doors now. The match had just started; in Stuttgart they were chanting. One young man at the bar was wearing a green Afro wig. A cloud of purplish cigarette smoke had formed under the fluorescent lights.

The volume was jammed up high, making the commentator's voice buzz as he named the players putting together a speculative English move. 'Stevens ... to Sansom ... to Peter Beardsley ... To the mighty John Barnes of Liverpool.' People were sitting around the room in groups, most of them wearing green shirts, hats or scarves. 'Beardsley to Wright ... To Robson ... England advance ... But it's a free kick to Jack Charlton's Ireland ... Free kick to the Republic in the sixth minute … A little … debate about it from Stevens. But referee Mr Kirschen very definite there.'

'How's it going?' Eddie asked the barman.

The barman shook his head in a doleful way. 'All over us like a rash,' he scowled. 'Running us ragged so they are.' He filled the glass and placed the pint on the counter.

'On the house,' he said. 'You look like you need it.'

And then a deafening ROAR exploded through the bar. It was almost as though a bomb had gone off. People were on their feet, wildly punching the air and screaming. A table overturned, sending glasses and ashtrays rocketing across the room. There were hysterical screams, anguished whoops. Teenage girls in Irish dancing costumes ran in from the corridor. A fat man Eddie didn't know grabbed him and kissed him. He pushed his way through the room and towards the television, dimly aware of the urgency of the commentator's voice, but the cheering was so loud that he couldn't make out the words.

The stadium was a forest of fluttering green flags. The camera was panning along the front of one of the stands. Then it cut to a scrum of green-shirted players hugging each other. Players were running and diving into the pile of bodies, followed by training staff and substitutes, still in their tracksuits. A linesman ran onto the pitch and bawled at the players. Peter Shilton picked the ball from the back of his net and swung a boot desultorily at the goalpost. Ray Houghton broke from the scrum and tottered like a man drunk with joy to the touch-line, where he stood with his eyes closed, arms held out wide towards the ecstatic crowd. He jabbed at the air with his fingers. A new shot showed the back of his body, the swaying mass of green, white and orange before him. He raised the hem of his shirt to his lips and kissed it. Packie Bonner was down on his knees, staring at the grass, shaking his head from side to side in helpless happiness. He closed his eyes and made the sign of the cross. Jack Charlton's face looked like it was carved out of granite. There was a long, lingering close-up of his craggy profile. He looked absolutely dazed, stunned into silence. He turned around and gazed at the shrieking crowd. Then somebody in the dug-out gently nudged him. He turned slowly towards the camera and gave an almost embarrassed half-smile, followed by the smallest of nonchalant shrugs. People in the bar screamed with joy.

'*Goarn, Jack, yeh man yeh*!'

A close-up of the scoreboard now filled the screen.

REPUBLIC OF IRELAND 1
ENGLAND   0

'*Yessssssss.*'

And then the slow-motion replay began. Kevin Moran's free kick drifted down near the touch-line. Stevens and Wright appeared surprised, confused. Sansom sliced at the ball, sending it skywards. It seemed to fall to John Aldridge as though guided by some invisible filament. He nodded it to Houghton, who headed it powerfully past the flailing keeper and into the net. The crowd in the bar roared with cheers once again, as though seeing the goal for the first time.

Eddie could hear applause and cheering from all over the building now, from below and above, from outside in the street. In an upper window across the way, a middle-aged woman was frantically waving a tricolour. The bride's father was standing in the doorway with the young strip-wearing boy from the Registry Office in his arms. The little boy was weeping with happiness.

A heavy man with damp-looking broken-veined eyes grabbed Eddie by the lapels and roared in his face. 'That'll fuckin' teach them. That'll teach the cunts, won't it? *Teach the fuckin' English a lesson for themselves!*'

Eddie had the feeling that if he pointed out Jack Charlton was English, the man might actually headbutt him.

*

It was half-an-hour later when he finally got through to his father and gave him the news about Patricia and her leg.

'My Jesus, Eddie. That's absolutely shocking.'

'Yeah, I know. Look, Dad, don't you think you should go over or something? Do Ryanair fly to Paris?'

'Well, to tell you the truth … I'm a bit busy at the minute, son.'

'Busy?'

'Well, it's just … you know. I'm watching the match.'

'You're what?'

'Yes, I'm watching it here with your Uncle Joe and George from the office. Mighty goal, wasn't it? D'y'think we can hang on till the end?'

'Jesus Christ Almighty, Frank. I'm saying your only daughter just lost a fucking leg, man.'

'Well, I know but — *oh Jesus* — *oh feck!* — *oh Jesus CHRIST!*'

'What?'

'My God, son, Packie just pulled off this MAGNIFICENT save. I'd never seen anything like it in my life! This is really a game-and-a-half, isn't it?'

'There's one or two factors kind of interfering with my enjoyment of it, Dad.'

'Oh well *obviously*. Some of the refereeing decisions have been controversial, to say the least.'

There was silence for a moment or two, and then his father started to snuffle with guilty laughter.

'I'm not seeing the humour of the situation here, Frank.'

His father suddenly howled with mirth. 'Sure Patricia's as fit as you or me and fitter,' he chuckled. 'One leg, me arse.

Sorry, Eddie, son. I was in on the caper all along. The two girls hatched it up between them. They wanted to play a bit of a joke on you.'

'… What?'

'I thought you'd cop it in thirty seconds flat, Eddie. Otherwise I'd never have gone along with it.'

'You thought I'd cop what?'

'Well, Siobhan and your sister cooked it up between them. I was sure you'd see through it straight away. Did you not know they were winding you up, son, no?'

Eddie said nothing. His heart was thundering. Somewhere above him he could hear a large crowd, singing to the tune of 'The Campdown Races': *'Who put the ball in the English net? Hough-ton, Hough-ton.'*

'Eddie? … Son? … Did you not see through it?'

'Well, yeah, Frank. Obviously.'

'That's my boy. I knew you would.'

'I mean, Christ almighty, what do you think I am, Frank?'

One Packie Bonn-er: There's only one Packie Bonn-er.
Ooh-AH, Paul McGRATH, say ooh-ah Paul McGrath!
You'll nehhhver beat the Irish!
You'll nehhhver beat the Irish!

He put down the phone and lit a cigarette. Across the lobby, Siobhan was looking at him and laughing. An Ireland scarf was draped over her shoulders.

'You evil malicious wagon,' he said.

'I know,' she chuckled. 'I'm really sorry.'

'No,' he said. 'Mussolini was sorry … You fucking … unbelievable …'

'It was all Patricia's idea, I swear. I didn't think you'd get upset. I thought you'd twig it was only a game.'

He sat down slowly on the stairs and put his fingers to his

boiling face.

'Smile,' she said. 'Give your face a holiday.'

'I can't believe you did this, Siobhan.'

'Come back inside for a bop,' she said, taking his hand.

He pulled away from her.

'I am never in my life going to speak to you again,' he said.

'Come on, Eddie. Don't be like that.'

He held up his middle finger. 'Swivel on it,' he said.

She shot him a glower. 'I wouldn't waste my time,' she said. And walked away.

By the time he got back inside she had taken her shoes off and was dancing with the bride to 'Rosalie' by Thin Lizzy.

*

In the back of the mini-cab she held his hand. They sped through the empty streets of London, both of them tired and badly drunk.

Westminster Bridge had been closed by the police, and a long line of cars and lorries had built up. Plain-clothes cops stood on the pavement wielding machine-guns, while soldiers searched the boots of cars. The driver cursed under his breath, then turned out of the lane and sped back down the way they had come. Big Ben said it was half-past two.

'Do you think we'll ever get married ourselves?' Siobhan asked.

'Urggh, God,' Eddie groaned. 'I think I'm gonna be sick again.'

'Take it easy,' she said softly. 'I'll mind you.'

'Patricia only has one leg,' he giggled.

'She's bleedin legless,' Siobhan laughed.

'You're one wagon, you are.'

'Ah, I'm not. I'm nice really.'

When he rolled down his window cool air flooded the car. 'So Uncle Peter's never gonna speak to me again,' he slurred.

'Probably gonna have me knee-capped.'

'He told me he thought you were great.'

'Oh yeah. I'm sure he did.'

'He's dying, Eddie,' she said, very quietly. 'He's riddled with cancer. He'll be gone in a few months.'

The driver started to hum along with the radio.

'I'm sorry, Siobhan.'

She reached out and took his hand again. 'Something about a wedding though, isn't there?'

'Mmyeah,' he groaned. 'I'm gonna puke me ring up in about two minutes.'

A group of dejected-looking English fans came trudging down the street, Union Jacks wrapped around their slumped shoulders.

'So did Aisling enjoy her wedding day?'

'Yeah, she did.' Siobhan gave a fond laugh. 'She told me something strange though.'

'What was that?'

'She said she went home the other week to collect a few things. And her Da had moved out of his own room and into hers. She went in and there he was, asleep. And it's only a little single bed, you know? And all of his stuff was moved in there, and her mother was still in the other room. Aisling said he looked like a tiny baby. He had his thumb at his mouth, you know, the way babies do. And when he woke up and saw her standing there with her suitcase he started to cry. And he told her he loved her.'

'Yeah?'

She nodded. 'It was the first time he ever told her that. Imagine.'

As they turned onto Lancaster Place and onto the approach road that led to the bridge, the blue flashing light of a squad-car appeared in the rear-view mirror.

'I feel sick, Siobhan,' Eddie said.

But she didn't seem to be listening to him. She was staring ahead at the street and softly gnawing her lip. Then she turned to him and smiled and touched the side of his face. 'I love you so much, Eddie,' she said.

He gazed at her, as the tears began to form in his eyes. 'Yeah,' he said. 'I love you too.'

She nodded. 'Try not to get so excited about it.'

'Sorry. I get a bit scared, that's all.'

She rested her hand on his thigh. 'We'll be OK,' she whispered. 'I wouldn't ever hurt you.'

The police car pulled into the middle of the road and started to overtake. The Sergeant in the driver's seat stared in through the window at Eddie, with a worried frown on his thin, pale face. He turned to his colleague and seemed to say something. Then turned to look at Eddie again, motioning for the taxi driver to stop.

The London night was surprisingly cold. A fresh wind was whipping up from the river. Gulls whirled, dive-bombing the water, screaming and crying as if in complaint. Somewhere in the middle distance a burglar alarm was wailing. Down towards the East, the dome of Saint Paul's was watching over the sleeping city, and the lights of the Natwest Tower glimmered through the swirls of fog.

By the time they had finished searching the car, Siobhan was asleep in Eddie's arms, the two of them slumped on a bench on the pavement.

'Sorry about all this,' the Sergeant said. 'Had a couple of bomb scares earlier.'

'Yeah,' said Eddie. 'Don't worry about it.'

'You see the match?' the Sergeant asked.

'No.'

'You know you won?'

'Yeah.'

'Only a game, though, eh?'

'Yeah,' said Eddie. 'It's only a game.'

The Sergeant pointed his torch at him. 'Bloody get you next time though.'

'It's a date,' Eddie said, and the Sergeant gave a soft laugh, before stepping back into the squad-car and driving away.

Siobhan stirred. He held her tightly and kissed the corner of her mouth. She murmured and twined her fingers through his. She looked so beautiful, and so happy too, that for one long moment he didn't want to wake her up and take her home. But the taxi driver said he was in a hurry to get on, and anyway, it was a little too late for love.

The Irish Male Gets A Life

*Physically there is nothing to distinguish human
society from the farm-yard except that children are
more troublesome and costly than chickens.*

George Bernard Shaw,
The Personal Sentimental Basis of Monogamy

Pins And Needles In Downtown Limerick

One afternoon not so long ago I was doing my shopping in a supermarket in Limerick — please don't ask — when a strange and significant thing happened to me.

There I was, wandering the aisles in my tracksuit and trainers, scrutinising all the delicious things I'm not allowed eat now that I'm on a diet, and merrily stuffing my basket full of nourishing lettuce, delicious beancurd and mouth-watering cucumber (*mmm-hmm*!). Anyway. This was not a supermarket with which I was familiar, and so I didn't really know where anything was, relative to anything else. A bit lost, I happened to turn a corner and drift into a section that had a large notice announcing HARDWARE over the aisle.

Now, ignorant reader, you might think the HARDWARE department of a Limerick supermarket would sell sawn-off shotguns and semi-automatic assault rifles, but you would be wrong. For this is actually the section where they sell corkscrews, light-bulbs, gas in bottles, sexually titillating novels with young floozies on the covers, wearing the kind of contorted facial expressions that would make you think they were under attack from some terrible intestinal parasite. You know the kind of thing, I am sure,

Anyway. I had a bit of time to kill, so I ambled around the section for a while. What a new and fascinating experience! So *this* was where a person bought cutlery and plates, towels and blankets and all that stuff. Being an Irish Male, I had naturally assumed these articles were simply supplied by the Mammy when one finally left home and moved into a bedsit. I figured the Mammy got them straight from God or the stork, or perhaps found them under a cabbage. It had never occurred to me that anyone at all could just enter a shop and purchase said items without even having to show a Children's Allowance book. This, my dears, was a fascinating development.

I ambled around for a good half-hour, as enthusiastic as a necrophiliac let loose in a funeral parlour. (Casserole dishes — *Phwoarr!* Bags of anthracite — *Woof!*) After a while I came upon a rack which displayed cute little packets of needles with multicoloured threads, and tiny boxes of drawing pins. One of each I purchased. These would come in handy, I thought.

Motoring back towards Dublin, I contentedly pondered all the things I would sew and prick, when suddenly I was gripped by a strange blinding terror. Good Presley in Heaven, *what had I done?* When I was younger I had always regarded supermarkets as good sources of cheap own-brand alcohol and dehydrated curries in plastic tubs. But now, here I was, buying needles and pins! I mean, only a few years ago, needles and pins were what you had in the backs of your legs when you woke from a drunken coma in somebody else's bathroom with an eerie feeling of inexplicable guilt. Now I was buying them by the box!

After all, needles are pretty significant articles, when you think. They imply domesticity, maturity, financial rectitude; long nights spent by the crackling hearth, darning old stockings and sipping Horlicks while listening to 'Ceilidh House' on the wireless. You wouldn't catch, say, Keith Richards buying a needle, would you? Unless it was to tattoo 'Born To Be Wild' across his chest or briskly jab it into one of his forearms. And drawing pins? What in the name of Christ did I need *drawing pins* for? Was I turning into the kind of person who snips recipes for left-overs out of the newspapers and pins them neatly above the cooker? Heavens to Betsy! Where had my youth gone?

I stopped the car somewhere on the outskirts of Toomevara, Co Tipperary, and began to take stock of my life. OK, so I'd started with the relatively harmless stuff. It was only a few needles and a box of drawing pins. I could handle it, man, once it didn't happen too often. But I knew soon, if I didn't watch myself, I would graduate to the heavy 'gear'. Like buying tiny fridge-magnets shaped like exotic fruits. Trying to spot my neighbours on 'Crimeline'. Jesus, if I didn't get some help, I might even take up gardening or golf! A bit of re-potting on a Sunday afternoon! *Banging my balls around the golf course with the boys!*

The rest of the drive home was slow and reflective.

I had a vague but powerful feeling that everything in my life had begun to change.

Don The Dog Learns All About Golf

Later that week I heard a politician say on the radio that children were our nation's brightest hope for the future. This is something politicians say with some frequency. Indeed, in the anthology of political cliché it is right up there with 'I'm glad you asked me that question, Brian,' not to mention 'I didn't interrupt *you*, Vincent, so please don't interrupt *me*' and, of course, 'Politics is about the issues, Olivia, not the personalities — as I wish my opponent would sometimes agree (the ugly woffler/wife-swapping sodomite/Cork loser/mendacious pinko /glorified corner-boy/Provo lush, etc.)'.

Of course just because a politician says something, we don't have to assume it's a ridiculous lie. Even a stopped clock tells the right time twice a day. Children *are* our nation's brightest hope for the future. (They could hardly be our brightest hope for the past, after all.) But does that really mean we have to like them?

Some years ago my family acquired a dog. Don was his name. ('The O'Connor Don', one of my sisters dubbed him.) Don was a great big shambling beastie, with large floppy ears and the temperament of a lamb. The three of my nephews who were then aged six adored the ground over which Don padded. Benevolent and endearing mutt that he was, he would actually give them piggyback rides up and down the garden.

'Giddyup, Don,' they would happily call.

'Woof,' he would reply, in a gently cheerful manner.

One Christmas somebody gave the nephews a set of toy golf clubs. Out to the back they cantered, cooing like joyful seraphim. I strolled out after them a half-hour later, brimming with seasonal cheer or, at least, red wine, intending to do the avuncular bit.

There they were, the three little horrors, expressing their appreciation for all Don's love by thwacking him around the flowerbed with their plastic putters, cackling gleefully while they thrashed and smacked. And there he stood, faithful hound, a vision of canine stoicism among the rhododendrons, bearing their blows with rude good humour, resisting what must have been the considerable temptation to snap off their little heads with his enormous jaws. I can still see the expression on his stupefied face, his big cute eyes just saying … '*Huh*?'

Sadly Don is no longer with us, having passed to that happier land of eternal puppydom. But I suspect that in the Big Back Garden in the Sky, the angels will not be little children.

Before they are born, children are trouble. The birth itself is trouble squared. In the early months of your infant's life, you yourself will sleep like a baby, that is, you'll wake up screaming and crying every two hours. After babyhood comes the toddling era, wherein dog turds, hot ovens and cliff-edges become sources of endless fascination. Next is pre-pubescence, that seemingly unending nightmare of plasticine and glove puppets, that purgatory of poorly conceived school-plays full of tinsel, stuttering and recorder music. Oh, how you can't wait for the fruit of your loins to grow up a little. Hee hee hee. You poor sad fool.

Just when you think it can't get any worse, adolescence arrives, like a Special Branch officer kicking in the door of your parental *sang-froid*. Spots, atheism, sulks, anarchism, rap music, dirty magazines hidden under the mattress — none of these take your mind off your teenage kids and their antics.

Not to mention the endless questions required by law to be asked by parents of moody pubescents — the utter reasonableness of such gentle enquiries being in precisely inverse proportion to the sarcastic sneer of malice in which the answers are delivered.

The Catechism of Adolescence goes something like this:

Q: Do anything interesting in school today, love?
A: Yeah. Right.
Q: Is there something on your mind?
A: None of *your* business.
Q: Did you find the clean laundry I left on your bed?
A: Huh!
Q: Would you like if I made your favourite dinner?
A: LEAVE ME ALONE, I NEVER ASKED TO BE BORN!

After adolescence, things calm down a bit. Your child can now express more mature feelings of affection and respect. This it does by being embarrassed by you in front of its friends, disagreeing loudly with every political principle you have ever espoused and generally shrieking 'Oh my *Christ,* how can you even *SAY* that?!' whenever you have the temerity to open your beak and draw breath.

When this phase has ended — phew — at last they are adults. Finally *finally* they decide to leave home, fall in love with persons of spectacular inappropriateness, get married, have their own children, get divorced, marry again, ignore you, never come to visit, and, ultimately, leave you to die alone and unloved in the kind of Dickensian maximum-security Twilight Home where the sheets are damp, the food is overcooked, and the only thing you can get on the television is 'Ballykissangel' — which you have to watch all day and all night before getting caned to sleep by a wannabe Nazi.

Oh yes, children are the future of the nation all right. It makes you wonder how contraception ever caught on.

My Own Personal Irish Male

By now you won't be surprised to learn that for most of my life I've been sure I would never be a father. Nor, to be frank, did I want to be. The very idea was painful enough to make me generally avoid discussing it. When friends or even family members talked about their children, something inside me would simply click off and I'd find an excuse to change the subject. I'm sure one of the real reasons was that my own parents' marriage was unhappy and ended in the courts when I was thirteen. Even after their separation, we children continued to be the focus of their arguments, my father having to fight constant and bitter battles with a woman whose idea of good mothering was giving you the occasional ten-minute head-start into the woods before unleashing the hounds. So I grew up regarding marriage as a trap for the decent people, almost by definition an emotional torture which having children could only prolong.

Most children of unhappy marriages blame themselves for their parents' misfortunes. I used to also, from my earliest childhood. Therapists, self-help books and often your parents themselves will advise you against this, and of course they are right. But I found it hard to kick the habit.

The guilt I acquired in my childhood had odd effects in later life. I spent most of my twenties sternly reprimanding myself for things which on mature reflection were not really my fault — Shamrock Rovers having to move from Milltown, the rise to power of General Pinochet — while accepting no responsibility whatsoever for things which were, such as heavy smoking, would-be promiscuity and the frequent composition of derivative poetry. My personal life was so fiendishly complicated I couldn't keep track of which lies I was supposed to be telling to whom. In politics I developed a deeply irrational need to feel spurious affinities with other creatures who were suffering badly, such as whales, Guatemalans or the Irish Labour Party. I do not mean to imply in any way that everyone on the Left is motivated by low self-regard masquerading as comradely solidarity. Indeed most of my personal Irish heroes are people who work for social change simply because it is right to do so. But that's not the only reason I did so myself. In those days, feeling better was part of the mix.

And in those days marriage was just another thing to oppose, another weapon in the arsenal of the bourgeoisie. This suited me well; it made bachelorhood a *cause*. I was opposed to marriage like I was opposed to apartheid. 'Free Nelson Mandela' may have been written on my T-shirt, but 'Fight For The Right To Party' was written on my heart.

It wasn't until my early thirties that I met someone who gave me inescapable cause to question my certainty. A beautiful, intelligent, kind-hearted woman who would send me John Donne poems by fax, she was, basically, my kind of gal. And even my attitude to the prospect of having children softened a little during our courtship. To fall in love is to make yourself believe that almost any difference of perspective is either illusory or unimportant. I knew my beloved wanted to be a mother some day and I felt she would make a wonderful one. Whenever she asked if I wanted a family myself, I managed to project a kind of nonchalant agnosticism. And by the time we married, several years later, I had succeeded in dressing up my neurotic unease as a laid-back desire to trust in fate.

Fourteen months later my wife discovered she was pregnant. My initial reaction was one of amazement — not just that it had happened, but at how happy I felt about it. For several days I walked around in a haze of cheerfulness and positivity. But soon my feelings became more complicated. It wasn't that the exhilaration of the first week exactly

301

disappeared. It was just that beneath it something else was growing; that old gnawing sense of foreboding and angst.

We decided not to tell anyone our news for a while, for the usual reason — 'in case anything goes wrong'. (Impending parents become quickly adept at euphemism, a skill they will need for the next eighteen years.) The pregnancy felt like a shared conspiracy, a covert game being played by two participants who didn't quite know all the rules just yet. A lot of couples say this is fun, and in a way it is, though for me the secrecy had other uses too. It allowed me an amount of crazy denial. If we didn't tell anyone, it wasn't really happening.

After a short time I began to see that what I was doing was ridiculous, and I tried to confront the reality of our situation. But I found that the only way I could think about the baby was with that particular mixture of empathy and objectivity one might feel for the hero of a novel. And then I realized it wasn't the baby I was seeing in this way; rather that most unbelievable of all fictional characters — myself as a competent, loving parent. The Irish Male: From Lad to Dad.

How could someone as interestingly damaged as myself ever begin to cope with this role? Who was I fooling? Myself? My wife? Statisticians tell us that most children of divorce will end up in unhappy marriages themselves. What if that were to happen to us? It didn't feel likely, but how could you tell? And if things between us ever did go wrong, what kind of separated parents would we make? I can see now that the questions look utterly paranoid. But at the time they seemed logical, *completely* necessary — even if, perhaps unsurprisingly, I kept them to myself.

This probably sounds far-fetched, but in a way I think abject terror was good for our relationship. Certainly it forced me really to consider the promises I had made to my wife on our wedding day. I would silently repeat them, thinking about the words, and whenever I did that, the fear receded. Yes, our marriage might fail — but whose might not? In a way, the risk seemed suddenly the whole *point* of marriage — to make an act of faith with the world. As soon as I stopped worrying about my own painful childhood, I sensed my wife and myself become closer. There were no big chats about the future, we simply seemed to accept that suddenly it was here. If we were silent sometimes, the silence became more comfortable than heretofore. My wedding day was the happiest day of my life, but I honestly think the first month of the pregnancy was in almost every sense the beginning of our marriage.

But still I found it hard to express my emotions about impending fatherhood. I think that's because I didn't entirely know what they were. I had managed to stop thinking I was doomed to be a bad parent, but that isn't the same thing as believing you'll be a good one. I did find the first fetal scan affecting, but I didn't cry, as most of my friends had predicted I would, and I felt a bit guilty about that. As my wife and I walked down the street together afterwards, I felt as if there were a sign dangling over my head — The Fucker Who Didn't Cry at the Scan.

I approached the second scan in a state of apprehensiveness. The clinic in London which my wife attended is also a renowned centre for fertility treatment, and I remember feeling painfully conscious as we waited in the foyer that many of the other couples in the room would give all they had to be in our situation. By now some of our child's features were clearly discernible — an arm, a spine, a ghostly white face. But if I am honest, the sight still wasn't enough to make me feel like a father. The little creature on the monitor screen was more like a being from a faraway planet, some amniotic spaceman unimagined by science-fiction. He turned, he rolled, he moved his tiny head. But even as the nurse finished making her notes, and confirmed that he was doing well, it didn't feel like he had much to do with me.

It was what happened next that I found astounding. Almost casually, the nurse reached out and flicked a speaker switch on the monitor unit. There was a short crackling sound, a few watery echoes. The nurse smiled and raised a finger to her lips for us to be silent. A moment passed. A truck went by in the street. And then the sound of our son's heartbeat filled the small room.

My own heart actually seemed to stop. It was like having a spear of longing driven through me. I will remember that sound until the moment I die, that pulsing rhythm of extraordinary rapidity that called for nothing but to be loved in return. It was about nothing except itself; its own beauty, its own aching vulnerability. It was so very ordinary, yet it felt unspeakably sacred. Unable to speak, I stood still and simply listened, trembling with emotion as I held my wife's hand. More than any music I have ever heard, that sound changed my life as I listened to it. I left that room a father at last.

But in truth that sound implied darker things too, some of which I was grievously unprepared for. The night of the scan I had a dream of my own death, the next night the same; before long it had become a regular occurrence. I'd be drowning, sinking, endlessly falling. Sometimes I would hear the baby's heartbeat.

I'm not someone who often has nightmares, so I found the dreams disturbing in the extreme. I wondered was something terribly wrong with me? Had the fear I'd always felt of parenthood been well-founded, after all? Did I, in shameful fact, simply not want this child? But even as I asked myself those questions, I already knew they were the wrong ones.

When I was younger I think I honestly believed that somehow I would never die. Now, on the point of becoming a father, I finally realised that one day I would. It is the darkest secret of impending parenthood — how birth also gives an intimation of mortality. To bring a new life into the world is to face up to many things, among them the certainty of your own ultimate extinction. 'They give birth aside the grave,' wrote Samuel Beckett. I never knew what those words really meant until the pregnancy.

And yet after a few weeks the bad dreams simply stopped. They never returned, I don't know why. Neither do I have any explanation for what happened next. To say I began to experience a deep sense of calm and acceptance would be technically correct but it doesn't come close. I have no shred of religious feeling, but the language of sacrament keeps suggesting itself. Suffice it to say, if there *is* a peace that passes understanding, I think I know what it is now. It is the memory of nothing more than a child's heartbeat, the small persistent puttering rhythm which proclaims that life has triumphed over death, that you can stand up and walk out of the tomb of your own past. Even if that peace eventually fades from my life — even if it were to completely disappear — to have glimpsed it just once is miracle enough. And I owe that blessing to my wife and child.

But I didn't see the baby as anything supernatural. As the scans continued, and our son developed, I found myself pondering the awesome fact of his *physicality* — his bones, his muscles, his skull and internal organs, the two impossibly black shadows that were slowly becoming eyes. He didn't appear to *grow* as such; he unfurled, he sprouted, he seemed to take leaf. Like a loving heart in a John Donne poem.

Sometimes, in quieter moments, I would allow myself to imagine what it would be like to look into those eyes; to see them gazing steadily back into mine with all the tenderness of filial love, to watch as one day, far in the future, they convey the beautiful wordless message which every father finds so deeply moving: 'Give me some money, Baldy, or I'll invite my friends around.'

The last time I saw our son's face on the monitor screen, it sent a bolt of lightning through my chest. I felt as though I were seeing a ghost. But I was, of course — the ghost was my own. I looked at his face, then I looked at my wife's. She gave me a vaguely playful wink. I truly believe it was the first time in my thirty-seven years that I understood what it is to love completely, unconditionally. The child is father to the man, they say. I only hope I can return the favour — because even before our beautiful son came into the world, he had taught me more about how to live in it than anyone else I have ever known.

What a blessing. What a joy.

My own beloved Irish male.

Slaphead

Georgina Wroe

Terry Small wants a woman. And he's seen a cat-
alogue full of them. They're in Moscow, employed
by REDS IN YOUR BEDS marriage agency. Armed
with his best Calvin Klein underpants and his new
abdominiser, Terry, the most dynamic conservatory
salesman in Basingstoke, is on his way.

Awaiting him in Moscow is Katya, the agency's
Russian representative. The only mate Katya cares
about is her delinquent six-year-old, Sasha – and
Terry, probably her most unprepossessing customer
ever, isn't going to pose a problem for a woman who's
already despatched a redundant husband to Siberia.

But Katya hasn't bargained for the intervention of
Fate. Not to mention Moscow's latest entrepreneur,
Professor Modin, formerly Lenin's embalmer, now
specialising in providing a mounting pile of dead
Mafia bosses with the flashy, unforgettable funeral
they so richly deserve . . .

Fast, confident and fantastically funny, *Slaphead*
introduces a writer of anarchic brilliance to the
fiction-writing scene.

'A female Carl Hiassen' *The Times*

0 7472 6203 9

HEADLINE

Icebox

Mark Bastaple

Here's the deal.

Give Gabriel Todd your brain, and you'll live forever. Gabe'll freeze your head in a flask – and three hundred years from now, you'll be reborn in a new, perfect body. You will be immortal.

Unity Siddorn wants in. She has her own plans to save the world – with genetically pumped tomatoes, as you ask – but she's already thirty-bloody-one years old. In actuarial terms, her life is 41.3% over. She'll do anything – ANYTHING – for more time.

Don, her squeeze, is less keen. A pack of smokes and a gambler's shot at seventy years – he can live with that.

Suddenly, Gabe's theories are about to be put to the test – though circumstances are admittedly less than ideal. The police tend to take a professional interest in a freshly severed head. It's not something you can easily hide . . .

0 7472 6839 8

HEADLINE

Now you can buy any of these other bestselling Headline books from your bookshop or *direct from the publisher*.

FREE P&P AND UK DELIVERY
(Overseas and Ireland £3.50 per book)

Backpack	Emily Barr	£5.99
Icebox	Mark Bastable	£5.99
Killing Helen	Sarah Challis	£6.99
Broken	Martina Cole	£6.99
Redemption Blues	Tim Griggs	£5.99
Relative Strangers	Val Hopkirk	£5.99
Homegrown	Gareth Joseph	£5.99
Everything is not Enough	Bernardine Kennedy	£5.99
High on a Cliff	Colin Shindler	£5.99
Winning Through	Marcia Willett	£5.99

TO ORDER SIMPLY CALL THIS NUMBER

01235 400 414

or e-mail <u>orders@bookpoint.co.uk</u>

Prices and availability subject to change without notice.